THE FAITHFUL SEXTANT

a memoir

Robert Devereux McEliece

CKBooks

No parts of this book may be reproduced or used in any form without permission except for brief quotations used for articles or in reviews. You can contact Robert Devereux McEliece at robdevmce@gmail.com

Publisher's Cataloging-In-Publication Data
(Prepared by The Donohue Group, Inc.)

Names: McEliece, Robert Devereux.
Title: The faithful sextant : a memoir / Robert Devereux McEliece.
Description: New Glarus, WI : CKBooks, [2017]
Identifiers: LCCN 2017906798 | ISBN 978-0-9832984-4-1 | ISBN 978-0-9800529-9-2 (ebook)
Subjects: LCSH: Vietnam War, 1961-1975--Personal narratives, American. | Vietnam War, 1961-1975--United States--Biography. | Sailors--United States--Biography. | Male friendship--United States. | Alexandria (Va.)--Biography. | LCGFT: Autobiographies.
Classification: LCC DS559.5 .M34 2017 (print) | LCC DS559.5 (ebook) | DDC 959.704/3092--dc23

Cover image by G-Valeriy
Cover and Interior design by Christine Keleny
Copyright © 2017 Robert Devereux McEliece
All rights reserved
Printed in the USA
CKBooks Publishing
P.O. Box 214
New Glarus, WI
53574

Just as the arc of a sextant measures the circle of the heavens, so too will the small arc sections of this memoir demarcate some of the special people who helped shape the warp and woof of my soul. Herein lies the truth of these events as told to or recalled by me, knowing, as Ms. Wylie captures so well in her ode to "One Person," that members of the unfaithful clay oft contrive to deem them false. It was, however, my faithful family and friends, along with an ever-faithful sextant, that helped navigate this journey.

For:

1Lt. Frank Coffee Packer USAF
Cpt. Joseph Lewis Powell Jr. USMC
1Lt. Laurence Douglass Greene USA
Cpt. Peter Mansfield Clay USMC
FO James Henry McEliece Sr. USAAC
Cpt. Alberic deLaet USAAC
Lt. Robert Anthony Gallagher USN
Col. James Henry McEliece Jr. USA
Sgt. John McEliece USA
Pvt. James Wesley Adcock CSA
Cpl. William Washington Hart CSA

And

Lt. Christopher Michael Devereux McEliece USNR

Table of Contents

Preface vi
Introduction 1
Moving In 5
High School 18
Carole 34
Joe 43
Frank 48
Graduation 53
Moving On 69
The Shipyard 76
The Voyage 92
Typhoon 114
Keiko 148
The War Zone 178
Vũng Tàu 186
Sài Gòn 201
The Rex Hotel 213
Departure 236
Crossing to Home 241
Voyage II 247
First Lt. Frank Packer 260
Cpt. James McEliece 294
Cpt. Joseph Powell 300
Joani 311
First Lt. Larry Greene 313
Epilogue 316
Acknowledgment 324
About the Author 325

Although these words are false, none shall prevail
To prove them in translation less than true
Or overthrow their dignity, or undo
The faith implicit in a fabulous tale;
The ashes of this error shall exhale
Essential verity, and two by two
Lovers devout and loyal shall renew
The legend and refuse to let it fail.

Even the betrayer and the fond deceived,
Having put off the body of this death,
Shall testify with one remaining breath,
From eternity's demand to be believed;
These words are true, although at intervals
The unfaithful clay contrive to make them false.

Elinor Wylie
"One Person"

Preface

The object of contemplation refuses to stand still, the words bounce off the experience and in the end, pure contradictions stand on the paper. Words. A world of words. The author, because he has asked, understands that many readers will not know what the word SEXTANT is or means. The World Book Encyclopedia, a research tool rarely used in era of the Internet, has a picture and a half page article about the sextant. This information piece can be found alphabetically just behind Sex Education and before the word Sextillion—a number followed by twenty-one zeros. A sextant has nothing to do with either. The word sextant is from the Latin word 'sextans,' which means one-sixth of a circle. Thus the instrument's measuring arc is one-sixth of a complete circle. In simplest form the word sextant means a finely engineered instrument employing mirrors and a small telescope used to measure the arc between a celestial body and the horizon. It's just about arc, nothing more. An arc forming one of the three sides of a celestial triangle, where the sum of the three angles equals 360 degrees, not 180 degrees, like they taught in high school geometry. This difference is due to the fact that the celestial triangle lies on a sphere, the infinite sphere of the heavens, thus it is the word sphere that changes everything. Just one little word. Sphere!

So it is that I write. Words are only flimsy mathematics used by writers to capture the humanity of a story. But unlike mathematics, authors have only allegory, metaphors, analogies, parables, rhetoric, symbolism, and simile to stand in for the wonderfully explicit equals sign found in the algebraic formula. Ah yes, the perfection found in $A + B = C$. In living our lives, it just never happens that we can take something called (A), completely mix it with (B), and convince ourselves that it is exactly the same thing as (C). So we struggle to convince the reader that the simplicity of our metaphor will unlock the hidden meaning and emotion of the human condition the author so wants the reader to understand.

Robert Deverux McEliece
Seattle

Introduction

Of the thousand experiences we have, we find language for one at most and even this one merely by chance and without the care it deserves. Buried under all the mute experiences are those unseen ones that give our life its form, its color, and its melody. Then, when we turn to these treasures, as archaeologists of the soul, we discover how confusing they are. The object of contemplation refuses to stand still, the words bounce off the experience and in the end, pure contradictions stand on the paper. For a long time, I thought it was a defect, something to be overcome. Today I think it is different: that recognition of the confusion is the ideal path to understanding these intimate yet enigmatic experiences. That sounds strange, even bizarre, I know. But ever since I have seen the issue in this light, I have the feeling of being really awake and alive for the first time.

Pascal Mercier

The Circle Begins

Though here and there a man is left
Whose iron thread eludes the shears,
The martyr with his bosom cleft
Is dead these seven years.

Assuming an heroic mask,
He stands a tall derisive tree,
While servile to the speckled task
We move devoted hand and knee.

It is no virtue, but a fault
Thus to breathe ignoble air,
Suffering unclean assault
And insult dubious to bear.

Elinor Wylie
"Heroics" from
Black Armour

Moving In
The Making of Robert McEliece

Design engineers of the 1947 Buick Roadmaster convertible compromised the normal roomy Buick back seat to make space for the raising/lowering mechanism and the storage of the canvas top and its frame. As our family motored to its new home in the fall of 1952, the three children thrown into this compromised back seat were now ten, nine, and seven; growing pre-teens who no longer bounced around in this seat like three puppies thrown into a laundry basket. Driving across the country to our new home, I slumped in the rear seat against the protrusion designed to hide the convertible mechanism; trying to get some sleep and at the same time trying to keep my head away from the cold steel of the ragtop frame, all the while basking in self-made misery at the thought of once again being uprooted from a home just at the dawning of the promise of friendship and love. All I could think of was Pricilla.

Meanwhile, Sissy whined at the injustice of always being stuck sitting in the middle of the bench seat over top of the driveshaft hump—a most uncomfortable long-haul, middle seat assignment with little padding and no place to put your feet. Stops for lunch or potty breaks resulted in a three-kid mad dash back to the car in an attempt to avoid the middle seat, with the two larger bully-brothers physically forcing the smaller little girl to take the middle. Even my father, possessing The Great Santini-like skills, could not adjudicate this dilemma as someone had to sit on the hump. In spite of the injustice to the Princess, the longer legs of the two older boys simply did not fit. It was clear that this growing family's needs for transportation had outgrown a two-door, single man's sporty ragtop…a mundane '57 Chevy station wagon loomed in our future.

Driving from Kansas City to Washington, DC, just as the weary traveler thinks that the objective is near, a 280 pound linebacker guarding the goal line smashes the unwary right in the nose. This obstacle called West Virginia…or to be more exact, the Appalachian Mountains, appeared formidable. Even today there is no easy way through this barrier. In spite of the slowing of our journey adding to my misery, fall in these Appalachian Mountains was glorious, lifting my spirit and bringing a vision of wonderful things to come as my family once again became citizens of Dixie. We would soon be in grit Mecca, where okra was not some minor Indian tribe from Oklahoma and fried chicken came with a crispy crust.

House hunting for a new home near Washington, DC was going to take longer than our last two stops and there would be no rental home; we would be bound into temporary living for a couple of weeks. A motel found near US Route 1 in Alexandria was conveniently located within walking distance of an elementary school where our mother had us enrolled in class in nanoseconds.

About a week into classes a couple of the school bullies jumped my brother and me because we sounded like Yankees. Damn it…we were both born in Alabama, but as with this kind of misunderstanding, there was no discussion period for thoughtful intercourse and diplomacy; a fistfight followed. Ironically, about four years later we became high school football teammates with these same bullies, but in the meantime, two bloody noses at the family dinner table lent a sense of urgency to my parents' new home hunt.

At last my parents found a prospective family house. It was a newly constructed home in a section of Alexandria located just south of Little Hunting Creek, an area known locally as New Alexandria. Return visits to the house became of concern because of the worried look shared by my parents followed by hushed conversations away from the kids. We loved the house…why were they dragging their feet? Just tell the man we wanted it and let's move in, okay?

This house was in a very different neighborhood from our previous homes in Idaho, Kansas, South Carolina, or Alabama. Here we would live next to career military officers, government department managers, a top rocket scientist, and even Gerald Ford, a new congressman from Michigan. This was not the truck driver/preacher/librarian type of neighborhood of old and, although we kids did not understand, the price of the house would reflect the wealth of the neighborhood. Kid knowledge never includes information about family finance, and it is natural for the young to assume that people live wherever they want. Listening to my parents talk in whispers, I could tell that they had bitten off a big chunk of something, but try as I might, I saw no reason we did not belong in this house. I overheard them say that it was beyond their imagination that they could afford a new house costing more than twenty thousand dollars, ten times what the home in Idaho had cost. What the heck was this mortgage thing? Yes, twenty thousand dollars was a big number, but anything more than five bucks was a big number to me. My mother assured Dad that she could get a job to help out, and we would all pull our belts a little tighter.

With papers signed, we moved into a real two-story, brick Colonial house, and although I still had to share a bedroom with my little brother, the living space was sumptuous by our standards. An older single man had acted as developer, contactor, and master builder to several homes in the neighborhood with this representing the last in his development project. His modest personal residence was a small bungalow behind the last house in the project, serving as a home for him as he finished the project.

His last job to complete this house project was to attach his bungalow to the main house with a breezeway, turning the bungalow living room into the garage with the remainder of the small house serving as an extra living area and workshop. The bungalow, now attached to the new brick house, was sold together as a package. The bungalow had one more extravagance, a second bathroom. We now lived in a two-story house featuring two bathrooms, what luxury.

Almost before the ink was dry on our new house purchase contract, my brother, Jim, sister, Ginny (known within the family as Sissy), and I made an amazing discovery. Directly across the street from our new house lived a family of the same age as ours with three children, two older boys and a younger girl, a mirror image so to speak. The middle child, a son named Frank, was born a scant two weeks before me. The oldest boy, named Greg, was two years older and the youngest, a daughter named Nancy. Soon to become Sissy's best friend, Nancy was barely a year older than my sister.

We quickly learned that we were living next to the locally famous Packer family. It was hard to imagine a better match in next-door neighbor kids and friends, a girl friend for my sister and the makings of a small boy gang for my brother and myself. There was, however, one huge hurdle to overcome before any kind of initiation into this gang could happen.

For my brother and I, our bid for membership into this neighborhood started at a huge disadvantage. Slightly older girly girls had populated our previous Kansas City neighborhood, the kind Lucy Brown of *Peanuts* would have picked as playmates. "You two can help us set up the tea set in the dollhouse, but take your shoes off before you come in," these older girls once told us.

The Kansas City neighborhood came with rules. Our BB guns had been locked away. Hunting quail, baiting bulls, pulling up surveying stakes, and looking for baby rattlesnakes was now just Idaho history. We arrived in this new bastion of male mayhem from a foreign culture of Lucy Brown. My brother and I had been sissified.

The new boys across the street in Alexandria, as well as several others living in the neighborhood, were all boy. This rat pack filled its days with bully activities: sandlot football, baseball, archery, track events, war, mumbley-peg…all the boy sports. For them winning meant everything, even if the mumbley-peg knife sank into flesh. When these guys tired of sports with rules, they would turn to blood sports, no rules required. Down by the creek, where forts had been dug, teams led charges in mud ball battles with the intent of inflicting pain or blood to the enemy. The winning team leader got to be Robert E. Lee, a name unfamiliar to Jim and I…causing more pain until we learned he was the forever-hero of all boys in Virginia.

This gang was certainly not admitting any newcomers without proof of boyhood, especially two who said 'yeah' like a Yankee. Boys in the South did not say "yeah," soon earning my brother and myself the nicknames of "Big Yeah" and "Little Yeah," nicknames soon to be taken as fighting words.

Earning our way into this pack would be neither easy nor quick. But like all things requiring earned recognition, once these relationships were formed, they were built for life. It did not take long before I bonded for life with Frank Packer, and in some ways he became closer to me than my own brother. There is no question that the twist of fate that dropped me in the house across the street had every bit as much to do with the gelling of my character as the relationship in my own family. I was to learn that a guy picked to be Frank's wingman would always be tested over and over. If you could not make muster, you would have to find someone else to fly with. Our "double dog dare" tests always ratcheted up the level of fear until someone dropped out.

One example of these tests came about a year after we had been accepted into the neighborhood. A strip mall was being constructed near our house that looked to be a perfect setting for a game of Hide and Seek. Our Hide and Seek games often came with contusions, lacerations, or sprains.

One summer evening, when it seemed as if the setting sun was never going to slip under the soft Virginia hills, we had begun a game that lasted into the darkening shadows of dusk. This particular evening we had picked the top floor of the new shopping mall construction site as the playing field where home base became a pile of beams laid out at one end of the floor. Frank had slipped up in the proceeding game, now finding himself as the dreaded "it," meaning that the game would go on until dawn if necessary until a new person was tagged. He would never accept the disgrace of being the butt of the game. Twilight had set in and as a hider, I found myself needing to make a world-class dash for home base in order to avoid carrying the title of "it" over to a future game. No boy in our gang wanted to be "it" for a full week.

My run was good but my stop never happened. As I managed to touch home base ahead of being tagged, my attention suddenly shifted to the far side of the stack of beams where a dark form loomed. This dark form turned out to be open elevator shaft, an unfinished opening through the floor that had not been covered or fenced off. In the evening gloom I suddenly found myself plummeting into this open elevator shaft, falling three floors to land on a pile of gravel. I had missed the internal scaffolding by scant inches.

Laying on my back, barely conscious, I see two sets of eyes as big a saucers peering over the edge of the shaft from three stories up. "Do you think Bobby is dead"? is all I hear, followed by a scurrying of footsteps around to the back of the building and in through an unfinished entry door.

Frank and my brother revived me with face slaps, and then made a Boy Scout arm sling to carry me home. I could not walk. A trip to the Emergency Room found no broken bones but severely sprained and bruised ankles. Like a cat, I had landed almost evenly on both feet, avoiding broken bones or shattered body parts. The pain was terrible, but recovery came in about one week. A later visit from Frank to ask how I was doing brought an assertion that became part of legend: at least I had not been tagged "it."

In spite of close calls, the fear level in our playtime always seemed to ratchet up. Jump off the roof of the house into a bale of hay. Okay, now let's do it without the hay. Pick up that garter snake by the neck. Now, let's get into the swamps of the Potomac and find a Water Moccasin to capture. Learn to make and fly wire-powered model airplanes. Can we put two of us in the center of the circle with two airplanes and have dogfights? Increasing the intensity or the level of danger was a sure way to improve any sport or game. As each of these heart-pumping events became part of our lore, so too they became part of the maturation process, turning us into young men of self-confidence, young men who could stuff fear. Each event gave us a little more assurance to know where our limits were and how to lead others to have this self-same confidence.

Likely due to youthful energy, it had slipped my notice that Frank was always the author of our show-off dares. Frank was the shortest kid in our group. I mean shortest by much more than an inch or two. Boyhood treats short boys harshly; Frank was never going to let that happen. Dares he spit out to the gang involved some test he already knew he could win or perform without breaking a sweat; some test that perhaps one of the other boys would find too hard or worse, too scary; some test, which would once again solidify Frank's standing as the ring leader.

One afternoon, about two years after moving in, Frank suddenly pushed me into a test of leadership challenge, a trial that became a step past tedious, a trial that I had decided could not go unconfronted. This had pushed me over the edge. The result was a full-fledged, *mano a mano* fistfight in our back yard. My parents came running, with my mother yelling at my father to break up the dogfight. But he did not do it. Instead my father told her to stand back and let us work it out; and work it out we did. Four black eyes, two bloody noses, and ripped shirts later, we agreed to a truce. A week later we were back to best friends, bonds of respect renewed. Even a week later, I couldn't remember what the heck started the fight. Perhaps the time had come, the time to assert myself.

A men's magazine once gave a list of ten things young men should check off before manhood. For example, things like a night in jail or a trip to a warzone or a night in a whorehouse or an all-in fistfight, preferably for the right to a young lady's hand. In my memory,

I had checked off all of the ten boxes except spending a night in jail... though as of this writing, there is still time to make all ten.

On the subject of fistfights, I believe my lifetime record to be about 5-0-1. Years later there was a real bruiser at a young-adult drinking party where a big guy came running down a flight of stairs to sucker punch me, knocking me to the floor and breaking my nose. After I got up, two of my friends helped me beat the crap out of him, knocking him out and tossing him into the gutter in front of the house, all of this over a girl who had picked me over the sucker-punch guy. Two weeks later I dumped her. But I digress, and that is all I will ever have to say about fistfights.

Not all of our adventures to manhood involved unsupervised high jinx and life-threatening dares.

My biggest adventure with Frank was to come. We would challenge the breadth of this country in a long and testing trip by bus into the wilds of northern New Mexico. The two of us had saved our money from paper routes and lifeguarding to sign up for a Boy Scout trip to spend the summer at the National Boy Scout Camp at Philmont in northern New Mexico. This trip would become a huge step towards independence and manhood. Ties to parents, siblings, and friends were cut as the chartered Trailways bus left Alexandria in July of 1956 in the days before interstate highways, winding its way westward, mostly on two lane roads. Frank had no idea how far it was to New Mexico. He had never been out of Virginia or Maryland. I sure as heck knew how far it was, but had no idea how different this would be from family travel. The anxiety, as well as the thrill of distance from families and parents, was heightened as all of the other boys, including the Scout leaders, were from other troops around Washington; we were strangers all.

Each long day on the bus was followed by a prearranged evening as guests of the US Air Force at strategically located bases or in a dormitory college. This crossing took a full five days locked inside a 1950s Trailways bus—no bathroom included. Swigging down the free milk and orange juice for breakfast—provided free from the Air

Force—became an early lesson in painful bladder control. Arriving at the Air Force bases, we were treated like new recruits, standing in line at the chow hall with the eighteen-year-old airmen recruits and sleeping in bunk beds in the barracks. It was an eye opener, immersing us in the working apparatus of the military.

Somewhere in the state of Missouri, likely in Joplin, our bus driver joined historic Route 66, the classic federal highway running from Chicago to Los Angeles. We would follow 66 all the way to Santa Fe.

After pulling on to Route 66 and knowing that our destination for the evening was the field house at the University of Tulsa, our driver announced that he had a big surprise for our lunch stop. Just before noon, our travels passed through the center of the tiny town of Commerce, Oklahoma, population 938—including pets—when suddenly the driver pulled off to park next to a small roadside diner. Upon entering, to our amazement and glee, this little diner had been decorated like a shrine, honoring the small town's greatest hero, Mickey Mantle. This local boy was not only a world famous New York Yankee, likely the best switch hitter in the history of baseball, he was a veritable god to us. Was it possible that we were eating where Mickey had once dined? His pictures and autographs were everywhere.

After an evening at the University of Tulsa, we headed for an Air Force base near Amarillo, Texas. Early the next morning found us motoring through Tucumcari, New Mexico. Now the view of the country was changing fast, leaving a thought from an old movie cliché, "Toto, I've a feeling we are not in Kansas anymore!"

The real eye opener, however, was yet to come…the rugged Sangre de Cristo Mountains of the huge Philmont Ranch near Taos, New Mexico.

Arrival at the ranch headquarters brought with it a decision. The bus was to be split into two camping/hiking groups, one to go north and one to go south. Frank and I talked, agreeing that if we split up, we would get to see the most of this wilderness; I would go to the north. Philmont is about thirty miles from end to end, covering almost 140,000 acres, making it one of the largest ranches in the country. We would have much to see and talk about later. A school bus loaded my group to the northern base camp where our group was to quickly discover that this was not just another Scout camping trip.

Indoctrination into this arid, high-altitude wilderness included several days of day hikes, horse rides near the northern base camp, survival training, and daily coaching about the new experience of thin air hiking, stressing the need for constant hydration. Once this orientation was completed, our group packed up everything, including a carefully divided ration of food, and began our weeklong trek towards the center of the ranch. Adult leaders took us down wilderness trails, purposely designed to make sure that at least once a day we passed a source of vital and safe drinking water. There were, however, no options for restocking food. By mid-week we began to feel hungry…very hungry. Shortages were now on everyone's mind as the adult leaders aggressively rationed the food, one day at noon handing out one measly apple per boy; this was lunch.

I carefully inspected my apple, taking only small bites, chewing them until only saliva remained, then biting into the core seeds and all, chewing and chewing until only a pulp remained also to be swallowed and finally sucking on the stem for the next hour. We complained, we whined, we pleaded, but in spite of our protests, the trek continued through the terrain of the rugged Sangre de Cristo Mountains. Never passing signs of human habitation, we became young, self-confident men. For the first time the ache of real hunger became a constant companion. Conversation about the strange and wonderful new rugged terrain returned over and over to the dream of a trip back home to the Hot Shoppes for a juicy large "Mighty Mo" cheeseburger.

One evening just before sunset, we were almost swept away in a gulch by a sudden flash flood. Another day found us at the top of a mountain with no shelter, exposed to a vicious thunderstorm, huddled behind a boulder, away from trees as lightning struck the ground violently all around our bedraggled little group. Prayers were being mumbled; all of the boys had now found religion.

Of all the learning experiences, one found its way into my character as a life event. The Scout leaders decided the boys of our trekking squad would all be peers: a leaderless group. The adult leaders would pass down the basic order: make camp, fix dinner, start a fire, and so on. As a group, the boys were then required to cobble together the assignments, demanding that volunteers step forward to perform chores. It took no time at all to see who the slackers were. One evening I got called out for slacking. It became a most embarrassing event, one that still replays in my memory. Now showing in vivid Technicolor and surround sound, "Bob the Slacker" starring…Bob. Those boys drove home a lesson, a lesson learned for life and one that I believe can only best be learned from peers, buddies, and brothers in arms, rather than from authority figures like parents or teachers or even Scout masters.

The leaderless group is, of course, a fantasy. There is no such thing. All leaderless groups quickly gain leaders. One person or two will always initiate the delegation of needed assignments to get the job done, often times without the group even noticing but sometimes with a bit of friction when two or more strong wills conflict. Here was another valuable life lesson. How is it possible to make yourself the group leader, or perhaps, do you feel more comfortable playing the follower?

Today the Boy Scouts have taken hard blows from society and the media, some deserved, most not deserved. The finger pointers, most of who never experienced a Philmont wilderness trek, have little conception of the life-altering, character-building experiences imprinted on young men at the knee of the mighty Sangre de Cristo.

At the end of our trek, Frank and I met up again, looking at each other and laughing about our new skinny bodies. Then it was back on the Trailways bus for the five-day journey back to Alexandria.

The Faithful Sextant

Passing through childhood into our teen years, the tests and games became more organized with teams, including uniforms and rules, sponsored by schools and little leagues. We thought the testing was getting harder, yet we had not even begun our adventures with automobiles, guns, scuba gear, and real airplanes. It has occurred to me that perhaps we never quite learned where to set a limit. We had not learned how to just stop. Looking back on those experiences, I narrowly avoided death several times in our adventures, a trend holding ominous overtones for the future.

Life in Alexandria for me was just grand. School was full of plain kids as well as wealthy kids and kids whose parents were congressmen, senators, and generals. Alexandria was a great city. Seeing what a great place this was to raise a family, my father used his magic with the government, managing to make his next three promotions become flip-flop moves to and from Washington National Airport and downtown Washington, DC. This resulted in my being able to live in one place from the fifth grade through high school graduation, indeed a charmed and lucky life for a teenager. My mother pushed me to have good grades, and my father encouraged sports. These pushes were nothing, however, compared to the drive to keep up with Frank. This kid was born to excel in everything he did. As we graduated from elementary school at the end of our seventh year, the American Legion gave two awards to each class moving on to high school (no middle school in those days). There was a top award for academic excellence and a runner up award as second best. Frank won the top award and I won the runner up. As a balance to my disappointment my mother pointed out that no other child in our elementary graduating class had won any kind of American Legion Award except Frank and me.

The very next year my little brother, Jim, won the top award from the American Legion. Here was another source of dog-eat-dog competition. That smarty-pants younger brother of mine always got the better grades, going on a four-year run in high school with nothing but A's, never having a B grace his report card. He had his eye firmly on that grade centric reward system, eventually earning a doctorate degree from prestigious schools and a job as a university professor after a spectacular career on the dean's staff at West Point. All I had to point to was a full head of blond hair and perfect eyesight, two things gifted by luck of the genes while my brother Jim inherited Dad's bald head and my mom's poor vision…oh but we cannot have everything. Society typically values grades, brains, and titles more than blond hair and eyesight, and I always admired and respected and envied his accomplishments. I am not sure how he fared in fistfights!

High School

Frank and I began the eighth grade version of high school at Mount Vernon High School, a historic and eponymous Virginia school near George Washington's home. It was a beautiful brick building with a central cupola just like George's estate. This high school would be temporary. A bright, shiny new high school was being built near our neighborhood to be called Groveton; it would be ready for us as we became freshmen. We would be its first graduating class to have completed the full four years of classes.

The eighth grade year did seem like we spent a lot of time on school buses. Frank and I signed up for eighth grade football, both of us making the team, adding more stress to finding a way home after football practice in the days before activity buses.

More than just football and buses, this first year of secondary education held many changes in our lives. The newest and most monumental change was an old subject suddenly turned new; this new something was girls.

We knew about girls; we knew they were different...we had sisters after all. Growing up, we could not figure out what good a girl was. They couldn't run very fast or block an opponent in football or make a mud fort or throw a baseball hard...just what good were they? They were always selected last when choosing up sides for baseball and never asked to play football.

Stepping back in time to the pre-high school, early-teen days, the era that saw us on bicycle or foot—still mobile but with a shorter terrorism horizon—things had begun to change. We had by now begun to graduate from threatening the neighborhood to a revised worldview in which our evening roaming took us to spots where those pretty thirteen-year-old girls we had met in school hung out. This girl thing was for sure new excitement worth exploring, but without a driver's license and wheels, our scope was limited.

Franks' parents belonged to the Belle Haven Country Club, a spot within walking distance, so it was natural that we started seeing girls as frilly things at the little cotillion dances. It was not long before we moved on to the rec-room make-out parties found up the hill from the country club in Belle Haven. Dancing close to a soft, sweet-smelling girl released electric jolts. It felt so wrong, it felt so new, it felt so good. And then one evening came the first kiss. Lying awake later that night, sleep would not come, turning over and over at the wonderment of this new sensation.

The cause of it, the release from it, the understanding of it eluded me and there was no way to go to Mom pleading for guidance. Not long after the kiss quandary came the first accidental orgasm. Wow! Splurge! What the hell was this white, gooey, warm Elmer's glue ejecting as if it had a mind of its own. And wow again, never ever before had there been an experience of feeling as if a wave had crashed overhead, surrounding me in warm pleasure. Let's try that again.

What a turn around. Suddenly girls went from being picked last for baseball to being picked first for everything. Had the boy world turned over in its orbit?

As if to add momentum to the already speeding hormones, in the last year of our primary schooling, our seventh grade teacher, Miss Hite, a single lady not long out of Teachers' College, used youthful initiative to bend curriculum rules by having boy/girl dancing lessons in our classroom during the last hour of the day. This occurred several times a week. She brought in a 45-RPM phonograph to play Top 40 music both fast and slow, planning to teach us to jitterbug to the fast rock and two-step to the slow ballads. Slow dancing, the innocuous way adults rubbed together before kissing and whatever happened after that…she expected us to do that? Did the school board know about this?

The speeding bullet train had just stopped and told us to step on. Next stop, dating and adulthood. What did this mean?

It meant that all my little infatuations better have more to them than just daydreams. We all wanted to have a special girl, what the older kids called a girlfriend. I had thought about this and had decided in the sixth grade that Audrey Lynn Androus should be my girlfriend…but she never knew. Then in the seventh grade I made a change; it would be Katie Avery. She never knew either. And now I might just have to slow dance with Katie. Uh-oh, this might not go so well. How could I ever ask Katie to dance?

Here was the problem in condensed form: Boys and girls were being asked to touch each other and not in the normal way. This would not be the same as tapping her on the shoulder to ask for a pencil. This dance thing, especially the ballads, required that a guy actually look the girl in the eye and try to think of something to say. Then there was the touch. Touch…that enemy of bravado, of daring, of bluster with all of its codes and conventions and covenants. I had never held a girl's hand before, at least not with intent and with her permission. When it did finally happen, it turned out that some of those tender little hands were clammy, one or two were drenched in sweat, some hot and some dry, some were shaking, some were clenched and in an unexpected surprise, one or two hands were very normal, confident, and bold. Touch was scary; touch was new turf; touch did not come with a rulebook like baseball.

Several of the guys sat in the back row and refused to budge. Miss Hite let them stay. The girls uniformly participated, even if it meant dancing with another girl. Upon the command for the boys and girls to partner up, panic invaded the room. Guy talk had already mentally picked the one or two most desirable girls in the class, but shy little sheep that we were, finding the courage to walk right up and ask one of these princesses to dance was just too much.

Here, playing sticky in my mind is a vivid memory from one dance lesson afternoon. Karen Gravelle, a tall lanky girl, walked right up to me and asked if she could have the next dance. For the last two years, Karen had sat directly in front of me, assuming the full role of flocked wallpaper in my little boyhood world. And now she stood with imploring big eyes, hoping against hope that I would not embarrass her, nodding that it was okay. If she only knew how scared I was. Karen was several inches taller, a brilliant student, and a very attractive girl…why would she ever ask me to dance. She broke the ice for me.

Then I asked some of the sweaty-palm girls to dance, and then at the next slow dance, I asked Katie.

Then an unexpected thing happened after one or two sessions, the first part of the real learning experience of those lessons: the picture-perfect little Becky Thatcher turned out to be sort of a dud. Girls that we thought of as *one of the guys*, the ones that were picked to play baseball, the ones full of vitality and laughter, suddenly were soft and smelled good once your arms were around them for a slow dance. Now we were learning something that might be important for the rest of life!

Both Karen and Katie had confident, relaxed, normal hands.

Looking around the classroom in those first afternoon dance sessions, there was one more group of students, mixed boys and girls, who did not participate. These were the no personality, no confidence, no gift-of-good-looks group, huddled together on opposite sides of the classroom. These were the students who went on to become doctors, economists, and supreme court justices, along with a couple of hermits.

Moving up to the eighth grade, the school board had decided to ease the innocent lambs into high school by scheduling subject matter teachers in hour-long classes in the morning, followed in the afternoon by the elementary class format called ESSO, where one teacher would bore us to death for three straight hours, simulating, we supposed, some sort of transition from primary to secondary education. Again, thanks to alphabetical seating, Karen Gravelle sat directly in front of me for the tedious ESSO class. The non-vision of her as sixth grade wallpaper was now replaced by captivation and fascination, all because of touch: that enemy of not seeing, that nemesis of not caring. Now I had fallen in love with Karen... whatever that meant.

Today Karen is known as Dr. Gravelle. She is a well-known author of books written for young adults about growing up. She lives in New York City. Kate is now Dr. Avery, PhD economist. My thinking that only no-confidence, brainy kids went on to become smart and successful was also wrong. I had so much to learn about life, so much to learn about the roles we were to play and who might make that perfect mate for life.

Freshman year brought with it a wholesale move into our shiny, wet-paint-on-the-wall, unfinished sports facilities high school named Groveton. The school board had decided to leave the senior class to graduate at the old school, so we would have no seniors for the first year. That sounded great, until we realized that there would be no seniors on any of the teams. The varsity football team was perfect that year; we did not win one game. It was a strange year of change and newness and it went by very fast.

The summer following frosh year was to bring monumental change: change propelling us into maturity, into adventures never dreamed of, into a vastly expanded world of friends and girls.

This epic change was brought about by the laws of the Commonwealth of Virginia, which in 1957 allowed unrestricted drivers licenses to be issued to all juveniles over the age of fourteen. Thus it happened that one week after our side-by-side fifteenth birthdays, Frank and I were seen sprinting down to the

DMV together to take the driver license test. We might have bilged a Latin II vocabulary test, but there was no way in hell the DMV test would be flunked. We aced that little state–sponsored, bureaucratic trial, becoming licensed drivers before we were Gillette shavers... did this ever expand our world!

As a birthday present, Frank's parents bought him a used '55 Ford Fairlane ragtop. Boys being boys, our first challenge was to see how fast his Ford would go. The Fairlane came with the standard 272 cubic inch "Y" block V-8 and a two-throat carburetor. It was not going to beat many cars at a traffic light. We decided to pool our money that fall and order an Iskenderian racing camshaft and a Holly four-barrel carb. We had no idea what we were in for. A self-trained mechanic, my father agreed to let us use our family garage and tools.

Our huge overhaul dragged into the cold weather, but we got the car back together and running. The arrival of spring saw us heading over to the closest drag strip in Manassas, Virginia. The Ford never beat many hot-rods, but a boy learns a great deal about autos when he tears one down and puts it back together.

In addition to newly found four-wheel mobility, our social circle was now expanding in other ways. Both of us were honor society students, but to my knowledge none of the other nerdy honor society students hung at the drag races. Only the "hoods" and "JDs" (juvenile delinquents) raced cars. And we were just exploring the new wonders of the world of teen life.

Many years following our high school adventures, Francis Ford Coppola produced a low budget movie titled "American Graffiti." Even though this movie was set in the central valley of California (actually shot in Petaluma and San Rafael), it captured the essence of our weekend social life. The movie had Mel's Drive-In as the focal point to the social life of these California kids. We too had a drive-in named the Hot Shoppes. The resemblance of our drive-in to Mel's Drive-In was incredible. Years later I liked to think that Frank and I resembled the "Graffiti" characters played by Richard Dreyfus and Ron Howard (what chutzpah!). We moved easily between the "duck tail" crowd or the "Pharaohs Gang" from the movie, and the nerds and the rich kids. Having good grades, parents who let us use the family wheels, and participation in every major varsity sport gave us every advantage a 1950s teen could want.

With wheels, our newly automotive-centric world took us first to the drive-in. This drive-in scene was further enhanced in early 1958 by a new, cheap hamburger joint that opened about a mile from our high school. Sporting giant yellow arches, clearly visible from way up US Route One, this new hamburger joint was called McDonalds. Not only was this place fast, but a Coke, hamburger, and fries cost forty-nine cents, a cheap meal that fit just perfect into our fifty-five cent lunch money allotment—a marketing coup not overlooked by Ray Kroc. By the year 2015, McDonalds was reported to have over 36,000 hamburger outlets worldwide; the new one down the street from our high school was one of the first thirty ever opened. McDonalds was nice for a cheap in and out, but it was not a real drive-In. A real drive-in was the Hot Shoppes in downtown Alexandria.

Hot Shoppes, in a parallel universe to Mel's Drive-In from *American Graffiti*, was the literal expansion of a hot dog stand and the first big endeavor by the Marriott family before they ventured into the hotel business. Soon these drive-in restaurants were strung around the Washington, DC area as if Willard Marriott had received orders from a pimply-faced god to serve the teens of Washington, DC. A chef for the Marriott family had designed a double decker burger served on a sesame seed roll with a remarkable secret sauce; naming the whole thing the "Mighty Mo" after the battleship of the same nickname.

Approaching weekends sent my digestive juices flowing in anticipation of the taste of a "Mighty Mo." (A McDonalds franchisee blatantly stole the Mighty Mo sauce formula to create the Big Mac in 1967). The Hot Shoppes was where you showed off your (Dad's) car, celebrated the football or basketball game, and let the other guys check out the new girl in your life while she flaunted her new boyfriend with wheels to envious girlfriends. It was also the staging point and debriefing area for many other activities such as a "parents-out-of-town" rec-room party or scoring a six pack of beer over in the Negro part of town or often times setting up a drag race on a lonely back road. Drive-in life was running between cars, pestering the over worked/under tipped car-hop gals, bumming money for some food, all the while enjoying the new rock and roll blasting from the car radios at every parking place. No story of the coming of age of the kids of the 1950s is complete without including the story of the revolution in popular music. The drive-in and the music were just one big coming attraction for the movie *American Graffiti*.

The War had changed the world in ways too numerous to count; we determined to change it our way. We probably did not realize it at the time, but one change we could influence, even at our age, was music. And change it we did! The mushy ballads of Nelson Eddy, Perry Como, and a host of big band singers did not speak to us... they spoke to our parents. We had discovered a unique consolidation of Jazz, Hillbilly, Country, Negro Spiritual, American pop, and the bee-bop of the '20s. Bill Haley added big sound drums in the driving "Rock Around the Clock" and Jerry Lee Lewis pounded the piano. This music had a dance beat that our parents could not keep up with.

Missed by almost everybody, another sea change came with the end of the war. Electronics wizzes put their peacetime talents to work making this music come to life. Stereo was invented, Hi-fi was developed, long play records made of durable plastics showed up, and the car radio came to life with push buttons, multiple speakers, and transistors that would not drain the car battery. Our new pop music was affordable; it was everywhere we hung out; it sounded great, and it had our unique signature.

The love song or ballad also had new champions. Mixing the Negro blues singer with the simplicity of country lyrics over top of a Southern gospel background, created a sound new to everyone. A Mississippi boy named Elvis was right there with the talent to wrap all that up in one package.

Small radio stations were popping up everywhere, and they

needed a sound to make them different. The owners and advertisers on these stations may have cringed when a newly hired disc jockey found records from the Sun Records studio in Memphis, featuring a white boy who sounded Negro, or a Negro boy who sounded romantic or an older Bible thumping pianist who on his third marriage said I do to his thirteen-year-old first cousin, but they loved the ratings when every kid in the county was tuned to their station. So the owners turned up the power at the station and hired even stranger DJs.

Parked at night with our steady girlfriend on a lonely road, radio button set for a station a thousand miles away, found Wolfman Jack howling over the airwaves, playing pop music tuned to the very thoughts bouncing around in our hormone-driven teenage minds. Singers like Jerry Butler, the "Iceman", singing "For Your Precious Love," harmonized with the crickets chirping in the distant, sultry evening air. The Dubs' incomparable doo-wop version of "Could This be Magic" set the stage that no teen lovers could resist. Why, it felt as if these guys were saying, "Go for it; you can unhook that bra strap with one hand."

We began to think we were really hot shit. Our music had taken over the radio almost completely and then it took on the black and white family entertainment box of evil: the television. Ed Sullivan looked as if he might just throw up as he introduced his prime time variety television show audience to Elvis and his wiggling hips. What delight for my generation to see the way in which our music revolution caused so much alarm to the authoritarian generation: our parents and teachers.

It is impossible to separate my generation of the late 1950s from this music transformation.

The music revolution served as a backdrop for all of the other new experiences of my teenage life. Neither Frank nor I had any real inclination to take up any kind of musical instrument, though we loved the sounds. Our euphoria was found under the Friday night lights of the football field dressed in uniforms, with war paint, shoulder pads, and shoes with steel cleats, with an obvious intent of making some guy on the other side bleed. Playing a saxophone brought no danger or thrill of victory that we could see. The arrival of this new thing called rock and roll served us well as the backdrop for our adventures, where there was something new to titillate emerging teenage hormones every day...like fast cars and girls.

At about the same time as the transition to being a licensed driver of vehicles, our interest in girls went into full bloom; it was time to find a steady girlfriend. Even with cars, our girl challenge was still locally focused, aimed at the beauties living up the hill in Belle Haven. Not all of the Belle Haven (BH) girls were private school debs. For instance, one Belle Haven gal at Groveton, named Pam Dickson, soared in popularity by hosting parties after every football game in the downstairs rec-room of her parent's mini mansion.

As the sophomore year started (our first as drivers) and as Pam's post football parties became a frequent event, it was clear that I had taken a real liking to Pam, and I know that she liked me. But getting this romance thing going was all new to me. Pam and I went back and forth and back and forth...would she...wouldn't she? She would play kissy face, but she was not letting any guy get past first base, in guy terms. I just could not get a relationship started with this gal. By our senior year, Pam seemed more than ready to get serious with me, flirting and flipping her very cute eyes at me often in class, but it was way too late as I was "pinned" to a pert sophomore (soon to be introduced).

Many years later a funny story came back to tickle me; a story about Pam and me.

While serving in the Navy Reserve, another Lieutenant named Ron Goode and I had become close friends. Ron had started his own real estate development business in Washington, DC, where soon enough he was making big bucks. His newfound wealth sent Ron house hunting in my old neighborhood. Here he moved up the social ladder as he found and purchased a large Belle Haven house. In a never-to-be-lived-down opportunity of irony, Ron had bought *the* house where Pam had lived during our high school years, the very house where many a post-football-game party had been held.

Later, while doing remodeling, Ron had torn out floorboards in the basement rec room, the precise location of many a Friday evening post-game party. To his shock and amusement, he found a used condom apparently stashed under this flooring many years earlier by young lovers in a big hurry. Having heard of my youthful party night lusting after the young girl who previously lived in this house, Ron's exquisite sense of humor shifted into high gear. Several social situations presented humorous opportunities allowing him to hold court with the story that the source of this love-sock just might have been me banging Pam on the floor of the rec room and hiding my used rubber under the floorboards. Everyone enjoys a caught-in-the-act revelation. Little did he know, humorous story or not, just how remote were the chances that the lovely Pamela and myself ever had sex, much less that her perfumed and powdered naked princess ass ever touched cold floor boards down in that rec-room. Everyone had a good laugh except me.

These little growing-up parties were fun, but on the whole as our sophomore year began, not much serious was shaping up. I was perplexed; here I was a football stud, first-string defensive captain junior varsity, with the use of a car. Additionally, as the oldest child, there would be a one-year grace period without a sibling challenge for car sharing. My grades were good, teeth straight, hair blond, eyes blue, and except for a pimple or five, what was the problem? All of this manifest charm (well, maybe kinda average), it was hard to figure why I did not have a steady girlfriend. Maybe, just maybe, I needed to find someone new.

As football season ended and basketball games took over Friday night lights, my school day had slipped into a routine. The start of a usual day found me sitting with my buddies, Charlie Strauss (aka Fuzzy), Steve Lewis, and various other football guys, in the school lunchroom. Here we had a little breakfast, spun yarns about football and cars, and checked out the new talent in the eighth grade:

little sheep trying to adjust to a lunchroom full of upper-class wolves. The northern Virginia education system had still not begun middle schools, continuing to inject eighth graders directly into the lion's lair of senior high school. These innocent lamb coeds were thought to be easy pickings for sophomore boys using our crass motto, "If they are old enough to bleed, they are old enough to butcher."

One morning, across the lunchroom strolled a drop-dead-gorgeous new face escorted by her plain Jane wing-lady. We snagged both to sit at our table where we learned that they were indeed eighth graders. The looker introduced herself as Carole Pate. As the class bell rang and the two gals ran off, one of the guys at our table jumped up and called dibs on Carole. In guy parlance this is just like being the first guy to call "shotgun"—for reserving the front passenger side car seat—but as I sat there after the other guys had departed, I had already made my mind up that this was not the same as calling shotgun.

That afternoon, during the mindless rote of delivering newspapers—a better time even than sitting on the toilet to hash out matters of great import to my squalid life—it came to me that the next morning, not the next afternoon, I was going to break out of my submissive character; I was going to break "first dibs" rules; I was going to ask Carole Pate to the Friday night basketball game.

So okay, it took all morning the next day to fuel my courage, but just after lunch I walked right up to Carole and asked her to the Friday night game, figuring that there was little to lose, as she likely would turn me down, saying that she already had a date. Instead, she looked me right in the eye and said, "I would love to go. Pick me up at six."

I was stunned...I was elated...I did not even notice the lack of hesitation as this innocent little eighth grader took control, issuing orders to the upper-class idol to " pick me up at six," not "Would it be okay if you picked me up at six?" or "Sure, what time would you like to go?" Oh, but how the phrasing of our language tells so much about who believes they are in charge.

I picked her up and we went to the game where we had a good time as our basketball team won a rare game. After the game, in the crush of folks leaving the gym, she grabbed me by the hand, leading us outside. She suddenly turned, looked me square in the eyes, and blurted out, "Take me to the Hot Shoppes, I am famished."

I had already hoped against hope, that I could persuade her to do this, and now she had just fallen into my clever little trap. Showing up at the drive-in escorting a good-looking girl was the ultimate after-game coup for high school guys. But once again I failed to note who was falling into whose little trap. Unnoticed, Carole's take-charge personality was leading this parade.

Later, as we devoured two Mighty Mo burgers, she asked me how I felt about dancing. I bluntly told her that when it came to a "red-dog" pass blitz as a linebacker on the football team, I was pretty good, but that my dancing was pathetic. She told me that she had been taking dancing lessons for over a year and that she would be glad to give after-school lessons at her house. In fact, to make it more fun I could bring Fuzzy and Steve along as well.

I got very little sleep that night. *This gal is no normal shy, unconfident eight grader* I realized as I tossed and turned. *And, oh yeah...I have no intention of inviting Fuzzy or Steve to come along for anything involving Carole.* I knew better than to suggest dancing lessons to Frank; he would have laughed me out of the room.

Monday morning in the school lunchroom, facing the crowd knowledge that I had been seen out on a date with the lovely Carole Pate, the group informed me that I should not get too comfortable, as one date did not mean that Carole was taken. Shortly in walked the lovely Miss Pate, directing her smile and curvy hips right over to our table. She sat down next to me and began to tell the guys what a great time we had at the game. That was an ego booster! Then my heart sank as she looked at me and asked, "Bob, you did invite Fuzzy and Steve over for dance lessons didn't you?"

Crap, now the cat was out of the bag. Fuzzy immediately jumped on this idea, saying that he could drive over any afternoon. Steve looked about as excited as if he had just learned of a pop-quiz in Latin Class, but he still said yes.

We did dance lessons at Carole's house several times, with Carole paying most of her attention to me, sending Steve and then Fuzzy off to the showers early. It turned out that the warnings about Carole were toothless; she wore my letter sweater for the next three years! Soon enough, she even informed me that we were "pinned." My defiance of the guy code caused some minor tension in the breakfast group, but it was soon overcome when all of the guys found other attractive girls interested in dating a football player. Fuzzy and Steve were still the best friends a guy could have; the lesson having already been learned never to trade a long-standing guy-friend for a fickle dating relationship.

Frank and I never bumped heads over girls. He began dating a cheerleader named Ellen Shapiro our sophomore year. Ellen came from a family that was very different than Frank's or mine. Frank's father was one of the nuclear physicists from the Manhattan Project who had been in on the ground floor of designing America's first atomic bomb. Frank's mother was a medical doctor and champion swimmer.

Ellen's parents were artists, living in a unique modern house featuring a look I was to later learn mirrored a Frank Lloyd Wright design. I think I remember that they belonged to a Unitarian church—whatever that was. That summer one of Frank's uncles, keying in on Ellen's last name, asked him if he was dating a Jewish girl. He spit his accusation out something like, "You datin' a Jew, huh?" I could tell by this man's tone of voice that being Jewish was not good, but I didn't understand why. The only Jewish person I had ever met was a girl in our class at school named Joan Sissman, and she was a jewel: an active, smart, caring gal, always a welcome fit to our crowd. We stood up for Ellen, informing Frank's redneck uncle that she was Unitarian, and the matter was dropped.

Growing up in the South, kids learn their prejudices early. I could never understand what difference it made in what tray a person dropped their donation each Sunday. Mandatory attendance at Sunday church service had become near torture for me. My brother and I shared a large afternoon paper route that reverted to a morning paper on Sundays. This meant dragging our young butts out of bed on cold Sunday mornings at four, jumping back in bed for an hour to be again rudely awakened by our mother to clean up for church. I just could not see the point of it all as I sat on the hard pew bench dreaming of being back in my warm bunkbed. What difference did it make which one of those churches a person chose, they were all a pain. Here was another childhood lesson to stick with me for the rest of my life as I separated strong beliefs in a Supreme Being from church dogma.

Frank, Ellen, Carole, and I became very close.

There remains with me until this day one very vivid memory of a cold winter evening following a heavy snowstorm. With schools shut and roads barely passable, Ellen called Frank, inviting Frank, Carole, and me over to her house for nighttime sledding if we could get there. The severe weather led both Frank's parents and mine to use commonsense and prohibit our use of a family car, but this was not going to hold us back. The two of us grabbed our sleds and headed for Carole's house. Putting our risk-taking teenage minds to the problem at hand, we came up with a plan. Taking our sleds to the nearest main road, we lurked next to a stop sign. Although the roadways were covered in a thick sheet of compact snow and ice, cars with good snow tires or chains were still out and about, even making it up the long hill to the bluff where Carole lived. Upon finding a car going in the right direction, we slid our sleds out on the snow-covered street behind the car, ducked down beneath the driver's vision, and hooked our arms around the easy to grab 1950s-style rear bumper, taking a nice sled ride up the hill.

A few cars later we had covered the two miles to Carole's house, where we picked her up and slid downhill about two miles to Ellen's house. That evening we played in the snow near Ellen's house and later enjoyed hot chocolate followed by an hour or two of soft music and romance. I left in the wee hours to pull Carole home by sled in the starlight, followed by a blazing ride downhill from the bluffs overlooking the Potomac and Washington, DC, all the way to my house. What a night! It still stands out as one of my most romantic memories.

It would seem that Frank and I had hit the trifecta of steady sweethearts. A perky bundle of smiling energy, Ellen was the captain of the junior varsity cheerleading squad and well on her way to being one of the most popular girls in the school. In so many ways, Carole represented the polar opposite of Ellen. Carole Pate was a person who, for better or worse, shaped much of my future understanding of women. Here is the abbreviated story of Carole.

Carole

Carole had a late November birthday. It was a school enrollment, no-brainer dilemma for her mother: Hold her back a year, sensing that this would give her daughter a head start in development. And did Carole leap ahead of the acne-ravaged, training-bra-equipped, no poise, no self-confidence hoard of her female contemporary eighth grade classmates. No pimple had ever graced Carole's flawless skin; she had already graduated to a full "C" cup, and she had been enrolled in dance lessons for years, giving her body tone, grace, and poise. Even though she was only an average student, she was a 4.0, honor society master at skills not taught in the drab classrooms of high school. Her talent lay in an ability to flirt in many seductive ways as she looked deep into a man's eyes, telling him to control himself with the clarity of one who was in charge. She thought like a man, not a girl. She liked men and most importantly, she wanted to be noticed by men. Robert Browning most famously wrote, "Ah, but a man's reach should exceed his grasp, or what's a heaven for?" Carole was firmly footed in things more earthly than ethereal, never letting her reach exceed her grasp.

If a child's family environment found at home is everything, then forces far removed from those found in Ellen's, Frank's, or mine, shaped Carole's. Her father toiled as a low-level clerical worker, a plodder in some obscure back section of the federal government.

Her mother did not work and her little sister, Shirley, was to me just weird. They lived in Bucknell Manor, a Levittown type development of cookie-cutter, 1100 square foot, wood frame houses thrown up right after the War to accommodate the hordes of new government workers flooding out of wartime service. Carole's mother and father were salt-of-the-earth folks from the outer banks of North Carolina, plugging away in the American dream. Mom made a career out of shaping the lives of Carole, Shirley, and her husband, Carl. An oddity to me, Carl was never addressed as Carl by his wife, he was always just "Pate." "Pate, are you cutting the grass today? Pate, I need some bread and milk from the store." Pate this, Pate that! The poor bastard

I stuck with calling him Mr. Pate, a small show of respect he seemed to appreciate as if there were few other sources of such sentiment in that feminine-dominated household.

Her mom, always wearing the pants, crusaded weekly to move every stick of furniture to some new location in the living room, the only room other than the bedrooms and a kitchen in this bungalow. This was quite a feat, considering how little room she had to work with. Nevertheless, every week, the couch was on a different wall. Her need to move large pieces of furniture from one side of the room to the other just might have satisfied some deep-seated psychological need for her, but I am sure it sent a strong message to her daughters that she was no person to trivialize. Later, Carole was to tell me that time after time Mom pounded into her head, "Never and I mean never, let one of those boys have sex with you, making you pregnant, until you have in hand two documents":

(a) Certificate of Marriage and
(b) His financial statement

Knowing that the process of filling in the blanks for marriage and finances with a mature, wealthy man might require time and patience, Carole decided to draw her own road map of what Mom meant by "no sex." Since there was no question about her ability to control men, thus preventing any possibility of one of those pesky little sperms ever reaching her monthly egg, Carole accordingly decided to allow any other form of sexual expression as her personal pleasure saw fit. And see fit it did!

Carole joined the school dance team named the Golden Tigerettes and later went on to become the drum majorette for the school band. A smile always came to my face as out of the corner of my eye, I caught her sashaying through the school hallways, giving me a strange feeling of masculinity watching hormone-driven freshman boys drool as she passed. At gut truth level, however, there was never any doubt in my mind that I hardly possessed superior masculinity, money, wit, personality, or other chick-magnet qualities to attract a superstar girl. I was just an average guy learning that persistence and determination can count for a great deal, and determined I was.

Carole wore my letter sweater most days and we became known as a "couple." However, with her strong personality and my determination, there were bound to be sparks.

Saturday, October 3 of my senior year, a hot and sultry early fall Virginia day, our football team took the home field, playing an early afternoon game against a new rival, James Madison High. The coach figured that JMH would be an easy game, and after pleading my case as a departing senior, he put me in to play both offense and defense, a wonderful experience sure to leave a guy drained. Meanwhile, up in the stands, Carole, along with her fellow Golden Tigerette Baton Corps team members, cheered on both her boyfriend and the team. Coming off the field drenched in sweat late in the game, I grabbed a ladle of drinking water from the team bucket, swished it in my mouth, and spit it out behind the team bench in front of the hometown stands. This was what we always did in those days; the coaches forbade the drinking of water…it would give you cramps (sports medicine later reversed that thinking). Behind Frank Packer's fine quarterbacking, we won the game sixty-one to nothing. Later, after showering and changing out of the football uniform, I met Carole in the parking lot to head for the drive-in. She was furious, and it was written all over her face. I was thinking, *what the hell, we had humbled the other team in what I thought was the best game of my high school life. Where is the congratulatory hug?*

She squinted at me demanding, "Don't you *ever* spit water on the ground in front of me. You embarrassed me to tears. What an uncouth thing to do. If you ever do that again, we are through."

I was suddenly mad. It sounded like she was offering a choice between football or her, so I told her to call me when she grew up and walked off.

We both suffered, but two weeks later, everything was forgiven.

Like all immature affairs, there were times when Carole and I would have a fight and agree to date others. When word spread that the lovely Miss Pate was back on the market, it upset the male equilibrium of our school. To the great dismay of the male-bachelor, high school herd, Carole usually found some older guy who had passed through high school some time back. These breakups always treated me harshly. As I stumbled around to find a new lovely to date, I was branded as Carole's ex. None of the high school sweeties wanted to invest time in me knowing that I would likely dump them in a New York second to get back with Carole. In practice, it turned out that this was always what happened.

Ginny Lynn Pierce, Karen Vest, and Jill Hutchins were top-notch ladies I managed to date during these breakups, later to conclude that any of these top personality gals would have made a better long-term partner than Carole. The moral found in those seventh grade dance lessons of not always picking out the most beautiful flower in the garden had not set in. In truth, however, unless some ailment or genetic flaw sucks the testosterone out of a young man (there are some like this!), valuing female traits promising a lasting mate is just not something that young men are predisposed to see. What the hell, I was still a technical (in legal terms) virgin and maybe that was the fault of it all.

In spite of hormones or young girl romance novel plots, a breakup between Bob and Carole had a chiseled in stone pending date. The second week of August of our dreamy senior summer was going to find me departing for New York to report to the United States Merchant Marine Academy. Although the practice is currently under attack, the five service academies have always had a no marriage policy for cadets and midshipmen, a policy which most of the guys secretly thought was okay as it made saying no to the amorous gal back home real easy. Carole was not a fan of this policy.

High school senior year ended with prom, graduation, and a wonderful summer until a totally unexpected and, for some family members, disastrous announcement from my father. The FAA had selected him for promotion and this time there would be no flip/flop back and forth between Washington, DC and National Airport; this time he was headed to Minneapolis. With one last trick up his sleeve, he was able to coordinate the move from Alexandria to Minneapolis to coincide with my reporting to the Academy in New York. In this way, the driving trip from Virginia to Minnesota could be by way of Kings Point on Long Island, New York, kicking their oldest son (me) out of the nest, so to speak.

My brother and sister were the two really getting screwed. My brother had been voted in as the vice president of the student body and would have probably been a football team co-captain. My sister had been voted into the number one sorority and had a trail of male suitors. They were two of the most popular kids in the school, and now they would walk into some strange high school in Minnesota expected to quickly put together alliances and friends to match those left behind. This is a tall order for teenagers.

The announcement of the move, when added to the austere rules of the service academy, really threw Carole for a loop. The way she saw it, I would probably not return to Alexandria ever again. With great emotion, I tried to convince her that I would return on my leaves from the Academy as there was an understanding with Frank's parents that I was always welcome to stay in his room, an offer which indeed I did later use.

Our last night together before our family departure to New York was like something out of a Greek tragedy. At the time it felt something like the gods had shifted the order of the universe, however, later I was to see the drama in a different light. Had I been a better student of Shakespeare, the oft quoted line from *Hamlet*, "The lady doth protest too much, methinks," might have come to my attention that fateful evening.

Sitting once again in the back seat of the family car as it moved off to a new home was most certainly a much different emotional experience for me than for my catatonic little brother and sister; I was headed off to a magnificent new life—I was leaving home. As our Chevy passed over the George Washington Bridge with a view of Manhattan and the huge ships in New York Harbor, my eyes were as big as tennis balls and my adrenalin-fueled imagination could not begin to grasp the wonders of this new world. Alexandria and even Washington, DC seemed so bush league; this was *The City*, soon to be my apple.

Arriving at the Academy, there was a formal check-in, a speech to the parents and family by the Admiral, and some warm goodbyes, all of which seemed to take only a few minutes. Then my mother, father, brother, and sister were back in the car in the parking lot heading for the front gate and a trip to their new home in Minnesota. At least now my brother and sister would have the backseat to themselves. As for me, I had a new guardian—he was an upperclassman. Pleasant is not a word I would use to describe the look on his face.

My graduation from Groveton and departure to Kings Point brought me the clarity that Carole was not going to wait four years for me to graduate from an institution whose refusal to countenance the other institution, that of marriage, was well documented and established. I believe that she was already mentally formulating a "Dear John letter," when a little twist of fate intervened.

In November of 1960, just as my plebe year got underway, John F. Kennedy was elected president. I quickly found out that one of the perks of being at a military academy was marching in at least one inaugural parade before you graduate. Not all of the academies bring their entire brigade or regiment to the parade, but since it was only a bus ride for our group the entire regiment was required to attend. We would ride a bus to Bolling Air Force Base, be berthed in an Air Force barracks, and the next day transported to the parade assembly area in downtown DC where the five federal academies would form the first five echelons of the Inaugural Parade. That evening after the parade, the cadets and midshipmen were invited to attend the inaugural ball with guests. Learning this, I quickly called Carole and asked if she would like to be my date for the inaugural ball, just the two of us along with JFK and Jackie. The answer to this question was quick and affirmative.

We had a wonderful evening at the ball, full dress uniform for me and dusted off prom gown for her, and indeed, the president and Jackie showed briefly. Following another impassioned goodbye, it would be many years before we saw each other again. Carole did send a "Dear John" letter to me shortly after the inaugural evening, and like most of the others received by midshipmen at the Academy, it was posted on the company bulletin board amid what was beginning to look like dead-letter wallpaper, for all to read. The letter toasted our relationship, an event likely well foretold, as I began the all-consuming task of making my way through the treacherous academics and regimentation of plebe year at a service academy.

Many years later, when I was in my '60s, I made contact with one of Carole's male classmates, who had found me on the Internet and was looking for information about one of my classmates. When the subject of Carole came up, he filled me in on stories I had never heard, stories that had taken place after my graduation and our breakup. From him I learned that Carole had targeted a new guy who had transferred in to finish his senior year at Groveton. There was a picture in the yearbook of Carole and this new transfer student named Jim Jones, arm in arm as who's-who in the homecoming king's court. I do not know any of the details, but Carole should have grabbed Jim, although he too had a flaw: he was going into the Marine Corps, heading off to Vietnam. Jim became arguably the biggest-name graduate of our high school, rising through the ranks to become a four star general in the Marine Corps, then later the commandant of the Corps and the 22nd national security advisor to the President of the United States, the first one to fill this position for President Obama. An occasion to get together with Carole did occur just after I returned from Vietnam. As fate would have it, I was between ships and Carole was between husbands. I traveled down from New York, and she became my escort for my first "formal" visit to Arlington Cemetery. Much more about that experience later.

Miss Pate was a beautiful lady destined to run her own life. Her goals were strong and important to her, but it seemed to me that they led her to the unintended consequences of failed marriages, no children, and a very lonely end to her life.

In September of 2006, Carole located my email address (never hard to do with my rare last name), sending me a note saying how nice it was after so many years to reconnect. She told me about her life along the outer banks of North Carolina while living life as an artist. Common to human nature, the real reason for her contact was found in the last paragraph, where she informed me that a backache had become more severe, leading to a trip to a doctor. His diagnosis had been a very aggressive pancreatic cancer, the same medical condition that had taken her father, Pate, at the young age of fifty-nine. She sadly notified me that the doctor had given her four to six months to live!

I thought I would hear from her again with a cancer update, but it never came. It turned out that she did not make even the four months, dying of cancer ten weeks later, all alone in an apartment outside Washington, DC two days after her 63rd birthday. She had no obituary, no funeral service, no memorial festivity full of friends, family, and well-wishers, and certainly no teary-eyed son or daughter or grandchildren. So unnoticed was her death that I only learned of her passing through a check of obscure social security records one year after her death.

I had always believed that Carole was my first love. That word loaded with all of society's imperatives implying marriage and baby carriage and damning invectives such as until death us do part. But I am not talking about that "love" word. Carole and I never got that far; others years later were to fill those roles. And in spite of both of us parting as sexual virgins, she will always be first in so many ways. She was the one who taught me to value any and all bonds with others and especially those who earn the position of loved one.

It seems so much more than unfair that she never had a four-year-old expectantly look up to tell her, "I love you, Granma," but then Carole always acted as if she knew where she was going and what was best. She taught me so much, and I left a large part of my soul alongside the trail we traveled. I will never forget her for that.

Joe

I met another guy just after the move to Alexandria who was also to become a close friend forever.

Moving into a new school is trauma for young students; our move from Kansas came with more than its fair share of burdens. Our nation's capital in the early 1950s was experiencing the most extreme part of the leading edge of the baby boom as new government workers flooded in to fill jobs in the post-war federal government expansion. The education systems of the suburbs simply could not build schools fast enough to meet this flood, leading to temporary school buildings surrounding the capital. South of Alexandria, next to the Potomac River, a large apartment complex named Belle View had been developed to house the increasing numbers of middle-class families who could not afford a single-family house or who were on temporary assignment. A school was being built on the west side of this development to serve both the apartments and the surrounding single-family homes such as the one just purchased by my family. Until this new elementary school was completed, our area would hold temporary classes in one of the apartment buildings that had been left vacant. This was the poorest excuse for a schoolroom I had ever experienced. There was no cafeteria; the students had to eat a brown-bag lunch at our desks.

By moving from Kansas to Virginia two months into the school year, my family had broken a cardinal rule of a kid's schooling. This poor timing sent me walking into a dingy classroom facing every student's nightmare, a room where all of the little fishes had "schooled" together with the ones they want to call friends.

The day I entered that classroom I would become either the new kid from Kansas City or a hick from the cornfields of Kansas; only time would tell. My first new experience came the second day when, as a relief from the brown-bag lunch routine, the teachers had planned for the class to have Mexican lunch day. Several parents had brought various casseroles of Mexican food, a serve-yourself lunch, which was laid out on tables in the classroom. I had never eaten Mexican food.

Waiting until near the end, I watched classmates in front of me select strange looking dishes while discussing what to put in this half-round thing they called a taco. As I stood at the taco table trying to figure out just what one did with this strange food, it must have started to look as if "hick from the sticks" was the winner. Suddenly, a guy walked up to me saying, "Hi there, my name is Joe. What's yours?" Thus it was that I met Joe Powell.

Joe made light of the foreign food saying, "Just stuff some of this and that in there," inviting me then to come sit near his desk where he introduced me to some of the other guys in the class. Whereas gaining admission to Frank's rat pack would require being tested, Joe was the kind of guy who brought you into his group with no questions asked. Joe was another natural born leader. Unlike Frank, Joe led people by gentle persuasion rather than Frank's smack-you-in-the-face-with-a-two-by-four style.

Moving to high school, Joe was not always leading the pack, but he was always nearby, lending a helping hand. Joe was an only child; his father a very high-ranking official—the assistant to the undersecretary of defense. His father would become our high school graduation speaker.

As an only child, Joe's perhaps over-caring mother had asked him not to play football. She was not entertaining the thought of her only baby becoming a cripple from playing some stupid high-testosterone sport. Years later, Joe's announcement to his mother that he was becoming a helicopter pilot in the Marine Corps must not have been her happiest day.

Failure to try out for the football team was not a killer for guys, but if you wanted to be a player in the top tier of the high school social structure, you needed to have something to make up for not being on the team. Working his people skills, Joe had no trouble finding a niche in the clique. Come spring, Joe tried out for the track team, becoming the lead runner in the 880-yard race. Joe was the guy who always had a smile on his face, the guy who never spoke ill of anything. If you were walking through the cafeteria and Joe had a seat near him, he would wave you over. As we ended our junior year, Joe was elected to become the president of the student body. This rise to stardom never changed Joe's warm nature.

No high school is an egalitarian society. Perhaps this is part of the matriculation that prepares students for the real world. It is likely that the kids in what was sometimes considered the premier clique were not aware that any such thing even existed, there certainly was no membership card, but I will bet the ones who had to drive the school buses to help support their families knew who was in and who wasn't. Joe was guy who could walk out of an Honor Society meeting and later find time for the less gifted kids, a trait that got him the votes to be elected school president.

This clique thing in high school deserves a few more words. All high schools have cliques. Here is how one formed in my school.

One evening, early in our senior year, found five guys and two girls gathered at the house of one of the girls. The five guys were mostly the usual suspects from this story: Frank, Joe, Charlie (aka Fuzzy), myself, along with the most gregarious guy in our rat pack, a guy named Bob Purvis. The two gals were Katie Avery (my secret seventh grade girlfriend) and Beth Arbogast, who was pinned to Charlie and who I considered to be the smartest student in our class, and who was to become a lifelong friend. This ad hoc group had decided our high school lacked pizzazz and school spirit. It was our senior year, it had to be special, and we were going to change everything to make it special. Before the evening was over, we had drawn up a plan and given assignments to turn things around. Our school mascot being a Bengal Tiger, thus was born the "Bengal Seven." We were going to run a media campaign in the school hallways to get the students interested in supporting the school. Football season was just beginning, making that our first target. We would show everyone that the Tigers were not to be dismissed. The guys came up with an idea to leave a large message in lime on the opposing team's home field. This would boost spirit and be great fun.

The night before two away games at McLean High and Mount Vernon High found us sneaking into their football stadium to lime big messages on their field of play. Team spirit began to soar. Our fifth game of the year would be an away game against city rivals, the Hammond High Admirals. We drew up plans to visit them as we had with the others. This time a surprise was waiting.

The county school administrators, it turned out, were not at all happy about our little team-spirit activities. Pouring lime on their football fields was, in their eyes, the same as destruction of school property. And they knew how to read a football schedule; next time they would be ready. The administration decided to end this little graffiti spree and to do it at Hammond High. They called in police guards on overtime.

That Thursday evening as we crept up to the stadium, two policemen walked right past us as we hid behind a hedgerow, carrying two bags of lime. We were scared shitless, but after some discussion, a plan was hatched. With watches synchronized, Frank departed to the lower playing field carrying a garbage can, with instructions to make a diversion noise in ten minutes. Joe, Fuzzy, and I then hurried over to the main field where we began laying down our message ten minutes later.

Later that evening at the Hot Shoppes, we laughed ourselves

silly, even knowing that we had dodged a night in jail for vandalism. We decided the greater the risk, the higher the thrill.

We went on to mark-up all the other away games, in spite of the schools knowing that we were coming. We saved our biggest deal for our last home game.

Our football field formed a natural amphitheater, with a steeply sloping grassy hill, where the band often stood. Late in the evening two days before the big game, our entire group of seven crept in with buckets of premix concrete. A very large seven was dug into the hillside and filled in with concrete. By the next afternoon, our new monolith had set up very well, now serving as a permanent monument to our clique. It was a thrill the next day hear kids in the corridors gossiping and trying to guess who the seven were. I never shared our identity with anyone, including Carole.

Frank

Frank's experience with high school romance was very different from mine. One day at lunch and quite out of nowhere, he said, "I'm moving on from Ellen." I was shocked. Ellen was a small sprite of a girl with off-the-chart energy; she was stunningly cute, genius-IQ smart, and by far the "Miss Personality" winner of our school cheerleader squad. All of the guys in our group wanted an attractive, steady girlfriend, and having Ellen wear your letter sweater would have been an *exploit of legend* for any guy.

In spite of the legend of Ellen, Frank had decided that it was time for a breakup. He gave me this information, offering no explanation and with an implied imperative that no more discussion would be forthcoming. This led me to assume that something heavy-duty had to spinning in the background…perhaps something like sex. Many of us who had been in committed romances for lengths of time had only one last step in our relationship. In 1950s teenage parlance this was known as "going all the way." You needed no more explanation than those four words. Everyone, and especially the girls, understood where "all the way" and that was where all the boys wanted to "be going." For the teenage girls, their mothers most likely had not braved the dreaded "birds and bees" conversation; nevertheless, these mothers had been clear on what "all the way" meant. One other thing was obvious, in rural and even suburban schools, birth control techniques were non-existent. Two other things were almost certain in those days. First, all the young boys wanted to brag that they were getting laid, and second, it was possible that one or two young girls were going to get pregnant.

The school system had just started teaching Sexual Education (SexEd), but the only thing accomplished in those classes was a dose of embarrassment for the physical education teachers. These educators were usually newly minted teachers who thought they had been hired to teach soccer and to check that students showered after mid-day exercise. Instead, they now found themselves with no training, answering questions about sex movies, knowing the only outcome was a hallway of tittering students charging off to warn later classes what was coming. The school board had mandated that the sex movie viewing audience would not be coed. This meant that the same movie seen by the girls came with a very different interpretation by the female teacher than the same movie seen by the boys and interpreted by the football coach. I know this to be true as Carole and I had great sport as we laughed about the same information being dished out with different interpretations depending on whether the student got the boy version or the girl version. Carole's mother had taught her daughter in depth about the birds and the bees. On this subject, Carole was an A+ student, though I never, ever admitted this to her.

This new education in no way changed the "all the way" goal. For the teenage boy, pulling "Mr. Happy" out of the Garden of Eden at the last second just before he erupted was still the accepted way of preventing pregnancy. Mr. Happy, a frisky organ with a mind of his own, was, of course, never in favor of this tactic.

Just the day before Frank's announcement, one of the Bengal Seven guys sat next to me in the cafeteria when in walked his cute-as-a-lollipop girlfriend. Approaching our table, clearly she had a grin from ear to ear as she whispered big news into his ear. He told us later—as a result of badgering from the boys—that she had just come from the showers in the girl's locker room after PE with the news, much to her anxious relief, that her period had whooshed out bright red in the shower, somewhat the same locker room scene made famous by Stephen King in his blockbuster book and movie "Carrie." My friend's expression of not having to face early fatherhood was etched deeply into the look of amazed relief on his youthful face.

Talk about implied sexual conquests often came up amid snickers of disbelief, but direct specific information about details such as spooky missed "M" cycles were never discussed. Revealing deep personal information was believed to offer way too much leverage, perhaps impacting a guy's standing in the group. In spite of this widely held tenet, it was hard to hide the terror followed by relief upon learning that our friend had survived the missing menstrual period bombshell.

Frank never talked about his exploits. I had always assumed, from our years of close proximity double dating, that he got to first and second base all the time, with the implicit assumption that from the vantage point of second base, stealing third was easy and home runs were possible. However, in thinking back on life in those days, Ellen, just like my girlfriend, Carole, was never going to allow the tagging of home plate. Anyway, all of this was conjecture on my part and really none of my business.

It seems to me, however, that two things were in play for Frank. First, he wanted to get laid because listening to the stories it seemed that all of his friends were getting some—although he might have been shocked at how many implied that they were but, like me, were still waiting to join the virginity conversion club. And secondly, he was after all, Mr. Everything. Frank was the president of our senior class. He was the quarterback and captain of the varsity football team, captain of the baseball team, first-string varsity basketball player and the star of the pole vault on the track team. He was the only guy in our senior class to letter in four sports. He was in the sweetheart dance court, in the honor society, and on every committee known. For him, it was simply time to cash in on some of the chips from his hard work, and he was, after all, just another teenage boy full of curiosity and very active hormones.

With all of this working for him, and having been released from the steady girlfriend contract, he began swooping though the pretty and very eligible underclass coeds. Frank never told me if he was scoring home runs with these beauties, but I will bet he did his best to convince them to give one up for the team. To my knowledge, none of these gals stuck with him during his academy experience. He too would be attending a service academy where cadets were prohibited from being married. We would both leave our high school romances at home, although as we will see later, Frank was to come back and revisit GHS after Academy graduation.

After the Frank and Ellen breakup, it became unavoidable that Ellen and I would have some classes together, in addition to seeing each other in hallways and the lunchroom. Being the perfect lady, she tried very hard to stay friends with me, but this became a problem. What in the hell was I to do? Ellen either did not know or understand the "guy code." There was no way I could remain good friends with my good bud's ex. There was no way I could ask Ellen to sit next to me in the lunch room and then have Frank stroll in playing cute face with a pick-of-the-litter young co-ed. There was just no wiggle room to remain close friends with both. Almost sounds like the adult-divorce-friend split-up game!

Persistently one of the cutest and smartest (graduating third) gals in our class, Ellen graced the halls and led cheers on the sidelines of sporting events. I do not, however, remember her having a serious dating relationship after Frank. In the warm late spring days just before graduation Ellen sat next to me in a teeth-grindingly boring American history class, where she would ask me nice questions to which I would not reply, blow off the answer, or just make some half-assed response. What was I to do? I really wanted to take her in my arms, hold her tight, and tell her how special she was, but that just could not happen. Just before graduation, Ellen wrote the following in my yearbook—quoted here verbatim.

"Bob, It's been great for 4 years and remember the 10th grade! I'll even forgive you for all the hard times you and 'others' have given me. I still haven't figured out why! Well, good luck and success always!" [signed] Ellen W. (Witch) Shapiro.

Where did the term "witch" come from? If she wanted to make a point about my poor behavior, she certainly did.

Oh Ellen, I do so hold you dear and cherish you. You will always be on my very short list of folks to whom I owe my sincerest apology. You are one of the most quality folks to ever enter my life; it is beyond excuse that egotistical, immature high school boys treated you harshly. The time that Frank and I spent with you will always be special. As I traveled through life, waiting until my mid-thirties to settle down, there were at least three ladies who could have been Ellen look-alikes. Hmm, was there a message? In my fading memory, I wonder if Ellen ever forgot Frank. I certainly wouldn't.

The coming of age of Frank and Bob, two neighborhood kids learning the lessons of life, had been pushed into a higher gear by the teenage antics of high school life. But little did we know how soon things were to become so much more serious. Little did we know how little time remained!

Graduation

So this is how it ends. Stories near death say that your life flashes before your eyes. I don't see a damned thing. Nothing but dark and the stone wall...that damned wall reaching to eternity. All right, now I am scared.

Shut up. Just shut the hell up. There has to be a way out of this mess. What am I going to do with this water in the hose?

How about if you drink it? Just lean your head back below the hose, shut your eyes, and drink it. Just little sips. No gulps. Just drink it. Make your lips press hard on the hose; bite the mouthpiece hard and drink. There is no other world, there is just that water in the hose. Now drink you stupid bastard or die!

❈

A blossoming of high school senior year with all of its promises and advantages flew by in a rush of clear skies and smooth sailing. Playing in the background, however, was a tune sung by parents, teachers, guidance counselors, and well-meaning adults. The name of this tune was, "Where are you going to school next year?"

Frank and I, once again, were charging ahead, looking for the brass ring. A service academy looked really cool. The Air Force had started a federal academy just four years earlier in Colorado Springs, and this looked to be the coolest of the lot—you know, go fly fighter jets.

We both made application to all of the academies with particular emphasis on Air Force. Our congressman was very candid with us. He had already filled West Point and Navy applications with political nominations (very common in those days), and his one unselected nomination to the Air Force was likely to be a hard-fought competition. It seemed as if every young guy I knew wanted to fly aircraft. Later, it seemed strange that in light of my father's lifetime flying career, my brother Jim and I, the two kids raised flying small aircraft and playing in dark corners of airport hangars, did not become pilots. It turned out that Frank grabbed the Air Force Academy gold ring. Having my best friend snatch the one nomination did not rock me with disappointment; I was happy and proud for him, and as it was, I had other attractive options on the front burner.

Having learned that the country ran two smaller service academies, I had made application to the Coast Guard Academy and this other academy called the Merchant Marine Academy at Kings Point on Long Island. I learned that a Kings Point graduate would receive a commission as a Navy ensign and would be eligible to go to Navy flight school immediately as an officer. The Coast Guard Academy was a fine school, but graduation there offered only one choice: the Coast Guard. I covered myself by applying and being accepted at Virginia Polytechnic Institute (now Virginia Tech), the engineering school where my grandfather's brother, and the man for whom I was named, was a well-respected professor.

My congressman and senator both gave me nominations to Kings Point. Now the waiting began; would the Academy tender an appointment? At last it was clear that both academies and VPI had accepted me. Now the choice was up to me. Of the three, Kings Point offered by far the most options at graduation, making the choice to attend the Maritime Academy an easy one.

With the decisions made and appointments tendered, my senior summer took off in full force. Just before graduation, when honors were being handed out, Frank and I struck duality again. Two awards were given at graduation that year to the two seniors who had excelled at both academics and sports. Frank got one, and I got the other! This time our graduation award was shared equally.

At our insistence (pleading), our parents gifted Frank and me with a full set of scuba gear as a graduation present. This was an extravagant expense for my parents, but their relief at my appointment to a full scholarship school swung the deal.

Earlier in the year Frank and I had done some diving in flooded rock quarries in West Virginia with borrowed gear. Now we were fully equipped, salivating over underwater fortune hunting, and ready to do the deep dives. Confidence in our abilities was not a question; there was neither time nor perceived need for professional instruction or training.

Right after receiving our graduation gifts, I sauntered over to Frank's house to see what kind of excitement was being brewed. Very excitedly he let me in on a cracking good story circulating at the dive shop about a flooded quarry in West Virginia, a quarry that we had not visited. There was an enticing twist to this new quarry; it was said to be very deep and rumored to have bombs on the bottom. The story told of the WWII Navy testing Hedgehog depth charges in this quarry by dropping them from aircraft. Divers had reported finding parts of these depth charges on the bottom—an instant challenge to our boyhood-adventure-driven minds.

The Navy Hedgehog had a warhead on one end connected to a shaft equipped with a set of tailfins for guidance. Guys at the dive shop had said that the shaft with tailfins often blew off upon detonation. There just might be some of these tail fins lying around on the bottom. Finding a WWII bomb sounded like the kind of exploit to complete our senior summer. Stories about people being killed by abandoned WWII ordnance that came back to life were shrugged off. This could never happen to us.

The flooded quarries of West Virginia were old hat to us. The point where the Shenandoah River runs into the Potomac River, forming the far northeast corner of the state of West Virginia, harbored formations of archaic plinths of solid granite, allowing a quarry industry to thrive and supplying stones for the buildings of Washington, DC. After years of digging, these quarries became deeper and deeper. Many of them had hit the water table and flooded. The economics of the business dictated that at this point it was best to abandon them. With the mineral rights exhausted, the owners of these quarries turned the land back over to the local farmers, who seemed ambivalent about trespassing, granting us the go ahead for dangerous challenges packaged around a great swimming hole. Several of them were located no more than a long hour's drive from our homes.

Our unsupervised visits to these quarries had begun earlier in the year with several of our rat pack friends. The first trip in January, using borrowed gear, had even involved breaking through a thin layer of ice. Later that year, once the weather warmed, we would dive until the borrowed air tanks were empty, spending the rest of the day swimming and playing on the rocks. There was a choice of two flooded quarries, but our favorite had the advantage of easy access along a sloping road built earlier to allow trucks to enter. This ramp formed a sloping beach, which coincidentally was about fifty yards from a main rail line carrying passenger trains between Pittsburg and Washington, DC. Upon hearing an approaching train, we would hurry out of the water, drop our swim trunks, bend over and "moon" the passing train, offering a change in scenery to the passengers who had been looking out their windows at the pleasant West Virginia countryside. Ah, what great juvenile fun!

The rumor of WWII bombs involved a new quarry, allegedly located farther to the west, near Martinsburg. Another new twist was that while our favorite quarry ran about fifty feet deep in places, this new one was reputed to be much, much deeper. We immediately filled our twin tank sets and packed off the next morning, hoping to bring back a souvenir.

Following some searching up and down country lanes, we found the deserted and flooded quarry. These quarries were never marked, and technically, we were trespassing on private property. The owners of the land around these quarries began to have a dim view of city boys arriving with new fancy scuba gear once they realized they shared liability by allowing us to risk our lives on their property. Years and criminal negligence lawsuits later, all this diving was to be prohibited by those rotten, fun-destroying, law school grads. But that afternoon we were the only two people there.

This was going to be our deepest dive ever so we had taken special precautions. The length of time an air tank lasts is directly proportional to the depth of the dive, a dilemma we had foreseen by insisting that our graduation gifts be dual tanks. Additionally, we carried depth gauges and diving watches, allowing the calculation of time versus depth. And since it is always very cold in the dark depths, we would be wearing cold-water wet suits. This dive would take us to a depth where the water pressure would force carbon dioxide and nitrogen into the joints of our limbs, potentially causing the excruciating pain known as the bends. Anticipating this, we had calculated the needed stops during our return to the surface, allowing time for these gases to be absorbed back into the blood stream. Yes, this was going to be a whole new experience in the cold, dark unknown.

On a bright, sunny West Virginia summer day we arrived at the water's edge, double-checked our equipment, and mentally ran through contingencies. Next came the tedious chore of wedging into a form-fitting neoprene rubber wet suit, a pulling and tugging job aided by sprinkling talc powder inside the suit. The neoprene used in these thick rubber suits was imbedded with tiny air pockets, serving as insulation to protect us from the deep bottom cold—just like with the Styrofoam in your beer cooler. The small air pockets in the neoprene, however, made the suit much lighter than water, meaning that when a diver is wearing a wet suit, he would float on the surface rather than sink to the bottom, a problem overcome by wearing a belt of lead weights. Learning just how many lead weights to wear on the belt was a trial and error problem solved by each diver testing his own buoyancy until he discovered his best setup. This perfect buoyancy thing, however, was a nasty moving target because as the pressures on a deep dive compressed the neoprene, essentially eliminating its buoyancy, the result was more force acting to pull the diver deeper. There are a lot of changing things that can make a deep dive very hazardous.

Once into the form-fitting wet suits, the eighty-five degree summer day turned the diver into a "pig-in-a-blanket," heightening the sense of urgency to get under the cool water. As we stood chest deep near the exit ramp, completing our equipment protocols, little relief was offered by the sun-warmed surface water. But we knew that in spite of our current serene yet steamy conditions, it was going to be very cold and very dark where we were going.

Leaving the gravel entrance road, our descent took us farther and farther out and deeper into the large quarry. Somewhere near the middle, maybe 500 to 700 yards out from the entrance, our descent suddenly ended as we floated just above the bottom of the quarry. Here it looked and felt as if we were on the abyssal plain at the bottom of an ocean. I checked my depth gauge, noting we were 110 feet down and the bottom still sloped gently deeper. At this point we began moving laterally along the deepest part of the quarry. Unlike swimming horizontally in the middle of a column of water, a diver's instinct near the bottom is to walk along upright. This human instinct to walk when near a horizontal surface is silly and inefficient. Nevertheless, we walked—as best we could with frog flippers—farther and deeper into the quarry. The bottom was featureless except for an accumulation of silt. The crystal-clear water visibility was about twenty-five yards, except when our movement accidentally stirred up the silt on the bottom.

The world at this depth is unearthly, bearing no likeness to that sunny, calm, relaxing, summer day taking place a mere 120 feet over our heads. The compressed air we breathe has a very metallic taste. The sounds made by our regulators metering air from the high-pressure tanks, as we sucked in its life-giving gas, makes a new high-pitched, tinny sound. This is followed by a noisy exhale of the unwanted carbon dioxide as it pushes out the left side hose to escape behind our head in the form of large bubbles racing upwards to the surface while making strangely muted gurgling sounds. We now passed into a twilight zone. These new sensations were due to the tons of water pressing in on us, muffling all sound, changing the chemistry of elements, and trying to squeeze the life out of two young thrill seekers.

The human body is mostly solids and fluids, materials not compressed by forces at one hundred twenty feet. But where air-filled cavities exist in the human body, they become a problem. Air in these cavities is easily compressed, just like it had been compressed in our tanks and in our suits. Where these air sacs exist, they must be pressure compensated or they may bleed, burst, or become injured. Counter-intuitively, the largest of these sacs, the lungs, are the easiest to equalize. This happens as you exhale. The real equalization problem comes in the sinuses and inner ears. As we descend, there is constant yawning and squeezing the nose while blowing out, just the kind of things you might do by chewing gum while on takeoff or landing in an airplane.

As we descend, I glance down at the sleeve of my three-eighth-inch neoprene wet suit, noting that the pressure has compressed the rubber neoprene as if I were wearing only a thin dark sheet of paper. It is dark and very, very cold…warming sunlight up at the surface but a dim memory.

Continuing to move along the silt-covered bottom as it slopes deeper, the surroundings become darker and darker as the water depth blocks the sun's rays. Suddenly, as if coming upon a trail marker left by aliens, we spot a metal tube sticking out of the silt at a forty-five degree angle; this might just be it! Slowly moving forward so as to not stir up silt, we close in on this object until we can see fins on the end of a tube. It has to be the tail end of a Hedgehog. We look at each other, both thinking the same thing: *Is this an unexploded charge with a warhead buried in the mud?*

Again, staring at each other while making hand gestures, we try to make a decision about what to do next. Suddenly, Frank shrugs, reaching out for the tailfin of the bomb. I instinctively cover my face with both arms as if to protect vital body parts from the imminent explosion, soon bringing a smile to my face at the realization of the futility of this defense. Frank pulls on the fin tube, and it slips easily out of the mud, the warhead missing. I look deep into his facemask where I see a grin from ear to ear; a feat hard to do with your teeth clamped down on a solid rubber mouthpiece. My face was probably petrified, my heartbeat racing towards 200. Quickly my brain tells my heart and breathing to slow down, at a later time I will need that precious air I am gulping. A quick check of my diving watch validates the need to begin our return, so I turn and signal to Frank that it is well past time to leave.

It is clear that we have overstayed our bottom time, leading us to change our route back to the beach. Rather than retracing the lengthy winding gravel ramp, we decide to shortcut directly to the nearest sheer rock face of the side of the quarry. Once there, we will head to the surface and swim around the perimeter to the beach. Why we did not just decide to surface in the center of the quarry and snorkel back to the edge, I have never figured out, but our decision to cross the quarry on its bottom rather than on the surface will have dire consequences.

The traverse across the bottom to the vertical rock face takes about ten minutes. At the bottom of the sheer rock wall, we stop, do a thumbs up, and begin kicking to the surface. Frank is carrying the depth charge tail souvenir.

Ascending a sheer vertical rock face deep underwater is a strange sensation, as if we are rock climbers pulling our way to the top of El Capitan without ever touching the face. Try if you will, standing very close to the bottom of a twelve-story building and then turn your face upwards. Looking along the side of the building all the way to the top, try not to feel vertigo and try not to feel the need to reach out to touch the building. This is somewhat the same sensation the diver experiences alongside a sheer wall. A lifetime of fighting the pull of gravity does not come with an on/off switch, leaving the diver to feel that if he stops kicking, he falls from the face. Everything underwater is about the third dimension.

As we start the assent, Frank begins having difficulty with the climb due to the extra twenty or so pounds of steel tail fin. In just seconds everything about our nice leisurely dive begins to change. Frank abruptly and with some urgency, taps on my shoulder, signaling that he has run out of air. Even in those early days of scuba, this is not a crisis as the valve on the tank is designed with a safety relief. Once rotated, this valve provides a reserve of air, allowing the diver to safely surface. While the idea of this safety reserve is excellent, the engineering of the placement of the release valve on these early models was not so great. A diver had only to pull on a rod to open the reserve, but this was difficult. Designers had located the rod around on the back of the tank, probably to keep it out of the way of actions on the front of the tank. Reaching it was difficult. It becomes virtually impossible if you have both hands on the tail fin of a Hedgehog.

Following Frank's request for help with his reserve rod, I reach over, give the reserve rod a pull, and he hands the souvenir tail fin to me. In one of the worst knee-jerk decisions of my life, I grab the fin from him as he begins kicking hard for the surface.

Boys and war souvenirs...sometimes I wonder just how many young men have died or been injured in the pursuit of some war trophy. What the hell was I thinking right at that moment? Had it even crossed my mind that if Frank was out of air, Bob could not be far behind? Of course not! This was our trophy and we were damned well going to have bragging rights.

Taking a second, I check my depth gauge, seeing that the surface is still about seventy feet above my head. Then begins the laborious swim up to the surface, still lugging the bomb fin. About twenty seconds later, adding proof to the old adage that the first time a sailor thinks about reefing sail is the correct time to reef sail, I too suddenly ran out of air. With a firm grasp of the bomb fin in my left hand, I contort my entire body around to the right and am able, with one last strenuous twist, to yank down on the reserve lever. *I'll show him, I can do this damn reserve rod by myself*, I proudly think!

This twisting motion set in place events, which were to become, to this day, one of my closest calls with death.

The scuba regulator rigs we used were the original Jacques Cousteau models. This classic gear featured two large, yellow, flexible hoses connected to a regulator whose job it was to allow the diver's normal breathing to control the flow of reduced-pressure air from the tanks. The suction from breathing opened the regulator, letting air flow through the right-hand yellow hose to the diver's mouth. Exhaled CO_2 would then flow into the other yellow hose, around behind the diver, where it would be released as bubbles. Connecting these two hoses was a soft, rubber mouthpiece with attached soft, rubber grip that went into the diver's mouth to be clamped by his teeth. This mouthpiece acted as an air collector and held the one-way valves insuring that fresh air came in and CO_2 went out. The twisting of my head around to the right as I completed pulling the reserve, had the unwanted outcome of pulling the entire mouthpiece from my mouth. Immediately and perhaps fatally, the mouthpiece collection hose had filled with water.

Now, I am in very deep shit and here are the facts. I am still about fifty feet down. My buddy has left me for the surface; I am alone. There is reserve air available to breathe because my reserve is now turned on, but my mouthpiece collection hose is full of water. I cannot get to that fresh air in my tank because the collection hose is full of water between that air and my lungs, which at this moment are sending panicky signals to my brain pleading for just one large gulp of air. I am much too deep to hold my breath and sprint to the surface. I will pass out before I get there. This air I desperately crave can be found on the other side of a one-way valve in the right-side yellow hose, just waiting for some suction to pull it through the valve. But here is the problem: that same suction will first draw about a cup of water down into my lungs, sending me into a coughing fit, leading to the spitting out of the mouthpiece, followed by death by drowning.

Years later in his marvelous book *The Perfect Storm*, author Sebastian Junger spends the better part of one chapter outlining vivid descriptions of the two very distinct ways to die by drowning. Who knew that there are actually two separate ways to die by drowning? In one case, the lungs do become flooded with water, quickly preventing any oxygen from getting to the blood and heart, leading to death. However, for the majority of drowning victims, the brain is so attuned to not allowing water into the lungs that the victim experiences paralysis of the windpipe, quickly leading to blackout and death. That afternoon there was no time to think of the finer nuances of drowning, but this is not to infer that my brain had shut down. Only seconds remained to determine if I was going to live or die

My first reaction is to drop the Hedgehog fin. Grasping just how desperate this situation has become, I force my brain to stop thinking about fresh air, forcing all thinking to shunt into little boxes where each part of the problem can be inspected. All time slows to a standstill. Step by step I organize the totality of the problem at hand, reaching a decision that just might save my miserable life.

In spite of having my lungs screaming for air and a brain threatening to blank out like your hard drive crashing, I slowly rotate over on my left side, placing the mouthpiece back between the teeth and begin to slowly drink all of the water out of my air intake hose. Gravity has to drain each drop of water slowly and surely out of the rubber air hose, down my throat, and into my stomach. Not one drop of water can be allowed into the windpipe. One small swallow followed by one more small swallow until there is nothing left to drink from the inhale hose. I have no lungs. I have no reason to breathe. I live only to drink in this cool water. There is no fear, only a total determination to see this through.

An eternity later, just before blacking out, there seems to be no more water in the hose, so I suck in a huge gulp of air. Naturally enough, several small drops of water come in with this frantic slug of air, but I had already mentally warned myself that this might happen, and by biting down on the mouthpiece so hard that I almost break a tooth, I am able to stifle a cough. At once my legs began pumping those frog-like fins, using leg muscles not put to this test since the previous fall during two-a-day football workouts, sending me spiraling up towards the sunlight above.

Breaking though the surface, I roll over on my back, pull out the mouthpiece, and experience an orgasm of sucking in warm, fresh, West Virginia mountain air. All is at peace; the quarry water surface is a flat mirror as my heart rate comes back to normal.

Insects hum and a bird chirps; no sign exists that the world above my head has taken any notice of the drama recently occurring fifty feet below the surface. Gently I reach behind my head, pull a snorkel around to my mouth, and while lying on my back, begin slowly kicking flippers to propel me over to the beach, where I expect to find Frank.

In our pre-dive planning, Frank and I had known that we needed to allow time during our ascent to stop in stages for decompression due to the depth and time of our dive. But our running out of air had failed to allow time for this decompression. Now we were going to pay. As we lay exhausted on the pebbles of the road leading to the quarry, we began to hurt all over from the bends. Frank rolls over, looks at me, and asks, "Where's the bomb?" Then in a slow voice, I tell him the story.

We lie there quietly for some time before finding the energy to collect our gear and head home. On the drive home we critique our mistakes, deciding that it was shortsighted of us not to have brought along an inflation device to help lift the bomb. We stop at the dive shop on the way home, fill our tanks, and buy two CO_2-activated, Mae West life vests. Now we have lifting devices!

Early the next morning we headed right back to West Virginia. The two of us knew exactly where to go to find that souvenir bomb fin! Using these new CO_2-powered inflation devices we had no trouble getting this trophy back to the surface. The Hedgehog fin was to sit as a proud souvenir, whose epic saga of acquisition was known only to us, in Frank's garage for several years until the angel of death came to take one of its owners.

There is no way I should have lived through my dive. That day should have been the last of my short life. Years later when some self-pumped-up corporate manager was in my face spouting off some particularly odious brand of corporate bullshit, I walked away smiling, remembering that day and others later in places like Vietnam or typhoon infested waters south of Japan, experiences giving me the pleasure of knowing that nothing he could do or say meant a damn thing. I had received the gift of living longer than I had any right to expect and no pointy-headed corporate hotshot was going to take one minute of it away. It also revealed a trait later validated on several more occasions: that I could and would, in truly extreme situations, spin into fear hibernation.

Two weeks later I had found a sweet union job for the summer, working grounds maintenance for the county, when one evening Frank came over and asked to borrow my dive equipment. He had asked our friend Andy to join him for a dive to the bottom of this same quarry. Andy had never used scuba equipment.

Andy nearly died that day. The boys became separated in a flooded shack at the bottom of the quarry. Andy panicked and blacked out at one hundred feet down. Frank saved him by inflating his Mae West life vest and later doing CPR on the beach.

Later, we figured out that an accidental switch had saved Andy's life when he had donned Frank's Mae West instead of mine. Frank had changed his CO2 cartridges but had forgotten to change the ones in my vest...the one he had worn. Had Andy worn my vest with the rest of my equipment, he would have died that day.

Andy was never told this story, a story I promised not to tell until the actors involved were gone!

Frank and Andy's near death calls were not quite over.

Growing up, our parents gave Frank and me lots of latitude and trust. Our fathers had spent some time teaching us gun safety, then permitting us to have and use .22 caliber rifles as we wanted. The bedroom shared by Frank and his brother, who occupied the entire upstairs of the family house, had windows looking out in all directions. The rear dormer windows of this large room overlooked the chicken coop behind the house. About twenty chickens were kept, serving as a source of both fresh eggs and money from selling excess eggs. The hen house keepers, that being the two teenage boys, approached the cleaning and feeding of the hens in a characteristic teenage, laissez-faire manner, providing a home and food source for a steady population of rats. Infested might have been an apt description. And boys being boys, that is, boys armed with rifles being boys, killing rats had become a favorite pastime.

We would put small piles of chicken corn outside the hen house directly under the second-story bedroom window, where rifle shots from the bedroom window down to the corn bait soon became like shooting "rats in a barrel." With practice, we could hit the rat in the head, causing reflexes to make it jump about a foot into the air before it fell dead on the ground, getting high fives from the guys. Poorly aimed gut shots, leaving entrails dragging on the ground, were roundly booed.

On this particular day of that senior summer, several of the guys were "hanging out" in Frank's room. I was working my county job and was not to hear about this day for several years. Our friend Andy, the one from the diving accident, was there that day. Andy had never been blessed with a father role model, and this boy-cave was like paradise to him. This unsupervised haven was full of guy gear, including goodies like WWII souvenirs given by one of Frank's uncles, such as a real Luger pistol and a German Wehrmacht helmet, Civil War battle gear, large model airplanes, and an assortment of engines to run them set up on test blocks; various parts of automobile radios, speakers, engine spares and hot rod equipment and, of course, real rifles. We had turned the bathroom into a photo shop darkroom where we developed and printed our own snapshots. There was always something going on in Greg and Frank's room. Many a day I had spent more time there than in my own house.

Sitting on his bed, Frank curiously looked up to see Andy sighting one of the rat-hunting .22 rifles at his head. Frank immediately chastised Andy with the old parental, "Andy, didn't anyone ever tell you never to point a gun at a person unless you intend to kill them?" Andy, who was now very unhappy at being rebuffed by his idol, quickly replied, "Be cool, Frank, it ain't loaded." Frank shot back that this was not relevant. "Never aim a gun at anyone!" Feeling further miffed at again being chastised, Andy walked over to the window to look for a rat.

As Andy found a comfortable spot to sit where he could rest the rifle barrel on a windowsill, he slid the bolt open so as to insert a .22 caliber round in anticipation of seeing a target rat. Shockingly, the bolt ejected a live round that had been housed all along in its deadly little chamber. Andy grabbed the live bullet and slipped it into his shirt pocket, closed the bolt and sat there by the window for about ten minutes while every nerve in his body tried to deny what had just almost happened. Unwanted adrenalin flowed into every corner of his young body. He had just come within a split hair of killing his best friend and his idol.

Soon, Andy got up, set the rifle down, and told the guys that he had to go. Later he told one of the guys that it was almost impossible to drive home due to shaking hands and that it took him a week to get his nerves under control. As one might imagine, Andy did not make this story common knowledge. I only heard about this event sometime after Frank's death, but it was years before I again saw Andy, allowing me to ask, no, to demand to know what happened. Andy became very agitated, not wanting to tell me what had happened. After I persisted, he finally confessed that it was his intention that day to do a "dry fire" as soon as he had the sights squarely between Frank's eyes. His finger was on the trigger and had begun the slow pull back, only to be stopped by the sudden reprimand from his intended target. Later that day with me, Andy swore, as tears swelled up in his eyes, that he believed the gun to be unloaded. But the fact was that he was less than one second away from splattering his best friend's brains on the wall of his bedroom. Frank was never told any of this story: the live round or the planned dry fire.

Growing to maturity, these events now seem like little pieces of a jigsaw puzzle, whose finished picture never avoided tragedy. However, living through my teen years, all of it seemed like a normal childhood. Upon leaving high school, I was not aware of how many more life-threatening events were yet to play out on the center stage of my life.

Moving On

Growing up in Alexandria was like living in a history laboratory. Visits to the Smithsonian, The Capitol, the monuments, the White House, the fortifications built around the Capital to defend it during the Civil War…were all taken for granted; it was just the neighborhood.

Hanging around Washington's estate at Mount Vernon became the same as a trip out to the backyard. We became very adept at finding small back roads behind Mount Vernon to park our cars at night and make out with our girlfriends. What is now known as Olde Towne (the affected "e" warns that it is "e"xpensive) in Alexandria has today become a tourist mecca, but in our high school days it was old, dilapidated warehouses. At the foot of King Street, before the Potomac River begins, now stands row after row of pricey restaurants and fancy revolutionary war-era curio shops. During our time in high school these buildings were the remnants of old, unused warehouses, a boarded up building used to make torpedoes during WWII, and the interarms warehouses full of guns headed to third world countries. One of the rundown buildings housed a very low-class pool hall, the kind where some shady, semi-legit deal was always simmering in the back room. A game of pool cost a dime, where the minimum bet was for the loser to pay the dime with other bets finding the "rack boy" holding wads of money. We knew this establishment as "Mom's."

"Going to the library to study, Mom," really meant, "Going down to study at Mom's"; the words just got slurred. Senior students with good grades were allowed a punch card that granted six class cuts per grading period, a privilege meant to help research college choices. We figured out how to duplicate the cut card records, cutting classes many times above our allotted allowance. Exercising care so that no one teacher took notice of our excessive cuts, we were often found wheeling out of the student parking lot, down to McDonalds to avoid the cafeteria poison, and then downtown to Mom's. My personal record was an eighteen-hour, nonstop pool hall day.

What the hell did we care about being the class valedictorian? Any without-a-real-life, bright nerd who studied could do that. Putting out the minimum amount of work to get grades good enough to get into a federal service academy and at the same time acquiring the skill to run the table playing straight pool…now that was saying something! The life lessons taught at the rail of a pool table in Mom's, lessons we studied assiduously, were never covered in high school social studies class!

One last life lesson made our teen experience different from that of many other kids around the country. This life lesson found its genesis in the unique occurrence that the drinking age in Washington, DC in 1960 was eighteen. There were other states such as Wisconsin where a kid could get a beer at eighteen, but our nation's capital let anyone over seventeen drink anything they wanted. Alcoholic beverages served to what would be a minor in any other state is reminiscent of the story of our national seat of power and bastion of ethics turning a blind eye in the early nineteenth century to slavery within its city boundaries. Washington, DC's reduced drinking age meant that a fake ID only had to have a two-year built-in fudge factor, turning pimply-faced sixteen year olds into new customers now eligible to buy beer and shots of whiskey. I do not remember how we constructed a fake ID card, but amateurishly comes to mind. Acceptance of these blurry, not quite right, identity cards was more a commentary on the greed of bartenders in dives where soaking rich kids from the burbs was an accepted diversion than a statement about our forgery expertise.

Dee Curtis, a football teammate and stalwart rat packer, had a rusty 1951 Dodge beater that he named "The Buzzard." One evening just after graduation, Frank, Andy, Dee, and I piled into The Buzzard and headed for a bar in a poor neighborhood in Southwest DC, a dive we had been to many times. This joint was known as Pop's (notice the family trend in the names of our joints). Many beers and a few sloe gin fizzes later we headed back to Virginia early in the A.M. A traffic stop would have found nary a single sober soul aboard The Buzzard that night. Just after crossing the 14th Street Bridge back into Virginia, we came to agreement that the evening was too young to call it quits and further, we needed to head back into DC for more beer.

Dee yanked the steering wheel, turning The Buzzard sharply through the center island of the George Washington Parkway, tearing out a whole section of bushes and plantings, and headed us back into the city. Someone in the back seat started hitting and beating on one of the guys up front, a melee that got wilder and wilder as we crossed the bridge back into DC. Nearing the Jefferson Memorial, Dee again wrenched The Buzzard over the curb and up upon the grass directly in front of the Memorial. All four of us, quite drunk, piled out of the car, onto the lawn in front of the stately memorial, directly under the stony, stern vigilant eyes of Thomas Jefferson himself. Once on the grass, we began to beat the crap out of each other with our fists. We were laughing so hard that I could not tell if the stream of liquid coming down my face was blood or tears. Turned out to be both!

On so many levels this melee was out of control, but what the hell, it was our town, we had all graduated and had no idea when or where we might again meet; surely Jefferson would understand. There were deep tire tracks in the front lawn of TJ's memorial for some months after this legendary event. Thankfully, Lady Bird Johnson had the plantings on the George Washington parkway replaced some years later. The next morning, when my mother found my very bloody shirt in the laundry, there was an inquisition; she simply could not believe the truth that this had all been good fun.

I really loved those guys! One of them would not live to see age twenty-five, one left us in his late forties, and one passed away in his fifties…how could all three of them have died so young? A famous professor, André Aciman, once wrote that "regret is how we look forward to things we've long lost yet never really had. Regret is hope without conviction. We're torn between regret, which is the price to pay for things not done, and remorse, which is the cost of having done them." I am often torn by regret that I no longer have these special men in my life, yet have little remorse that I escaped the terrible price they paid for the lives we lived.

I vividly remember an occasion sitting with a buddy, drinking a beer on a warm summer evening, while shooting the bull on the porch step at Gatsby's Tavern, the very spot where George Washington had delivered his Farewell Address to the nation. We had played around the house where Lee had grown up. All of these hallowed places were our playgrounds with the exception of one: Arlington National Cemetery. We had visited the tomb guards once when I was a Boy Scout, but the whole place seemed spooky. Little did I know of the shared future between myself and the 1100 acres that had been the Custis Mansion: Robert E. Lee's home. The land surrounding the Custis-Lee Mansion was to become a most important repository of the histories of the men and women who made America the home of the brave and the land of the free. It was also to become repository to some of those who help make up my life story.

Now, however, the time had come to leave my boyhood home, to leave behind those childhood memories, the adolescent friends, the wonderful events that had prepared me to live in a more unforgiving world of men and adult demands.

The last chore, before leaving Alexandria for the academy and the new life it would bring, was to pass an intensive medical exam. My academy medical qualification exam would be given in the naval medical center at what was called "Main Navy"; a string of temporary plywood WWII buildings in Washington, DC sited alongside Constitution Avenue, next to the Reflecting Pool. Following a couple of hours of proving to these old men what a fine specimen of young manhood stood before them, my last chore was to have a dentist check my teeth. As I lay back in the dental chair, the doctor looked down at me saying, "Going to the Merchant Marine Academy. So, you want to become an old salt, huh?" My first thought was *What the hell is an old salt? I just want to get a good education, learn to be a man, and serve my country.*

As I reclined in that dental chair, I had no inkling of the turning of future events, when some twenty-two years later those temporary Navy buildings would be torn down and a 246-foot long trench dug some several feet directly under where my skinny butt then resided in that chair. And in that trench would be erected a wall of shiny black slabs of gabbro, a dark grained plutonic rock entwined with stains of olivine. And on those slabs more than 58,000 names would be inscribed. And I would know many of the names chiseled into that cherished wall, and two names would be those of guys in this story.

SS Exhibitor

*For this you've striven
Daring, to fail:
Your sky is riven
Like a tearing veil.*

*For this, you've wasted
Wings of your youth;
Divined, and tested
Bitter springs of truth.*

Elinor Wylie
"Fire and Sleet and Candlelight"
from
"Nets to Catch the Wind"

The Shipyard

One-of-a-kind, a prototype for the future, she looked like nothing else afloat; in the mid-1960s the *USNS Taurus* was the largest floating parking lot in the world. A class of Navy landing ship now converted to commercial service to carry truck trailers, she was ugly when berthed alongside the classic "stick" ships of that era. While lacking grace and beauty, she could do something that no stick ship could do: she could be completely unloaded and reloaded in less than the blink of an eye; all of her cargo was on wheels, allowing it to roll on and off over ramps. She was both my home and my workstation. The military loved her…the sixty-nine-man crew on board, not so much.

Well over a year had now passed since my graduation from the Merchant Marine Academy. With New York City as a homeport, I had become an experienced mariner with two dozen crossings of the Atlantic under my belt. My employer, The Military Sea Transportation Service (MSTS), had been selected mainly to avoid joining the Masters, Mates, and Pilots (MM&P), the largest maritime union for deck officers. Just out of school I had had a bad experience with the union. I had been selected for a job on an oceanographic research vessel operated by Woods Hole but had not gotten the job, as the MM&P was trying to unionize this ship. In a call from a leader of the MM&P, they had thinly threatened breaking my kneecaps if I took the job without joining the union. I quickly decided that the MM&P would never see any of my money in their dues coffers.

I had been serving as the Third Mate on the *Taurus,* a special operations ship in the MSTS fleet. The ship had been built with a flat bottom, allowing her to move in close for beach assaults. But soon the military need for beach operations diminished, leaving a surplus ship in the fleet. As a roll-on/roll-off, where the cargo rolled on wheels, this old amphibian was born again. This ship was to become the first in a large class of popular vessels that came to be known as "RO-ROs."

A long low engine room located just above the flat bottom allowed low ceiling decks to run the length of the ship, and when connected to ramps...voila, a parking lot. Without a traditional deep keel and with vehicle cargo loaded high above the center of gravity, this ship was going to roll in ocean waves, and roll she did. Sailing in the North Atlantic between New York and Germany brought her into the teeth of nasty weather, insuring that her crew spent most days bracing as she hobby-horsed around the ocean. Although I never experienced seasickness, the *Taurus* was no ship for crewmembers with sensitive inner ears.

In addition to the quick turnarounds, the stress of the North Atlantic was becoming tedious. Voyage after voyage, we played dodgeball with icebergs south of Newfoundland followed by a fight through freezing storms in the middle of the Atlantic. Approaching Europe we often found dense fog in the English Channel, making for long watches glued to a radar screen looking desperately for high-speed ferry ships, while trying to ignore SOS calls from small fishing boats and avoiding things rocky. Next, it was into the mouth of the Weser River, docking at special ramps at Bremerhaven where trailers and vehicles rolled off, only to be followed by a turnaround to do it all over again. The worst of this ocean-going hobbyhorse came during payoff at the end of the voyage, when I found I was drawing lower pay on this Navy-sponsored experiment in fast cargo ops than any of my classmates. They were making much more money, feeding at the breast of union wages, as they served on ships plodding the sunny Mediterranean or sailing lazily to Asia through the calm Pacific. Maybe it was time to rethink feelings about unions. But one thing was for sure, eighteen trans-Atlantic crossings on a military troopship followed by six more on this ship had provided plenty of time to become tired of that ocean. It was time for a change.

❖

A warm and calm late September day, 1965, saw the crew of the *Taurus* slowly backing into a dock in New York Harbor next to specialized piers where her ramps would work—something the captain of the ship likened to "sticking a wet noodle up the rear end of a wildcat," when suddenly my spirits lifted. There, as I looked down on the massive pier apron, sat my new midnight blue Mustang convertible, driven by a perky blonde driver named Joani. Who doesn't have their spirits lifted by having a welcoming party after a long trip, especially when it is a steady girlfriend waving to you with her top down (the car's, not hers). Having already asked the crewing manager for some time off, I had packed my bag, not knowing whether I would return. Ideas making light bulb-like appearances in my head were to enter Naval Aviation at Pensacola or, in another very different plan, to become a certified Navy/civilian diver by attending Basic Underwater Demolition School (BUDS) run by the Navy or, as a final thought, perhaps look at jobs with commercial steamship companies.

In any event, until this was sorted out, it would be nice to have time off. So down the gangway I went, sea bag over my shoulder, to the Mustang and a trip to my apartment out on Long Island. What relief to know that when once again we were back ashore in my cozy shared house in Queens, my bed would not be rolling from side to side, well at least not as much as on the *Taurus*.

❖

A couple of days later found me shucking down beers with Phil "Tuna" Tomlet, one of my favorite classmates. Through the haze of Budweiser enlightenment, Tuna began explaining that there was a way to increase my pay by more than the girth of a hippo and not spend another winter in the storms of the Atlantic. This plan offered two additional benefits: there would be no dealing with the thugs at the MM&P, nor would I be forced to pay an outrageous initiation fee to join their union.

Tuna had signed on with a company-sponsored, no-initiation-fee-necessary union called the Brotherhood of Marine Officers, giving him the opportunity to find a billet as a deck officer with American Export/Isbrandtsen Lines. He was making the big bucks while sailing on their Mediterranean run, enjoying the pleasures of Lisbon, Cádiz, Barcelona, Naples, Venice, and many other sundrenched, romantic ports of call. Additionally, the company had agreed to charter a small fleet of ships to the Navy transport service to carry war cargo to Vietnam. They would be begging for ship's officers.

The very next day I was pounding on the doors of Export Lines in New Jersey with the result that within one week I found myself signing articles as a third officer. I would be taking an Export Lines ship on what was called a coastwise trip, to unload and reload exports and imports, prior to a foreign voyage. This would be a short five-day trip, at which time I would be assigned a deck officer position on a "new Vietnam ship." At payoff from the coastwise trip, I noted a sizable increase in my daily rate of pay, but the icing came when I confirmed that crewmembers on all ships in the war zone around Vietnam received a double pay, war pay bonus. Now I was going to be making some big dough, more than my own father, a senior level manager with the Federal Aviation Administration. It must be remembered that this pay was in addition to the free room and meals always provided for crewmembers. Not bad for a twenty-three-year-old single guy, fourteen months out of school. It felt so good that I phoned my stockbroker on Long Island and told him to expect more money.

This war zone pay rule really got the monetary juices flowing. News reports from Vietnam said that there were huge delays getting ships in and out of the war zone due to the ever-typical Army joke referred to as wartime logistics. Rumor had it that ships were sitting in the Vietnam waters for months at a time. This was going to more than double my already large paycheck, while giving me a nice vacation in the sunny tropics of the South China Sea. The remembrance of this South Seas vacation dream was to later remind me of a family story where my great-grandfather and his fellow Yankee recruits thought that signing up for the Civil War would bring a sunny vacation down to the plantations of South Carolina.

Arriving back from my short coastwise trip, I again checked with the Export Lines office where I confirmed that there was a job waiting for me on a new ship named the *SS Exhibitor*, a ship sitting in a shipyard in Camden, New Jersey. The Export Lines manager tendering the promise of a position on one of the Vietnam ships, perhaps failed to adequately explain his understanding of the meaning of the noun "ship" when combined with the adjective "new" or perhaps we both realized that the only thing "new" was what was about to happen to me.

That evening as I excitedly spread this good news to Joani, she looked anything but excited. She thought it was great that her boyfriend would be making big bucks. And she loved the idea that my shiny new 1965 Ford Mustang convertible would be left in her care…but she did not like this idea of me being on the other side of the globe for an indeterminate time, in a place where the evening news was reporting ever-growing hostilities. I shrugged off her worries and saw the whole thing as a great lucrative lark. At least one of us was using some common sense.

Three days later, having stuffed my sea bag, in full knowledge that it might be a year or more before my return, I headed the Mustang down the Jersey Turnpike to the Navy shipyard in Camden, New Jersey, Joani serving as a co-pilot.

That fateful day began the next phase of my "life education."

The Faithful Sextant

What compliments can a reasonable person find to say about Camden New Jersey, a working class city abutting the cultural and historical, classy city of Philadelphia. Camden's mean streets have bred gang and drug warfare in cycles matching the economic cycles affecting blue-collar employment. In my life experience resume, I had already checked off the box of having worked in a shipyard. They are damned dangerous places, where big steel structures move through the air just waiting to crush human body parts. Lesson number one to be learned in Camden: there was more danger outside the shipyard gates than inside. Camden has kept its record as the murder capital intact for some time.

It was now November. The weather had turned gray and cold, and the landscape had put on a drab mantle of approaching winter in this industrial city, one more distraction from finding anything nice about this side of the Delaware. *No wonder those pitiful Philadelphia Eagle fans just across the river have the reputation for booing Santa Claus*, I thought. *It's the Camden Eagle fans doing the booing.*

Joani, myself, and the Mustang wound our way through the city streets of Camden, eventually locating the weary motel where rooms rented by the steamship company served as temporary housing for crewmembers until berthing conditions on the ship met minimum living conditions. I quickly removed the gear from my car, said goodbye to Joani, and watched her and the shiny new Mustang disappear around the corner as she headed back north to New York. The adventure had begun.

Camden, I thought, would be just a small irritation; after all, the crew would be quickly moving onboard the ship and departing for sunny weather. But if my first impression of Camden as a tired, dirty, dangerous, decrepit city was alarming, the next morning was to bring an even bigger shock to my expectations when I met my new workstation and home, the *SS Exhibitor*.

The Faithful Sextant

❋

The first glimpse of this aging maritime vessel of commerce, lying alongside a pier on the far side of the Camden Shipyard, sucked the breath from deep inside my gut. She was more than just an old and rusty relic of pre-WWII commerce; she was ugly. She had been put together with ancient rivet construction rather than welding. Her lines were sharp angles. There was no grace to her design, but mostly, she was just worn out. Built in the mid-1930s, the *SS Exhibitor* had served many years in the India trade, primarily hauling grain to the hungry masses of the sub-continent. Her life had been hard, and the elements had not been kind to the steel of her soul.

Export Lines knowingly let scheduled maintenance slide as she aged, and when there was almost no life left in the old lady, they traded her back to the Maritime Commission for a new ship under America's wonderful Maritime Construction Subsidy Program. The old ship was then sealed up (mothballed), towed to a wide spot up the James River where she rafted with aging sisters—monuments to the past maritime power of a nation never quite dedicated to its seagoing heritage. Holding on to this dowager fleet made congressmen feel good that the subsidy program was not a total giveaway.

Knowing that these ships were really nothing but scrap (more accurately drop the "s"), I am sure that the shipyard workers originally tasked with sealing them did so with the intent that the only group to ever unseal them would be some poor "ship breakers" in some third world place such as Chittagong.

A long-standing cliché has it that old ships, when scrapped, are cut up and made into razor blades. Most certainly no representative from Gillette was interested in recycling any part of the antiquated steel of this sad old lady. In order to protect what little integrity was left to the hull of these ships, the sealing had been accomplished using some of the most diabolical gunk ever invented through the ingenuity of chemists at Dow Chemical Company.

Not only were we going unseal this worn out old ship, we were going to challenge her remaining life in some of the worst of oceanic weather, the winter typhoons of the North Pacific. It was going to cost millions of dollars just to unseal one technologically antiquated vessel that had a market value measured in thousands of dollars. An obvious abuse of taxpayer funds, this program nevertheless gave our congressmen the ability to say, "See, I told you that saving those "trade-ins" would be a good idea one day!" Even a dimwit could see that this was throwing a great pile of money down a rat hole, but without the foresight of history's lessons, this country had allowed its maritime fleet to reach a point of not having the capacity to carry normal trade, in addition to the surge needed to fight a foreign war.

After a few minutes of apprehension from the shipyard pier, I turned and bounded up the gangway, trying to keep an optimistic spring in my step, before I reported to the captain's office. There I met Captain Winebrenner, a middle-aged, steely-faced mariner; a man I would come to like and respect. He sent me to meet the first officer (aka chief mate, aka first mate) who instructed me to grab a cup of coffee and settle in for an experience. The coffee was regular old shipboard gunk, the experience began immediately, and it was indeed new.

Removing the sealing gunk from this ship was new even to the shipyard workers. These skilled shipwrights often had no better answer than we did about how to strip off and bring back into working order various parts of the ship. Starting from the outside, the ship's hull was covered by a mad chemist's wet dream of the toughest gunk designed to prevent corrosion to the ancient, riveted steel plating. This gunk had to come off. No problem. Shipyards have high-powered sand blasting guns designed for tough jobs. Working from scaffolding in the dry dock, the shipyard men quickly encountered a serious problem: the steel on the hull of the ship had rusted to the point that sand blast equipment could easily punch holes through the hull plates. Sand blasting was stopped and not used again.

Problem noted…solution found! Just slather over the "gunk" with several coats of standard Navy gray paint and move on to the next challenge. Some months later, this interesting solution to the gunk problem on the ship's hull had this side effect: As the ship steamed through thousands of miles of ocean, the salt water managed to work its way in between the thick coat of Navy-gray paint and the sealant gunk. In so doing, large pimples were created under the paint, several of which had grown to over a foot in diameter, containing perhaps a quart of seawater. Later, following our arrival in Saigon, we found it was great sport to stroll along the wharf at shipside, poking these pimples with a stick, jumping back before an eruption of seawater shot out. It was sort of like puncturing a teenage zit. We noted that the salt water whooshing from this pimple was a dark rust color, containing small particles of the ship's hull as it continued to rust away beneath both the Navy gray paint and the gunk. Soon there would not be enough steel left to fabricate even a cheap Bangladeshi razor blade for later sale in Chittagong.

Many corners were going to have to be cut no matter how many tax dollars were thrown at this problem, corners that the crew hoped would not come back to later select a spot for a watery grave. However, of all the short cuts and gunk solutions, one stood out above all others for audacity, folly and even a twist of humor.

The halcyon maritime days of the *Exhibitor's* design and construction had seen the installation of teak wood flooring on the external decks of her bridge wings, an exquisite flooring found today only on luxury cruise ships due to the high cost of solid teak. When teak gets wet, the grain stands out, providing very effective footing, and if kept clean, it looks very classy. When the ship was laid up and sealed, the ham-handed workers laid gunk over everything, including the beautiful teak bridge wing decks. Following years and years at anchor in the reserve fleet, daily exposure to the sun's UV rays had forced this chemical gunk down into the beautiful grain of this wood as if it were purposely infused by a high-pressure injection system.

The gunk over the bridge wing teak could not be allowed to remain atop the teak decking as it would be slick as snot in a cold rain and sticky like Br'er Rabbit's tar baby in the sun. Everyone could see that there would be no way to lift the gunk from the teak short of stripping the top half inch of the wood, resulting in degrading the strength of the wood while costing thousands of dollars and wasting a week. The "costing thousands" bothered no one, but the added week was just not possible as an Army battalion waited specifically for this ship to move their mechanized equipment to the war zone. The gunk could not be removed and yet it could not stay as it was, so in the spirit of getting this damned ship out of the shipyard, a very simple shortcut was approved.

A roll of heavy duck canvas was lifted aboard so two large pieces could be cut in the pattern of the bridge wing floors. The patterned pieces were then laid over the teak decking and secured by nailing strips of wood along the edges. A statement of the expectations for the life expectancy of this old ship was illustrated when we noticed that the fasteners used to secure these wood strips to the teak deck were plain old iron nails, not brass screws. Given our environment in saltwater spray, I figured the iron nails for maybe a year before they became powdered rust. In the wintertime shipyard of New Jersey, even the ship's officers overlooked this half-baked idea as the chilly weather left the gunk a solid mass allowing for firm footing over top of the heavy-duty canvas. None of these shipyard geniuses were thinking any farther ahead than getting this old rust bucket past the sea trials at the mouth of the Delaware River, forever out of their lives. Life on board the Exhibitor months later in the tropical sun at the mouth of the Saigon River was of no concern to them.

Turned out this quick fix became a real problem long before we arrived in Vietnam. No sooner had the ship reached the tropical sun of the Caribbean than this sloppy idea began to unravel. The dark canvas laid over the gunk absorbed heat from the sun as if fired by some sort of solar steaming machine, making the underlying gunk turn into a viscous jelly. Walking on the bridge wings quickly became a squishy event.

Any five-year-old boy knows that oozing gunk never likes to be trapped inside something like a canvas bag and we didn't have anything near as good as a five-year-old-boy's canvas bag. The oozing gunk, fully determined not to stay trapped under hastily laid down pieces of canvas, quickly found its way to daylight. Up it oozed. It found edges. It found seams. It found weak places in the canvas. But mostly it found our shoes.

Then it was tracked into the wheelhouse, then into the passageways, then into the dining room and then into our staterooms. Soon enough it felt like we were being gunked over and laid up just like the old *Exhibitor*. After a while, this just became one more part of the whole patois of life somewhere over the edge of maritime sanity.

Back in the shipyard, a new crisis seemed to arrive almost hourly, providing the experience of playing a giant game of "Whack-A-Mole." For example, one of the ship's engineers found that there was hardened concrete in the bilge piping system. Turns out it was not actually concrete; it was something just as bad. Noted above, the *Exhibitor* had been in the grain trade for years, where she had carried both bulk and bagged grain, a foodstuff which, when crushed as it seeped from burlap bags, became a flour powder. This fine-grained powder, when mixed with moisture (rain, seawater, condensation, longshoreman urine, etc.) became a slurry able to slip into the bilge piping system where it became a sort of glue, hardening into a mass stronger than concrete, almost as solid as the steel piping itself. New plumbing was out of the question, so quick fixes had to be found.

The clogged bilge piping may not have had the humorous profile of the tar on your shoes up on the bridge wing, but it was far more dangerous; a serious problem lurking in the bowels of the ship just daring the ship's crew to pump large amounts of seawater out of a lower hold some dark night in a storm. A mariner did not need to be very prescient to know that such a dark, stormy catastrophic night lay in our future.

As we began to wrap up the shipyard stay, tragedy struck!

Painting everything was the last job. We had swung the two lifeboats out over the side of the ship to make sure the antiquated davits still worked and while the boats were swung out, an older shipyard worker was given a brush and a can of paint and told to slop it on thick. This old man had probably been a new hire, picked up to handle the extra workload. Paint can and brush in hand, the worker had climbed into the starboard boat; it was the one swung out fifty feet over the shipyard pier. The shipyard project supervisor knew that he did not need a lot of skill…just paint everything inside the boat.

Launching a lifeboat is by no means an easy task. Try to imagine a huge open boat full of fifty scared-to-death crewmembers and/or passengers. Suspend it out over the ocean well away from the side of the ship, which is itself rolling thirty and forty degrees from side to side, then try to drop the boat weighing a couple of tons into an angry ocean pushing around waves much deeper than the little boat. Under these circumstances, the lifeboat might be at the water's surface and within one or two seconds be ten or twenty feet over the water as the ship rolled and the wave under the boat moved from crest to trough. The absolute nanosecond in which the boat touches the ocean surface, it is critical that both boat hooks connecting the boat to the ship (called boat falls) be released together so that the lifeboat will be floating, no longer attached to the abandoned ship.

To make this happen, the lifeboat is connected to the boat falls by two large, open throat hooks. These hooks are then further connected by way of a universal joint to a long shaft that runs from the bow hook to the stern hook. In the middle of this shaft there is a welded handle. The idea is to rotate this handle, thereby rotating the shaft and the hooks so that the open throat of the hooks comes up and the shackle connecting the boat to the lowering wires and both hooks fall free simultaneously.

Whew!

This process is not as complicated as the untrained reader might imagine. Just understand that when the boat commander orders the crewmember to rotate the handle, the hooks must fall free and the boat must also immediately fall free into the ocean. A non-synchronized release of the boat can be disastrous, where one end of the boat is released and the other isn't, dumping all of the occupants into the sea.

The "quick release" lifeboat fall device is a well thought out system that has been around for a long time. But it is a loaded gun. The entire launching of the lifeboat depends on these hooks *not* opening prematurely. After lots of accidental, premature, lifeboat drops, use of this dropping shaft became the most stressed part of training for lifeboat-qualified seaman.

Coast Guard rules further require that this handle be located just above one of the lifeboat seats (thwarts) and this thwart must be painted red. Large block letters stating, "WARNING: HANDLE DROPS BOAT" must be clearly stenciled in white paint on the thwart next to this handle. This rule had been followed on the *Exhibitor*, but after years of bleaching by the sun's rays, it is doubtful whether this warning was readable.

The elderly, temporary shipyard worker did not have lifeboat training. He knew only one thing; they gave me a can of paint, a brush and told me to be sure the entire inside of the boat was painted. When he got to the dropping handle, he grabbed it and rotated it to be able to paint both of its sides, an action that instantly sent the lifeboat

The Faithful Sextant

plunging to the pier below. The old man was standing in the middle of the boat when it hit the pier.

I had been sitting in the officer's salon, having a cup of coffee, when a noise roared through the ship. I sprinted out of the salon to the transverse passageway, over to the pier side of the ship where I looked down to see a lifeboat laying on the shipyard pier with what looked like a human form slumped over in the center of the boat. Out of the corner of my eye appeared movement above my head. I quickly looked up to see the ends of two sets of boat falls with sheaves and shackles, empty of their burden and gently swinging in the breeze. My brain, not wanting any of this to be true, was forced to put the whole thing together; this was *our* lifeboat smashed on the pier surface below me!

Workers were now swarming around the boat as shipyard supervisors began screaming for help. Soon an ambulance arrived, taking the man to a trauma center. The old man would linger for two days in the ICU before dying.

We now had our first fatality; it would not be our last!

Later, while inspecting the inside of the boat, I noticed something shiny on the bottom bilge between the floorboards; it was several of the old man's teeth. Carefully picking them from between the floorboards, I placed them in an envelope for the family.

This tragic event struck me hard. As the officer of the deck that afternoon, I had walked by this boat during its painting, noting the worker moving around in the boat while it was swung out over the dock. How could I have let this man get into a pre-deployed lifeboat without instruction? What the hell was I thinking? As an officer of the deck, the safe operation of this ship was my personal responsibility. I had been trained and now it was time to become a man, to become "the" man, to become responsible for the lives of others.

A fellow ship's officer dryly noted, "We were lucky. Someone could have been walking on the pier beneath the boat, killing more than one worker." I didn't feel lucky, and I am certain that neither did the old man's family.

The shipyard wanted no part of making a big deal over the lifeboat incident. They put a patch or two on the old boat and lifted it back up to its cradle with a shipyard crane. It was a quicker fix that also had the side benefit of not needing to test the shipboard electric motors designed to recover a deployed lifeboat after required lifeboat drills.

Sometime later as we made our way south to the Panama Canal, we scheduled a mandatory weekly lifeboat drill. This drill was to include breaking out the boat and lowering it to the boat deck. Here we would have boarded the boat during an emergency real-life launch. Everything in the drill went fine until we began to hoist the boat back up to its cradle. The electric motors, whose job it was to pull in the boat falls, lifting the boat back to its cradle, heated up and began to smoke. We finally had to rig long lines back to a cargo winch and winch the boat back to its stowed position. The captain made a log entry and we never did another full lifeboat drill again. *Dear God, I pray that we are never in some terrible situation where we have to depend on this piece of shit to save our lives,* I thought. It turned out that this prayer wasn't to be answered.

It was now mid-November. Export Lines was anxious to get our ship out of the yard and on hire, and the Army was chomping at the bit to get their combat engineer battalion loaded and on the way to war. It was not possible to say who made the decision that the ship was ready, but out of nowhere, a Navy civilian worker appeared carrying an envelope containing orders telling our captain it was time to get under way. Several days later, inspections were completed, followed by shipyard workers removing the last of their equipment. Early the next morning a qualified inspector was boarded to travel with the ship down the Delaware River to Cape May for sea trials. Having never been on a sea trial, I had this notion that a crew of engineers would take the ship out on maneuvers, testing all systems, bringing the ship back to port to make any needed corrections, and indeed, this is how a real sea trial is supposed to take place. Ours would be very different.

We cast off from the shipyard on a day with a cold, northerly November wind blowing down the Delaware River. We navigated the ship down the river to Cape May while the inspector looked for equipment and structural deficiencies in the engine room, on the bridge, around the cargo handling gear and with lifesaving and emergency equipment. Finally, making several notations, followed by a logbook entry that sea trials were complete, he declared that the ship was fit for sea, and that was that! Showing a deep look of concern on his face, Captain Winebrenner, nevertheless, signed off that sea trials had been accomplished. My observation of the whole process: two hours down the river and we were still afloat; what the hell could go wrong with this picture?

A boat put out from Lewes, Delaware to pick the inspector up, taking him ashore, where he could catch a ride home to Philadelphia. He had told us about the big Thanksgiving dinner planned for next week with many family members at his house in the suburbs of Philadelphia. He wished us well just before descending the Jacob's ladder to the small boat. I swear that I saw him shaking his head as his boat sped away, leaving us to begin a very long voyage. It turned out that once we had rounded the Florida capes, it did become a kind of one-way trip. We did not know at the time, but destiny had already sealed the fate of the old *SS Exhibitor*. She would never again sail in the waters of the Atlantic Ocean.

The Voyage

Calm down, take some deep breaths, I tell myself. But my right eye will not stop twitching. Deep, deep...breathe deep. You have seen this all before. But a little rat voice is telling me that reverse psychology just might fail this time. Maybe, just maybe, we have pushed lady luck over the edge this time! No, you have been in storms this bad before, and it always got better.

Then the rat voice again. No, you have never seen anything like this.

Wham! I am thrown violently against the edge of the chart table; I grab for the edge to hold on and miss. Slammed against the chartroom floor, I slide to the other side and bang into a wall as a large book flies across the room to hit my head. Damn, that hurt...no one asks if I am okay; they are out in the wheelhouse barely holding on, and I am just one more nasty noise in the background. Then as the ship begins to right itself, the second mate looks around the corner to ask if I am okay.

Hell no, I am not okay. Okay would be sitting in the Buena Vista Bar in San Francisco sipping on an Irish coffee with friends.

This piece of crap rust bucket of a ship full of war material is sinking. It is becoming real hard to see a way we live through this night. I am a damn long way from okay!

A course was set southbound past the stormy seas of Cape Hatteras, to the calm waters of Charleston, South Carolina. As a frontal weather system passed, a chilly clear wind blew out of the north, bringing puffy little cumulus clouds and clear weather, forcing us to hug the coast in an effort to avoid the strongest of the northbound currents of the ever-present Gulf Stream. A steady northerly wind, coming in with the cold front, was a sure way to double the size of waves found in the Gulf Stream, giving us a nice coating of Atlantic salt from the spray until we turned the corner at Cape Lookout, passing close to Frying Pan Shoals, just abeam the North and South Carolina border. Suddenly it was summer time again with smooth waters and warm zephyrs…now this is what I signed on for.

The following morning, on a clear, warm fall day, Fort Sumter and the beautiful harbor of Charleston showed up. Our orders took us into the harbor, past the old city, and up the Cooper River to the Charleston Army Terminal. There we would begin loading all the mechanized equipment needed to support an Army combat construction battalion: trucks, jeeps, bulldozers, and all of the other support equipment needed to make up a fully functioning reinforced Army battalion/regiment in South Vietnam. This would take more than a week.

Charleston is a very quaint, old Southern city, home for a time to my grandfather Lloyd McEliece during WWII. I was very much looking forward to a nice, relaxing visit in this lovely antebellum Southern city with its unmatched mansions in quiet neighborhoods. In my mind, a person could find very few places in the world to live that would be more charming than the mansions near the seawall in old Charleston.

In spite of our rushed schedule to get the ship loaded and on its way, time was found for a couple of evening trips into Charleston. The third assistant engineer named Bernie, a young man my age from Maine Maritime Academy, had by now become my new buddy. The two of us were to become good friends, drinking partners, troublemakers, extreme poker players, as well as wingmen.

Bernie shared the same watch rotation in the engine room as I had on the bridge, meaning we were always off duty at the same time. Bernie came equipped with a wicked sense of humor and a take-no-prisoners attitude—we were going to get along just fine.

One of Bernie's classmates had opted to exercise his naval commission, signing up for submarine school right out of Maine Maritime. His first duty assignment in the Navy was with a submarine squadron stationed in Charleston. Following a phone call from Bernie, we were invited to a party at his classmate's place in Charleston, a get-together hosted by several young naval officers our age who made up the "Blue Crew" for one of the submarines at the sub base.

Grabbing a cab, Bernie and I located their "frat" house, known in Navy jargon as a "snake ranch," in a quiet neighborhood outside Charleston. Joining into the guy-group telling sea stories, it was enlightening to grasp that the Navy guys thought we were nuts, sailing ships up rivers in Vietnam. We in turn thought the same of them. At the same time, the young ladies floating around the house party, mentally scoring the guys for looks, charm, and future income potential, thought all of the seagoing guys were nuts. They were impressed that we were officers with good educations, decent paying jobs, and bright prospects. But to a lady, each of them lacked acceptance for long absences by boyfriends (maybe future husbands) who would sail away, to who knows where, for months at a time. Needless to say, and in spite of our manifest charisma, none of the unattached girls had any interest in hooking up with Bernie or me, even for one night. Our prospects, in spite of our huge, war bonus paychecks, looked deader than the Navy guys. Ah, the life of a sailor.

Workday life aboard the *SS Exhibitor* now registered a new level on the misery meter. The Army had found a place to tie up our ship at the very far north end of Charleston Army Terminal. Just beyond our berth, farther up the Cooper River, was a large paper pulp mill, one of those nasty polluters for which this part of South Carolina has become well known. Air quality control at these plants was nonexistent as a constant supply of puny pine trees came in the front door and the smelly exhaust was sent out the back. In those days, people were expected to know better than to buy land downwind from a pulp mill; that bargain priced acreage had been saved for poor mill workers and sharecroppers. Someone forgot to tell the Army why the land was so cheap on this section of the Cooper River, or more likely, the general in the Pentagon, who won plaudits for saving budget dollars, never smelled a thing.

The air from our downwind location had a slight green haze, burning our eyes and throat, while adding a new misery to everyday life. Ducking through a door into the ship brought no relief to this acrid smell as it percolated into every interior space. Catching a taxi into downtown Charleston and its sea breezes would have brought respite, but such leisurely tourist activities were going to be in very short supply. Was this unhealthy fog a clever incentive to get us to work harder to get the ship out early?

Planning to get the *Exhibitor* out in a week, the Army began loading equipment round the clock. The third day after our arrival, we celebrated Thanksgiving with a large turkey meal served up with all the trimmings. In spite of the genuine effort put forth by the steward's department to create an old-fashioned holiday meal, the turkey and mashed potatoes tasted just like pulp mill acid.

This was by no means my first Thanksgiving away from home on a ship, but it became a new high water mark for loneliness. Later that afternoon, I found a payphone on the base at the foot of the pier, where I placed a collect call back to my girlfriend in New York. Not only was I in a lonely, smelly place, missing her and a family Thanksgiving dinner, but also added to my melancholy was one more little tune-occupying top spot on the dance card of my mind.

Maritime crews and officers agree to a contract called Signing Articles—a legally binding bond between a sailor and the ship owner that we will not jump ship in the middle of a voyage in some faraway place. Articles are historically signed for exactly one voyage, which runs from when a ship leaves a certain port until it arrives at another port, usually a round trip from home port back to home port. Wartime Articles are very different! You sign on for a voyage for a year, whichever suits the needs of the government and the shipping company. We had only a vague idea of where we were going or of what we were getting into and no idea when we were coming back or even in what part of the United States the Navy might pick for us to load a second voyage. There was even some chance we would not be returning to this country; some ships had been tasked to shuttle back and forth between Japan, Korea, and Vietnam. Try explaining this concept to a young lady who has marriage and family on her mind, and while you are at it, try to ignore scenes, as seen on television, of irritable little men dressed in black pajamas with guns and a penchant for shooting at nice, young, blond-haired, blue-eyed ship's officers. Added to the plight of her boyfriend, Joani's older brother, a naval aviator, had just been deployed on an aircraft carrier to the waters off Vietnam. There was little that I could come up with to be thankful for that afternoon.

I wasn't the only one concerned about this voyage. Just after arriving in Charleston, the chief engineer, a portly, gout-ridden man with an unquenchable thirst for cold beer, polled the ships officers with an idea to make a purchase of beer for the voyage. I was thinking in terms of six-packs and the chief was thinking in terms of hundreds of cases. I remember him once saying, "Hmm, twenty-four cans in a case of beer…twenty-four hours in a day. Just a coincidence? I think not!"

Insults thrown my way castigating my beer-drinking manhood caused me to up my order, resulting, along with the other officers, in a rather large order phoned in to a local beer distributor. The next afternoon found a beer truck making its way down the pier, where the longshoremen were nice enough to hoist the cases of various brands of beer loaded on pallets up to the deck outside the chief engineer's office. Nine of us had ordered 194 cases of beer. This order came to 4,656 cans of beer, which for nine guys, over what we thought would be a thirty day voyage, came to a little over seventeen cans of beer per guy per day. This was not quite the can per hour that the chief had in mind, but what the heck, a guy has to sleep sometime. It was a stroke of genius; someone was seeing this voyage to hell clearly.

Technically, United States Maritime Law does not allow drinking aboard merchant ships. This rule, however, is set and enforced by God himself, otherwise known as the captain. Well, this captain was one hard-drinking, hard-smoking, hard-poker-playing, old-time maritime officer named Winebrenner, a name I believe to have been Anglicized from *weinbrauer,* meaning wine brewer in German. How appropriate!

The captain did draw an enforced line when it came to the crewmembers drinking. This rigid non-drinking rule, applicable only to un-licensed crewmembers, was going to be a problem. This problem was highlighted when the fourth mate asked the chief, "Where we gonna stow this beer, and more importantly, how are we gonna keep it cold?" The ship had a large refrigerator that kept many months of food supplies chilled, but the stewards controlled the refrigeration, and as non-officer crewmen, they were not allowed to drink. That wasn't going to work.

The old chief engineer replied to the fourth mate, "Lad, you deck apes sure are slow in the engineering solutions area. You just leave that problem to the men who really run this ship of fools." The next day another truck pulled up alongside with a standard household refrigerator in its cargo bed. The dockworkers put a sling around the fridge and lifted it up to the door of a large fan room located just behind the bridge.

Again, the junior third mate, sharp as a tack, mentioned to the engineers that the refrigerator was a good idea but it would not work on this old ship. Household stuff like refrigerators use standard alternating current (AC), but all electrical wiring on these ancient ships provided only direct current (DC).

For a second time, the chief engineer was forced to put the mate in his place. Never underestimate the ingenuity of a group of engineers who daily are called on to perform miracles with mechanical stuff and who also have cold Budweiser on the mind. That afternoon the first assistant engineer and the electrician got busy in the spare parts bin. In no time they had built a motor/generator set using a DC motor to spin an AC generator, making good, old-fashioned, alternating current with just enough amps to run a household Frigidaire. The motor/generator equipment was then bolted to a wooden pallet, hoisted up to the same fan room, hard wired into the ship's DC electric circuit, and installed next to the refrigerator. This ingenious unit's sole purpose was to run the refrigerator, whose sole purpose was the chilling of the officer's beer, whose sole purpose was to make this lousy trip tolerable. All that was left was to weld a hasp designed to hold a large padlock onto the door of the refrigerator to keep out unauthorized nighttime prowlers. The ship's officers now had cold beer on demand.

Does 194 cases sound like a lot for nine men? It seemed like a lot to me, who usually preferred a cold gin martini, but not for the refrigerator-sized, beer-swilling chief engineer, who often consumed a case or more a day. We barely made it through the Panama Canal before the Charleston beer ran out, but as luck would have it, an unplanned stop on the West Coast let us refill.

On our next round-trip voyage, much to our pleasure and delight, the Army selected the *Exhibitor* to carry PX supplies, including almost 4000 long tons of beer destined for the troops in Vietnam. For those of you slow at math, that equals 9,000,000 pounds of beer or slightly over twelve million 12oz. cans. On that trip there was never a need to go farther than number four hatch for resupply, dealing a blow to black market beer activities.

Near the end of our load-out of Army vehicles, two sergeants boarded, to ride with us over to Vietnam as passengers. At first, this puzzled me. Did the Army think we would mess with their trucks? Or maybe these sergeants were put onboard to repel foreign agents! Anyway, these two men turned out to be real standup guys, blending in with the crew, even though they had no part in the day-to-day operation of the ship. In the weeks, which became months, that they were on board, everyone tried to visualize their wartime duty assignment, them included; the predominate thinking being that this whole thing would be a big lark, a real adventure. It never entered our minds that these guys would be in danger; they were just too nice to have anything bad happen to them. And since we believed this fairytale, it never entered our minds that any of us would ever be in danger or, beyond any belief, that this country could actually run away from this war without winning it.

The two sergeants became brothers and shipmates. When we finally debarked them in Saigon, there was heartfelt sadness in our goodbyes, and as with so many experiences to come, I would later regret not writing down these guys' names, hometowns, and unit number. In retrospect, perhaps it is best I did not remember their names. Finding either or both names on "the Wall" would only have added later to my personal burden of this war's real cost.

Once all the Army equipment had been loaded and secured, we cast off, heading south for the Panama Canal, a departure full of mixed emotions. Among the warm thoughts of historically beautiful Charleston, the unease of seeing all of this olive drab war material crowding our main deck, the pleasant thought of fresh sea breezes to clear out the acrid pulp smell, but most of all, the anxiety of leaving loved ones, to ply our way into the unknown and a war zone, were the mixed emotions crowding into thoughts of running the ship.

The Faithful Sextant

As the *Exhibitor* sailed south along the coast of Florida, through the Cays and across the Gulf of Mexico, a magnificent week of nice, warm, Caribbean air combined with calm ocean sailing, all framed what we all hoped would become an idyllic voyage. Leaving the bedlam, dirt, and stink of life in a port behind in our wake, the ship's crew began to reacquaint themselves with the comfort found in shipboard chores. Gear was stowed in its proper place, decks were swept and scrubbed, windows were washed, meals and watch schedules became repetitive, and daily life became predicable (all reasons sailors adjust poorly to the bedlam of life ashore). Crewmembers now found time to recount stories of that disorderly life just left behind, allowing us to get to know new shipmates. Life as a sailor, leaning against an outside railing while watching the full palette of colors of a Caribbean sunset, is an inspiring experience.

Arriving at the Caribbean end of the Panama Canal, we dropped anchor in the bay outside Cristobel to wait our turn for transit. A day later, having picked up a canal pilot, we began the transit of the canal.

Sliding silently in the night from one ocean to another, wedging our way through a man-made wound between the steep cliffs of the massive cordillera, itself preventing the mixing of these two great waters, feels like breaking some basic law of nature. In contrast to the dream of untold mariners for a way to avoid the cruel storms of Cape Horn, we now so easily pass through the continents. This realization of ancient mariner dreams was, however, a hard-won contest, pitting man against nature. Proving the cost of this fight, our ship now passed silently over swamped graves of thousands of workers who sacrificed everything in disease and the toil to make this dream come true. Transiting between Atlantic and Pacific in this canal was, and still is, beyond magical.

That night, as watch officer on the bridge, howler monkeys painted the airless, muggy atmosphere of our transit through the Gaillard Cut. Screaming, with the loudest voice of any mammal, while hanging in treetops only a short distance from our bridge wings, they gave warning to all of our intrusion into their sultry, green world. Landlubbers cannot begin to imagine the poignant disconnect of these sounds following a long sea passage. Imagination is strained when the ocean voyager is dropped into a dark night while steering a massive steel island through the sweltering sounds and smells of a narrow path within an inky jungle. It was as if I had become Marlow proceeding at night up the Congo River in search of Kurtz in *Heart of Darkness*, a feeling I was to have again, more vividly, in the near future in Vietnam.

Arriving at the Miraflores locks near the end of the canal, the ship's engine, as if smelling the Pacific Ocean, began its petulant ways. The ancient steam plant, making up its mind not to go a mile farther, quit no sooner than our clearance of the last set of locks. Calling for a tug, the canal pilot had us towed into a shipyard in Balboa—the seaport for Panama City—tying us up to a pier where repairs could be made. Since the deck crew had no function with the engine repairs, we took off for the wilds of Balboa and Panama City.

Naturally, the boys headed straight to the wrong part of town. By this time in my career, I thought that I had seen every kind of whorehouse, strip show, and sexual perversion imaginable as performed between consenting adult humans. Was I ever wrong! I found that Panama had taken depravity to new levels (high or low, depending on your life viewpoint), where whorehouses issued patrons a numbered receipt after payment at a cash register. In addition to girls in private rooms, the paid receipt also allowed the patron to see shows or become a participant. It is my understanding that performances in Balboa originated the term "Dog and Pony" show.

Dogs and ponies were but a few of the animals brought live on stage with human actors to participate in sex acts.

Years later, it always brought a smile to my face to be in a corporate meeting where some nice young female management understudy, newly out of Wharton, was asked by a senior manager to prepare a "dog and pony" show (a slide or power point presentation) for visiting corporate executives. My vivid imagination and visually oriented mind invariably chuckled as it drew a graphic picture of this fresh young corporate innocent performing in front of an esteemed audience, having sex with a small Shetland and a very large German Shepherd.

Many of the crewmembers on my ship partook of the delights of the flesh, but I decided to be a bystander. It wasn't that prudery or moral convictions came forward to guide this decision, it was simply that upon reflection, it seemed that Panama, being the true crossroads of the world, must contain a virtual cocktail of sexually transmitted germs left behind by worldly sailors. Additionally, the "meat on the hook"—mostly Indian girls out of the interior jungles—were ugly as mud fence posts. For the couple of days we stayed in Balboa, I became a sideline cheerleader, rooting the boys on and reminding them that I was the nominated ship doctor, meaning I had to stay healthy so that I could apply the sharp hypodermic needle waiting for them later. The crew did their best to leave their good will, earnings, and bodily fluids ashore in the economy of Panama. Ah, the life of a sailor.

Once we cleared the Panamanian capes, it was a straight shot to Asia. But my, my, my, what a long straight shot. A string, laid out on the face of our globe, stretching from the Panama Canal directly to Vietnam, was the Great Circle Route and would take a navigator so severely to the north from Panama that it would lay out over the mountains of Central America. Therefore, ships making this passage travel closely up the coast of Central America, staying as close to this great circle track as possible. The same string, if laid down starting at the North Pole, would touch Antarctica just short of the South Pole. Starting from Camden, we would be voyaging more than halfway around the world.

Again, the shipboard society quickly settled back into its well-worn, comfortable, long-passage lifestyle. It would be weeks before we saw land again; heck, with our unusual course track, it might be weeks before we saw another ship. It would not be fair or true to say that four-hour watches on the bridge of the ship were boring; that would imply a distaste for the whole life at sea. Often a four-hour watch went by with the ship on auto pilot, with almost no human contact, with no shipboard chores, with my eyes glued to that never-changing, never-arriving line…the horizon. My mind on those days pulled itself back into a zone, deep in thought, deep in memories, but very much finely tuned to any anomaly, to the sixth sense of experience where any small oddity brought me right back to the present. Alarms would ring in my head, and I would be ready to take action. Added to this sixth sense, I had been gifted with great eyesight. When something out there wasn't "right," the hair stood up on the back of my neck.

Plodding our way north along the coast of Central America one afternoon, found our ship experiencing a day where the Pacific Ocean lay smooth and flat as if it were a giant lake. As my eyes did a lazy circle in all directions, suddenly something on the horizon set off internal alarm bells. Rushing to look through binoculars, I saw what looked like a rock sticking out of the water almost dead ahead. I ran to the chart room, checked our position but could only find very deep water ahead. Still very concerned, I called the captain to the bridge. He took a long hard look and decided to alter the course of the ship, not wanting to take any chances that we could hit whatever it was out there. As we closed in on what continued to look more and more like a rock, a large seabird swooped in to gently land on the rock. Suddenly, likely due to the noise of our ship, the bird took off and the rock submerged. We began laughing once we realized that our rock was nothing more than a very large turtle, warming its shell in the tropical sun while giving a resting place to a bird. The water was deep, and we resumed our plodding course to the northwest.

Back into the tedium of a fourteen-knot crossing of the Pacific Ocean, our biggest concern had become the worn out condition of the ship's steam-powered engine. We carried thousands of gallons of bunker oil to feed burners in a large firebox, where it was ignited to heat water flowing through tubes. The water became steam and as it did so, it expanded greatly. This steam, under pressure, was heated again, causing it to expand further. The superheated steam under great pressure was then forced into a turbine, causing it to spin. The steam was exhausted from the turbine, condensed back to fresh water, and the cycle began all over. Engines powered by steam have been around since the nineteenth century, and while they work well, they have a great many moving parts. Moving parts wear out.

When I entered my maritime career, I chose to be a deck officer rather than an engineering officer. It took only one visit to the engine room of a large ship to help me with this decision. Steam engine rooms do not look like the space under the hood of your car. Instead they resemble a maze designed by a mad scientist who was given an unlimited supply of various-sized piping, told to contort it in every imaginable way, pump in heat directly from hell, add noise at a level of decibels designed to destroy human hearing, and cover everything either in an asbestos jacket or a film of grease and oil. And there you have it...the engine room of a steamship.

While I directed my career towards navigating and vessel operations, my respect for the officers and men who kept these maelstroms of piping, pumps, and gears running was immense. The imagination used by some of these men to keep complicated, worn out equipment running twenty-four hours a day, for months at a time, was truly amazing. When something gave up and stopped working from old age, there was no calling the Maytag repairman. These guys either had to find or cannibalize a spare part or fabricate one from scratch. It was a constant fight. In the case of the old *Exhibitor*, hardly a day went by without the phone ringing from the engine room to the bridge, informing us that they had to shut down the main engine in order to make some repair.

Ships without propulsion are one step away from being derelict. International rules refer to ships without means of propulsion as "not under command." The International Rules of the Road require that such vessels warn other shipping of their inability to move by showing a signal shape during the day and a pair of red lights hung in a line from the mast at night. As this voyage progressed, we found the ship sitting dead in the water so many times that eventually the captain ordered the permanent rigging of the two red lights to the mast with an on/off switch mounted in the wheelhouse. In my many years as a mate, I had never used not-under-command lights. Now it was a nightly event.

This constant breaking down of the propulsion plant finally got the undivided attention of the captain and chief engineer. They now believed that there was simply no chance of us making the Pacific Ocean crossing without first having shipyard repairs. Following the captain's teletype wire to Export Lines headquarters demanding immediate repairs to the old steam plant, an approval was given to send the ship to a yard. Working through the Navy, a divert order was issued telling the ship to change course to San Pedro, California, an order that the crew viewed as a gift from Lord Neptune himself. We were going to have liberty in LA, baby!

The port of San Pedro found a deserted spot to tie up the *Exhibitor*, a section of unused wharf on Terminal Island next to a federal penitentiary, as remote from normal human business as was possible in the Los Angeles basin. What was with this banishment? We had no diseases, not yet at least; that could not be it. The answer, of course, was that the Navy simply looked for the cheapest berth in California that could still be served by an engineering firm.

Guys in nice, white, starched jumpsuits were on the dock waiting to dive into our engine room and make a big fat fee, knowing in advance that we operated under a cost-plus contract. Cost-plus, what a great profit model! Extraordinary costs, such as emergency engineering, could be passed directly back to the government with very little audit. As usual, the deck department had no part of engineering, leaving us with what we thought would be time to sample the nightlife of Los Angeles.

At almost the same time that several officers had lined up a cab willing to haul us to some nice night spots, the captain informed us that we would sail at midnight, meaning we were back on watch two hours before that departure—not even time for what the Navy calls "Cinderella Liberty." The captain went on to inform us that the engineering company took one look at our "historic" steam engine and flatly stated that they really could do nothing for us. I believe one of them sarcastically suggested "Hospice Care."

The chief steward had been on the phone since our arrival and was able to acquire about three days of fresh milk, always a rare treat, but had no time to line up the delivery of fresh meats or vegetables, meaning we would continue a meal menu of thawed and canned food for our long passage. We knew that meals would become grim long before we tied up in Saigon, and then who knew what would be available. Out of all this gloom, one bright spot sprang up.

The chief engineer had been busy with chores other than the engine room. He managed to get a local liquor distributor on the phone, lining up an emergency delivery of several hundred more cases of beer for the officers. That, sports fans, is keeping your eye on the ball and prioritizing needs.

Just after midnight we cleared the Long Beach breakwater,

watching the bright lights of Los Angeles and Hollywood fade into the horizon. As always, I stood the midnight-to-four watch, so I found myself out on the bridge wing spending almost of the whole watch staring backwards at those disappearing twinkling lights as the bow of the ship plodded on into the gloom of the dark Pacific.

For many years in the early- to mid-1960s, it seemed that way too often as we left a port at night, my view was of brightly lit apartments full of friendly people, who I imagined were at some nice evening party in their cozy apartment. My despair came from knowing that my ship headed out into the black violence of some ocean. The bridge of a ship is always pitch black to protect the crew's night vision, and once underway, the bridge becomes as quiet as a tomb. Over and over I imagined myself back on the balcony at that party with a nice drink in my hand, watching this large mass of steel heading out into a vast ocean of charging waves and loneliness. In my imagination, I would stare intently from this balcony and then turn and head back inside to the brightly lit room full of folks laughing and making interesting conversation.

I reached the height of this imagined fairy tale one Saturday night leaving a port of Antwerp in Belgium. Due to their common trait of extreme tides, many northern European ports have their inner harbors guarded by locks, through which a departing ship must pass as it heads out to sea. Placing fancy apartment buildings next to the locks carries a romantic image.

On this particular evening, I was on watch after a cold winter's eve. There seemed to be parties and folks having fun on almost every floor of the nearby apartment buildings. The apartments were so close that it was possible to see smiling faces.

We knew that a raging storm in the North Sea lay waiting for us just outside the harbor entrance. There would be fog, howling wind, mixed snow and sleet and, of course, the usual SOS calls from some poor, unfortunate fisherman who would be left for the Coastal Guard to handle. I would be glued to the radar screen marking dozens of target ships moving in every direction of the compass, while giving orders to the helmsman in hopes of avoiding collisions. At 0400 when the watch ended, I would fall into my bunk dead tired with emotions worn to a frazzle, only to begin again a recurring "my ship is in fog nightmare," a repeating dream still sometimes plying my evening sleep to this day. Party animals, drink in hand, waved to us, but I could not wave back. Did they not have any idea the bleak evening waiting for me? There was no justice that a young guy like me had to go and they got to stay.

About thirty years later, long after my career as a ship's officer had ended, on an evening that found me attending a cocktail party at an apartment overlooking Puget Sound, a friend standing next to me noted the dark form of a large freighter headed out to sea and asked, "Now Bob, don't you miss being on the bridge of that ship?"

I answered with a preoccupied "Mmmm." I was already deep into memories of what it meant to test every skill I had worked so hard to hone to a razor sharp edge; of the memories of the responsibility born from life and death decisions; of what it meant to be a man among men at sea. Yes, I did miss it!

The December evening we steamed out into the Pacific from Los Angeles on the *Exhibitor* had none of the drama of the evening I faced in the stormy North Sea. Unknown to me, however, a new all-time-dangerous stormy night lay ahead just a scant two weeks away.

Now began the day after day and night after night of crossing the Pacific Ocean. The *Exhibitor* would follow a track well away from any recognized regular shipping lanes. The low latitude (near the Equator) waters of the Pacific generally reflected the pacified name given to this ocean, but our great circle route would be taking us to the stormy winter weather closer to the Aleutians than to the

The Faithful Sextant

tropics. Every day as we steamed to the northwest, the mid-ocean swells became longer and deeper, the result of having been pushed thousands of miles away from storms to the north. It was December; destiny would surely bring one of these regular winter storms into our planned line of track. About every other day, the engine would break down, leaving us to sit idly by as the engineers worked to rig a fix and get the propeller turning again.

Life aboard was mostly dull, except for cocktail time, the time when a group of officers brought drinks up to the radio room where happy hour would start. The "radio shack" drinking would last until dinnertime, afterward to reconvene in the captain's office. As mentioned, Captain Winebrenner was one hard-drinking, cigar-chomping, ace poker player.

Two poker games took hold most nights, one topside for the officers and one in the foc'sle for the unlicensed crewmembers. Our Chinese-American bosun, a man serving in many cases as the titular head of the unlicensed crew, ran the downstairs game. A nice diversion from mid-ocean tedium, these two games were played for money, and as so often happens, the stakes continued to grow until the friendly pots grew into life-changing monsters. The captain's poker games were working fine until one of those once-in-a-lifetime hands came along to change everything. Here is the story of how that happened.

The game is seven-card stud with no wild cards. I'm dealt my first three cards with two kings in the hole and a low card up, telling me to bet low to draw in some suckers. Across from me are two guys also with pairs hidden. The next three cards dealt up, so everyone can see, give me another king, along with three small cards—all spades—the makings of a flush. This is great camouflage to confuse the other players, preventing them from ever thinking that I now have three kings. The two other guys, however, both draw well-disguised full houses, a hand that beats almost any poker hand, including three kings or a flush. I am off everyone's radar screen.

At the sixth card, also dealt up and showing, the two other

remaining players start raising the pot like there is no tomorrow. A sinking feeling invades my thoughts, warning me that my three kings, or even my potential flush, are good hands but likely only the third best hand at this table. Still, a little twinge in my gut tells me to suck it up and stay in.

On the seventh card, dealt down and out of sight, I draw my fourth king. I now own three kings down and not visible, and one more lonely looking king of spades sitting next to three other spades, all proudly announcing the possibility of a spade flush. The four kings is a whale hand and now ranks as the second best hand of my forever poker life. The only two hands in all of poker that will beat me are four aces or a straight flush. Having paid careful attention to the cards discarded and showing, I see aces split; no four of a kind is possible.

In poker, the odds of drawing a straight flush are more than 700,000 to 1 or once in every two and half lifetimes for an active poker player. I refuse to believe this is my once in more than two lifetimes to see a straight flush opposing me. My four kings is one of those hands justifying a trip to the safe to pull out the deed to your house and put it in the pot. And I am sitting across from two guys who have very strong full house hands and who believe me to have a flush—a good hand but beaten by the full houses. My camouflage is perfect. Now the betting becomes insane.

Of the two guys betting against me, one is an irritable engineer I would love to bankrupt, but unfortunately, the other is my good friend and wingman, Bernie. The captain has dropped out and is staring at me with blue eyes piercing my soul. As good a player as Captain Winebrenner is, he has already figured out that I must be sitting on a whale. He is enjoying this until he suddenly realizes that there is trouble brewing. Bernie, now having correctly guessed that he has the higher full house, has just asked the captain to allow him to bet his earnings from the rest of the trip on this one hand. This is going to be big trouble and the captain knows it because he knows we are friends and this will certainly end our friendship. But he also knows there is a bigger problem. He cannot have Bernie bet and lose his paycheck.

Here is my problem. I do not want to take all of Bernie's money, but these two guys keep raising each other and I have to call or drop out and lose all my money; and I have the winning hand. And now Bernie wants to bet his entire paycheck, knowing this will force the other guy and me to fold. I cannot call and take Bernie's paycheck, nor can I ever fold this hand of a lifetime. This is a terrible dilemma.

Before the captain can answer Bern's request, I jump up and yell. "Hey, guys, this is enough. I have a hand you cannot beat!"

Lord, I might just as well have thrown nitro into the pot. The table explodes. "Just who the hell do you think you are, McEliece?" shoutes Bernie. "Who appointed you freakin' god of the poker table?"

Bernie thinks I am trying to keep him from taking the other guy's money. He has never even considered that I am still in the running to win the pot.

I look at the captain and ask, "If I turn over right now, can I keep the pot and end this before someone gets hurt?" The captain, who now knows for sure that I have a whale, nods that he thinks it will be okay under normal poker rules. But I damned well better have the winning hand, otherwise I am out and my money is forfeit and Bernie can keep raising the pot. Bernie and the other engineer snarl at me, letting me know that I sure am a cocky son of a bitch, but both have by now smell a giant rat trap about to spring shut on their dream poker hands

Laying my three hidden kings out alongside the one showing, left the room speechless. I rake in the huge pot and announce that it is time for me to get ready to go on watch. Captain Winebrenner is still staring at me with a smile on his face. He nods, knowing that what I have done to save my friendship with Bernie is much more important than taking all of his money. He also realizes that having an officer in the engine room for the rest of the trip working off a debt to another crewmember would not have been a good thing for the safety of the ship.

After that evening, the captain looked at me differently.

Several nights later, one of the very young ordinary seamen, a sailor assigned to my watch and serving on his first-ever voyage to sea, lost his entire paycheck to the bosun in somewhat the same situation at the downstairs game. The young sailor came up on watch about 0100 that night to serve as lookout on the bridge wing, when, after about ten minutes, he collapsed on the deck from the shock that he had lost his entire payout for this trip.

After we had revived him, the captain and I had a talk about the poker games. We agreed to set limit rules to eliminate the use of allotments. Later, the captain made some under-the-table agreement with the bosun to give the young man back his wages.

The allotment system we used was never meant to be a banking system to support games of chance. After these incidents, everyone calmed down and began to again act like shipmates.

A treacherous smiler
With teeth white as milk,
A savage beguiler
In sheathings of silk,

The sea creeps to pillage,
She leaps to her prey;
A child of the village
Was murdered today,

She came up to meet him
In a smooth golden cloak,
She choked him and beat him
To death, for a joke.

Her bright locks were tangled,
She shouted for joy,
With one hand she strangled
A strong little boy.

Now in silence she lingers
Beside him all night
To wash her long fingers
In silvery light.

Elinor Wylie
"Sea Lullaby" from
Nets to Catch the Wind

Typhoon

As we neared the Asian mainland, warnings of a major change to our dull routine began to appear on our weather fax. Moving in a huge parabolic track, a very intense typhoon was spreading her tentacles as she moved now in a more northeasterly direction. Our route brought us south of Japan, through the Philippine Sea and into the Straight of Luzon, just north of the Philippines, on a direct collision course with this storm. The recent weather synopsis made this typhoon out to be dangerous.

All mariners have a special place in their psyche for bad weather at sea. Weather soon develops its own personality and life existence, the kind of thing that makes mythology, fables, legends, and much superstition. Digging deep into my honesty locker, I cannot leave the reader to assume that merchant sailors spend time reading the Greek classics so that they will develop a kinship with mythological gods of weather. However, I have always believed that mythology has a bastard stepchild called superstition. Indeed, it is this untamed beast of ignorance that guides much of the daily life of sailors.

Take for example Samuel Taylor Coleridge's epic poem *The Rime of the Ancient Mariner*. In Coleridge's epic, a crewmember had shot and killed an albatross with a crossbow. Shortly after the killing of the albatross, the wind ceased as the ship entered the Pacific Doldrums. To quote,

The Faithful Sextant

And I had done them a hellish thing
And it would work 'em woe:
Ah wretch! said they, the bird to slay,
That made the breeze to blow.

And thus the killer of the albatross became the "Jonah" of the ship. In the *Rime*, the dead bird becomes symbolically hung around the neck of the sailor who shot it, leading to our current day rub of "having an albatross hung from one's neck."

Merchant sailors have changed little in the past hundreds of years, still superstitiously believing that one bad shipmate can bring bad luck upon the entire ship and her crew. Taking the place today of shooting birds with crossbows are other more contemporary offenses to the gods of superstition, seen in the current widely held belief that failure to pay a prostitute will bring bad luck or bad weather. Many times I heard sailors gossiping about the supposed guilty shipmate who ran out on his bar girl, causing us to suffer a particularly bad storm. This was carried so far that I once saw a sailor dropped off at the gangway by a cab so drunk he could not walk, but sober enough to hand a wad of dollars to a shipmate pleading with him to return to the New Texas Bar and give this money to Maria.

Humans, and especially poorly educated sailors, find that the stronger a superstitious emotion, the stronger the consequences of breaking the bond with the superstition. Aircraft pilots and sailors lead lives dedicated to the avoidance of serious bad weather for an obvious reason. Our inability to deal with Mother Nature's tantrums makes for a miserable day or, at the extreme, a life-threatening day when flotation becomes questionable. At sea it is all about floating. The sailor must stay afloat. A philosopher hundreds of years ago wrote, "Going to sea is just like being in prison, with the added risk of drowning."

Scientific knowledge can defeat the fear of superstition, and man has progressed a long way in understanding and forecasting bad weather, and we have learned many a trick to say afloat. Avoiding its inevitable misery is another story.

Steering the ship around the forecast path of a storm may sound like the answer, but in practical terms, very little benefit is found. Oceans behave nothing like large landmasses. Wind on the continent pushes dust and moves on; wind on the ocean surface pushes water, and it keeps pushing. And soon the real problem for mariners arrives as moving mountains of water.

There are storms, however, which come with more than a misery quotient; they are the ones able to alter human existence. Naming them memorializes the most terrible of storms, typhoons, and hurricanes, almost as if we could, for all time, accredit them with human emotions.

Regardless of a storm's name, weather forecasters recognize the bad ones by how closely the isobar lines are spaced near the storm's center. Isobar lines measure the gradient of distance between equal lines of pressure such that the closer the lines are together, the stronger the wind will howl. The isobar lines on our approaching storm fell almost on top of each other, the kind of low-pressure center that resembled a black hole. There was something else. This thing was immense, not only large, but out of proportion, like the sense of looking at Greenland on a Mercator projection chart.

We entered the outskirts of this wind metropolis just as the afternoon segment of my watch wrapped up. At sea it always seemed that the weather went from a nice day to an ugly day a lot faster than it went from ugly to nice, again reminding us how fast the ocean waves and the weather can change when both the ship and the storm are moving towards each other. Following dinner, I went immediately to bed, hoping to get some sleep, knowing my next watch—starting at midnight—would be a long four hours. Sometime around ten o'clock,

The Faithful Sextant

the violent rolling and pitching of the ship tossed me out of my bunk to the floor. The old dirty-weather trick of stuffing a couple of life jackets under the side of the mattress, forming a V-shaped sleeping pocket, gave some security from another toss to the deck, but sleep was not going to be my friend this evening. Giving up around eleven, I dressed for watch and joined the captain, the junior third mate, and the helmsman on the bridge.

Once in the wheelhouse, the radar provided the only light, casting an eerie green loom as the sweep rotated around the screen, its parabolic antenna expelling waves of electromagnetic energy into the stormy dark night, as if daring one of these pips to hit something and return screaming back to us at the speed of light. I instinctively grabbed for the radar housing. This would give me something to hold onto until the pupils of my eyes expanded. Expecting to see a blank radar screen showing only distance rings and the continuously rotating sweep, I was shocked to see two strong targets, one large blip out near the forty-mile ring and another smaller one in near the twelve-mile ring. These two blips got my immediate attention. What could possibly be on our radar on this stormy night in the lonely North Pacific Ocean? Breaking into the silence of the wheelhouse, I asked the captain about these targets.

"We picked those two up about four hours ago. The larger, more distant blip is the infamous island of Iwo Jima. The second, smaller and nearer one, is her little sister, Minami-Iwo or south Iwo, another volcanic island. There is a third little island in this chain, Kit Iwo (North Iwo), but it's just outside of our radar range."

Well, I gratefully thought, at least we know exactly where we are! Knowing your exact position back in the days of sextant navigation, when no one had seen a celestial body, including the sun, for days was a really big deal.

So much for good news.

Waiting quietly in a dark corner of the wheelhouse as my pupils expanded to capture night vision, thoughts wandered to a personal memory of what seemed like a long time ago and a night never to be forgotten. It happened two years earlier while serving as a junior deck officer on the bridge of a large military troop ship during a rather nasty, North Atlantic winter passage from New York to Germany. For a change, on this voyage we would transit over the top of Scotland, through the narrow Pentland Firth, and down to Germany. This particular evening just happened to be Christmas Eve, a night that found our ship in a vile snowstorm as we desperately searched to make landfall near a rocky island off the coast of Scotland.

Fresh out of the Academy, serving on my fourth voyage as a licensed officer, I was still learning. There would be many lessons taught that evening.

Lesson number one: Driving snowflakes can partially block pulses emitted by our old 10cm radar. We were flying blind through the blizzard. Lesson number two: The captain of the ship likes to party with the passengers on Christmas Eve. He was down in his fancy uniform entertaining passengers. My young mind that evening was visualizing New York Times headlines, "Troopship Hits Rocks on Christmas Eve. Over 3000 troops, passengers, and crew missing!"

It turned out that our dead reckoning was accurate enough to get us into Pentland Firth, a narrow two-mile-wide gap over the top of Scotland on Christmas morning, but what a night it had been for the young junior deck officer.

Back aboard the *Exhibitor* I am thinking, *great! Two uninhabited piles of glistening, black volcanic rock upon which we might find ourselves stranded while being pounded to pieces by enormous typhoon-driven waves.* Our steam engine on this old rust bucket has been failing almost every night. A ship with no propulsion would leave us helplessly adrift, just upwind from these deathtraps when the nearest help would be a Japanese maritime patrol aircraft over 500 miles away. And, oh yeah, it's almost Christmas Eve again. No mariner ever wishes for trouble, but this little thought of mine about our power plant was to turn very prescient later that night.

All mariners since the days of the sailing ship have a dread fear of rocky leeward shores. On some level we believe that the gods of the seas create a universal magnetism, drawing ships downwind to these rocky lee shores as if some apparition from Greek mythology sings a siren call to timorous mariners lost at sea. I can almost feel the pull.

With night vision now sharply tuned, I begin asking questions of the fourth mate prior to relieving him of the watch. His news is not good, the worst being the still-falling barometer, a sure sign that things are going to get worse before they get better. I repeat the ships heading and formally relieve him of the watch while finding a spot near the forward windows on the other side of the bridge from the captain. *Let's see if I can find a place to be comfortable for the next four hours*, I am thinking. On nights like this there is not even a helpful wake-me-up cup of coffee as everything is locked down or secured in some other manner.

The wheelhouse on a merchant vessel is not only very dark at night; it is, with the exception of storm noises, a very quiet place. Two crewmembers, the watch officer and a seaman acting as an additional lookout on the bridge wing, usually occupy this lonely place. But in stormy weather with huge waves, the seaman reverts to a helmsman steering the ship. The auto helm system, driven by a large gyrocompass, has no capability to anticipate charging waves or make corrections before the wave arrives. It also lacks the experienced eye of a skilled mariner. Nights like this would also find the captain in the wheelhouse. This setting of deep solitude leaves a man with only the darkness and his deepest thoughts as company. Even on a violent night like this, "awake dreams" creep back. As my mind finishes reviewing all of the horrors of what-ifs for this evening, it begins again to remember other stories. Spontaneously, the story of my good friend and Kings Point classmate, Russ McVay, comes strolling out of receded memories for a revisit of tales of destruction and death.

Not only was Russ a classmate at Kings Point, he was in my section, and we were both boat racers on the varsity sailing team. Being on the sailing team, Russ and I had the same sea year split, so that when our second year at the Academy began, we both joined ships and went off to sea for our maritime practical training. Russ left from New York on the *SS Pioneer Muse* bound, through the Panama Canal, for the Orient, and I left from New Orleans on the *SS Del Sol* with classmate Bill Long, for the east coast of South America. The voyage Russ took that training year was a mirror image of my current voyage on the *SS Exhibitor*. Even though the *Pioneer Muse* was headed to Manila and we are now headed to Saigon, the ocean routes would have been almost identical. We are following along right behind where Russ had been four years earlier.

On board the *Pioneer Muse* as a cadet, Russ had found himself on the western side of typhoon Violet, racing along with huge waves and seventy mile-per-hour winds blowing from behind them. Just after 0400 he was thrown from his bunk by a huge force as his ship ran directly into a tiny, two-mile-wide volcanic island by the name of Kita Daito Jima. Kita Daito, another one of these nasty pieces of volcanic rock, is about 200 miles to the west of our current position, right on the track to clear Luzon Island.

Even though the typhoon was moving away from the *Pioneer Muse*, there would never be a way to remove her hull from the cruel sharp volcanic rocks. The huge ocean swells remaining behind the typhoon would rip her guts out in a short matter of days; it was time to evacuate the crew to the island. In a true twist of fate, a US Navy aircraft carrier, the *USS Princeton*, was nearby, and would be able to collect the stranded sailors from this volcanic rock. Russ related this story later back at the academy. He added a postscript to the story that was funny. It seemed that Russ had never in his life ridden on any type of aircraft, and now he got his first ride by air as a Navy chopper lifted him to the safety of an aircraft carrier. Imagine the looks of disbelief telling your grandchildren that your first aircraft ride was in a Navy rescue chopper while being saved from a ship stranded on a rocky shore in a storm?

The captain of the *Pioneer Muse* remained on the ship to protect the company's salvage rights, but was removed the next day when the ship broke in two and became a total loss. She had broken up in less than forty-eight hours. My mind is just trying to imagine that. The *Muse* was a new mariner class ship forged out of modern steel with welded construction; we are just an old, pre-WWII, riveted rust bucket. How many hours would it take us to break up on the rocks of Iwo Jima; maybe two?

On the *SS Exhibitor*, steadily increasing wind strength, forming typhoon-sized waves, forces the captain to alter course into the wind as a precaution to the danger found in wallowing and uncontrolled rolling. Were we to fall broadside into the ever-steepening troughs and wave faces, the likelihood of damage to the ship and cargo would be serious. Even with this course change, twenty to thirty degree rolls become the new normal. And in spite of the efforts of every crewmember to secure every little coffee cup and piece of nautical gear, each roll brings new unsettling sounds of crashing cargo and equipment. Down on the main deck, in front of the bridge house, I can see the chief mate with a pair of ABs (able-bodied seaman), working to secure one of the gigantic Caterpillar D-8 tractors, part of the equipment we had loaded for the Army combat engineer battalion. In spite of the secure chains holding down these steel mammoths, the frantic motion of the ship causes slack in the chains, letting the huge bulldozer slide a few feet from side to side. As the ship takes deep rolls, showers of sparks are sent up from the steel of their massive treads grinding into the steel of the ships main deck. Shortly, the captain called these crewmembers back inside, knowing that the risks of working near these unruly steel beasts did not warrant the slim chance of stopping this bulldozer dance. Danger to the seaworthiness of the ship is another matter.

The barometer proves correct; the storm continues to intensify. Without wind speed measuring equipment on this old ship, only the experienced eye looking at the tops of the waves can guess the wind speeds. Indeed, based on the violence of foam blown off the caps of waves and the pitch of the shrieking sound in the ship's rigging, Captain Winebrenner and I estimate the wind speed at seventy to ninety knots, but later I was to learn that wind speeds recorded by meteorologists were 100 to 140 knots.

As for the height of the waves, this is a total guess, as it always is in storms because each wave has its own personality and shape. Oceanographers have discovered that large, mid-ocean waves will travel for days as they cross the breath of an ocean, with the length of period from crest to crest stretching out longer every day as friction and gravity separates the distance from one peak to the next. When new storms, such as ours, create new young waves with shorter periods, the two (or in some cases, three or four or more) wave trains will travel together but at different speeds and with different heights and widths. This differential in speed and length of the harmonics of waves will cause wave trains of varying age, strength, and period to form on top of each other like layers on a cake. This is how rogue waves are formed. A rogue wave has a very short life span as the multiple wave trains move apart from each other and begin to cancel out the wave height. The mariner who happens upon this short-lived monster, the rogue wave, has found himself face to face with a killer. Throughout history, many mariners have seen rogue waves, but those who have seen the biggest and the worst have rarely lived to tell about it. Where there are multiple wave trains running together, the harmonics are such that often times the seventh wave is much steeper than those before or after it, every forty-ninth wave (seven squared) becoming higher than that, and so on.

Storied height of waves as boasted by mariners and oceanographers can be as elusive as clichés about the size of a fish reeled in, and there is no need to try to top whoppers. But when our ship lay in the bottom trough of the largest of waves that evening, where the peaks towered over our highest masts, instinct and science told me that we were no longer in charge of our destiny; we were along for the ride.

With a solid grip on the rail below the pilothouse windows, feet spread as wide as possible, I stare out into a solid blackness where I see no visual punctuation in the form of a horizon or stars. The huge waves crashing over and around the forward bow area, strongly outlined by small phosphoric sea life churned to brightness by the crashing peaks, is to be the halo of my world for the next four hours. The effect of the brilliant flashes of phosphorescent sea life creates a feeling of finding oneself on an extreme new ride created by sinister technicians at Disneyland. The seawater at the tops of these huge waves, blown so hard as to create a frothy mass called "gray beards" sends spume flying as if seawater was no longer a liquid, now becoming a feathered beast.

The totality of flying though this maelstrom is constant motion in every direction without providing any perspective of actually making headway towards our destination. This intuition about lack of headway is confirmed by Iwo Jima, now a steady, unmoving blip on the radar screen. We are making little passage through the ocean, merely keeping our bow pointed into the wind while continuing to pray that we may see the dawn and better weather. The violence expressed through the battle of steel slamming into walls of water has no match in everyday human experience. The steel ship—man's creation meant to conquer the oceans—is supposed to always win the battle of steel versus water by making the water move aside, but watching the spectacle of this epic battle, twinges of skepticism and fear begin to creep into the core of my being.

Every fifteen minutes or so I struggle over to the radar to confirm that we are alone in this mess and that Mount Suribachi, last resting site for many fine young American Marines, is still on the screen and still thirty miles away. We are going nowhere, but by God, we know where we are, and by God, we are still afloat!

With no warning, the ship falls suddenly into the trough of a super wave, sending the hull into a violent roll to starboard and giving us the feeling that the deck below our feet had fallen from the edge of the world. This sensation is one of being on a rollercoaster having just crested the first big drop, except we are standing inside a giant ship weighing thousands of tons. How can something this huge just drop?

I am pitched to the far side of the bridge where I find that I am now standing on the wall not on the floor. This is confirmed by a glance over to the bubble inclinometer showing that the ship has just rolled beyond forty-five degrees. Playing in the background is the sound of many things, big and small, suddenly breaking their silent bond with gravity, now flying across open areas to find a new resting place. My heart rate has just passed 100; adrenalin is pumping through every fiber of my body. The *Exhibitor* slowly rights herself to begin a slow climb up the shoulder of the next wave as if to peek over the edge for a view of better weather. As this happens, the entire ship gives a shudder from end to end concurrent with a sudden stopping of noise. The *Exhibitor* has now slid to the bottom of an unusually deep trough of a monster wave; one so deep as to block the wind from shrieking through our rigging. Suddenly everything feels at rest, as if for a brief moment all has returned to normal.

As the *Exhibitor* slowly sheds tons of seawater to begin its long climb up to a new wave crest. Then I look below to the main deck and what I see freezes me in alarm. One of the huge Caterpillar D-8 Bulldozers secured by chains on the main deck between the hatch coaming and the side of the ship is sliding across the deck in a shower of sparks, having broken free of the chains that had secured the rear part of its treads. This is a serious problem. The partially loose bulldozer could smash through the coaming around the hatch cover, allowing green seawater to flow directly down into hatch number three, potentially putting the flotation of the ship at risk. The captain looks over at me with a troubled look on his face, one that says, "This will have to be fixed before it is out of control." There is no shouting or giving of orders; what are we going to do, send down some men to try to capture and subdue this iron monster doing a jig on our main deck? He then mutters, "Shit!" and looks at his watch so that he can record a log entry for the beginning of an event unlikely to have a happy ending.

The ship has now clawed its way to the top of the next wave crest and is beginning the sleigh-ride down into the trough at a new and more dangerous sideways angle. It is the force of water pressing against a ship's rudder that turns a ship to its helmsman's order, an effect that only works if the rudder is actually in the water, something pretty much not happening at that time. As the ship rises to the crest of a wave, the rudder and sometimes even the propeller are largely out of the water, allowing nature's forces of wind and waves to become our new steering mechanism. We have no control over these forces. Once the *Exhibitor* climbs to the crest of this latest giant wave and begins the ride down to the trough, the rudder loses its "bite" and sends us down the side of the wave at a crazy angle. At the bottom of the wave trough our bow digs in, once again sending tons of green seawater rushing over the deck, making all visibility disappear as seawater spray covers the bridge windows as if the ship were in the most violent of car washes.

Having once again been thrown across the bridge, I recover myself from a pile of books and charts collected on the low side of the mayhem. Intently looking out the forward window, after a sweep by a wiper blade, what I see freezes me. The brand new Caterpillar D-8 bulldozer is no longer on the deck of the ship. Tons of seawater rushing across the main deck had crashed into this 87,000-pound machine, snapping the last of its securing chains, sending it spiraling across the main deck, where it ripped out our safety chains to go tumbling over the side of the ship.

Traditional design of seagoing ships finds extensions of the ship's hull above the main deck as a way of preventing crewmembers and cargo from washing overboard. These barriers have a name; they are called bulwarks. The *Exhibitor* was never designed with strong, steel-plate bulwarks, instead being equipped with insubstantial, four-foot-long, steel pipe stanchions to be inserted into fittings in the deck. Running through these well-rusted stanchions were three lengths of chain running from the bow to the mid-ship house providing the only security to keep crew and cargo from washing over the side.

I never saw the D-8 bulldozer tumble overboard as it smashed into and through this feeble attempt at a bulwark, but as the wheelhouse windows clear, all that remains is a tangle of chain and stanchion and a deserted spot on the main deck where once a large earth mover had been secured before plunging into the depths of a dark ocean.

I do a double take. All of this just could not have happened in the last two minutes. As often happens with a group of large, violent waves, suddenly the ocean becomes very quiet and well behaved for several moments, giving me a chance to look over at the captain, who has a shared expression of anxiety and wonderment on his face as he turns to me, saying, "Now that's going to cause a whole shitload of paperwork, isn't it?"

Many months later, I spoke to a guy knowledgeable about bulldozers, asking, "So just how much does a new Cat D8 cost these days?" "Somewhere in the ballpark of about $75,000" was his answer. This valuation was, of course, couched in 1965 dollars.

Caterpillar has made changes to this most symbolic of its line of heavy equipment, but the D8 (t) is still the workhorse of their product line, and you will need more than one million dollars to buy the new model in 2015. The real shocker to our story, however, was that in almost the only time I can remember, it turned out that Captain Winebrenner's prediction was wrong. There was no big paperwork deal once we got to Saigon. As I remember it, the sergeant in charge of the cargo discharge in Saigon sort of shrugged his shoulder, took a pen, scratched through the entry on the manifest and that was that. The US taxpayers had just paid for a newly minted, million-dollar fish reef about three miles below the surface of the Pacific Ocean and about thirty miles south of Iwo Jima.

Later, in a dream, I visualized this huge bulldozer, its durable yellow Caterpillar paintjob replaced by military olive drab, taking some time to sink three miles to the ocean bottom where it plowed into the seabed floor, blade first, at about thirty miles per hour creating a nice long furrow; the only time in its short life that it was able to perform the job for which a team of skilled workers at the Caterpillar plant in Peoria had spent hundreds of caring man-hours to manufacture.

Meanwhile, our situation has not changed much except that now we have an ever so slight list to port due to the missing weight of the tractor. As my heartbeat and blood pressure slowly come down, the ship's bell interrupts the momentary lull with four chimes. Oh great, it's 0200; there's only two more hours of this watch to fight through. Within five minutes of the chiming of the ship's clock, our internal phone begins to ring. Grabbing the handset, the captain answers with a stressed out, "What now?" to the voice of the chief engineer calling from the engine room. Many "uh-huhs" later, spaced between periods of concerned silence, he asks, "How bad is it?" Then more "uh-huhs," and finally, "Keep me advised immediately. I will be on the bridge."

Once off the phone, he looks at me and with apprehension says,

"We have got to slow down. That last pounding has broken loose something in the engine room; there is a lot of water coming into the bilges." I ask him if he thinks we are going to lose the plant, and he just shrugs, saying, "I hope not, but this sounds very serious."

As the reduction in steam pressure to the turbines slows the propeller shaft, maintaining the ship's heading into the towering waves will become impossible. Watching the engine speed drop, we notice the bow hesitate as it climbs the face of the next wave, eventually losing the fight with the wind and falling off to leeward. My helmsman turns to me with a look of concern. "I have her hard over mate. She ain't gonna hold agin' this wind."

"That's okay, Jonesy," the captain interjects. "Leave your helm at twenty degrees to port; any more than that just slows the ship down and does little good to get the bow over."

We are doing the best we can, but soon the ship begins to wallow in the trough of the big waves as our rolling becomes unmanageable. The captain and I discuss turning the ship and running downwind as a solution to the rolling, quickly eliminating that idea as it would send us speeding towards Iwo Jima and her two little sisters. Dancing around this volcanic chain at night in a lame ship is just too dangerous; staying upwind is our best hope. The captain noted, "You know, in the time since Captain James Cook first landed a survey party on the beach at Iwo Jima two centuries ago, forces have raised the island a couple hundred feet. Who knows what underwater rocks in this poorly surveyed area might have risen to sit close enough to the surface to rip the guts out of this old ship. We need to stay as far from this nasty volcanic lee shore as we can."

Several minutes later found the captain once again on the phone with the chief engineer; my ears straining to overhear a conversation that told me that things were well past serious. The rate of seawater flooding into the engine room will soon put the boilers at risk of flooding, resulting in the total loss of the propulsion plant, followed by the very real possibility that the ship could be trapped in the trough of one these huge waves, forced over on her side past the point of recovery, and sent to the bottom.

My thoughts now turn to those two dilapidated lifeboats stowed on opposite sides of the ship. Each lifeboat has the capacity to hold the entire crew, the thinking being that redundancy leads to safety. Lifeboats are launched by gravity; thus if the reader visualizes a ship listing say thirty-five degrees to one side, the lifeboat on the high side would not launch as the force of gravity would pin the boat to the side of the ship, not allowing the boat to be lowered into the water. In that case, the boat on the lower side could be launched carrying all hands, an example of reasonable planning under reasonable conditions. Nothing is reasonable about our typhoon-driven evening. The ship is rolling more than thirty-five degrees to the starboard side, followed some tens of seconds later by a roll of the same amount to the port side. Now just how in the hell are we to pick which boat to launch?

In addition to the above conundrum, I remember that we have not lowered either of these boats for months because it was impossible to recover them. What if a boat cannot be launched? What if the straps holding the boat in its cradle are rusted closed? What if the lines needed to hold the boat-falls next to the ship for crew boarding cannot be found? What if the boat rudder is not in the boat? What if the bilge plugs needed to close the rainwater drain holes are missing? What if all of the other survival gear that we have never inventoried is missing? Of what use then will these things called lifeboats be to us?

Land, even though it is uninhabited, is only thirty miles away: a tiny speck in a huge ocean. What chance will we have of navigating through huge waves in a tiny open boat, trying to find a speck on the horizon? Have any of the officers checked to see if the boat compass has survived the fall to the pier in the shipyard? Why had the Coast Guard inspection officer not required us to do a lifeboat inventory prior to leaving the shipyard? Damn it…there are only questions, serious questions and no answers.

Even accounting for my youth, I have by now made over two

The Faithful Sextant

dozen voyages to sea, and I am beginning to feel and act like an experienced mariner. In spite of some demanding experiences, I have never even come close to having to abandon a ship. I have, however, several years earlier, launched a lifeboat at sea in the middle of the ocean, in what had become a never-to-be-forgotten experience. Suddenly, and without warning, my anxiety-ridden mind drags out this memory as if it were the RSVP to the lifeboat party we may be having later this night.

Following graduation from the Maritime Academy, I found the first step in my seagoing career as a junior deck officer on one of the last of a kind of specialized ship: a troop carrier. Falling in line with World War II tradition, this troop carrier is nothing more than a large passenger ship, taken over by the Navy, painted gray, and operated by civilian mariners. Outfitted to carry about 2000 Army troops, it is the same ship described in the Christmas Eve story told earlier. In addition to the troop compartments found deep below decks, there remain nice passenger staterooms left in place from her days of carrying fee-paying passengers. Now this sometime passenger ship/troopship could carry over 400 military dependents such as spouses and children, who were traveling to be with their deployed family members.

Trips on these ships were a routine of picking up soldiers and their dependents in Brooklyn, NY and taking them to Germany and England and returning with rotating soldiers and families. Often during these voyages the Navy would have their sealift ships, including the troop carriers, do things that commercial ships would never do.

One such chore was to test new lifesaving equipment for government contractors. This trip in question, several voyages after the Christmas Eve adventure, found us equipped with a new, high-tech buoy with a radio signal and a strobe light. This buoy was designed to be thrown overboard following reports of an accidental fall of a passenger from the ship into the sea—what mariners know as a man-overboard event. The purpose of this high-tech buoy was to help locate the person floating in the water. In order to test this new device for the Navy, the captain had planned to find a calm day mid-ocean and have a man-like floating dummy—kept just for such tests—thrown over the side, at which time we would proceed with a crew training event as well as an equipment test. Once the dummy was in the water and a report of "man-overboard" sounded, the buoy would be tossed overboard, followed by the launching of a motorized lifeboat to retrieve both the dummy and the buoy: a practical man-overboard exercise.

This exercise sounded like the greatest of fun to me, and I pleaded with the captain to appoint me the boat commander. I convinced him that my years of small boat experience would make me the perfect boat commander, an argument to which the captain agreed, green-lighting my command of the recovery boat. In the heat of the glamour to show off my skills to the nurses on board, and the eligible dependent daughters, it slipped my notice that none of the more senior officers showed any interest in this chore: a clear warning sign. Also failing to bubble to the surface was the long-standing advice from my veteran father: "In the Army, never, and I mean never, volunteer for anything."

Soon enough the weather moderated in the middle of the Atlantic Ocean, allowing for the announcement one afternoon that all were invited to witness this exercise. The chief mate had carefully picked the boat crew, filling it with grizzled old bosuns, ABs, and a couple of older engineers to run the boat's diesel engine, instructing us to report to the starboard boat deck launching area as the ship slowed to about one knot.

The dummy was then tossed overboard, followed by the deployment of the new high-tech strobe buoy as the appointed boat crew slowly began to lower the boat away. Standing in the stern, rudder tiller firmly in hand, I glanced hopefully at the crew and quickly realized that the boat commander (that's me), who had just turned twenty-two, still fighting the last wars of teenage acne, was by far the youngest person on board. Well, all of a sudden, this exercise became something for which I was not mentally or emotionally prepared. This was not going to be the same as pulling a launch away from the old Yacht Club dock to take fresh sandwiches to the race committee. *Oh dear God, please do not let my voice crack when I give my first order*, my mind was pleading.

Just before the life boat was ready to plunge into the ocean, I looked back up above to the troopship where I saw thousands of soldiers, hundreds of passengers, and what seemed like every officer on the ship, including the captain and chief mate, lining the rails of the various outside decks of the ship: a real festive atmosphere and a nice break from mid-ocean boredom. This was far and away the largest audience ever to have witnessed any event in which I starred. There were thousands of eyeballs focused on my every move, my every order.... This part of the officer in command thing had never been part of my expectations for this boat trip.

Buck up, man, you have done this lifeboat launching thing at the Academy many times in front of the toughest audience of all—your classmates. You are fully qualified, and this is no big deal, my little inner voice entreated.

As we lowered the boat to the water, the first of several surprises was just how huge the ship was and how small was our boat. The next surprise was about those calm waves as seen from the deck of the big ship. When seen at eyeball level, they were unexpectedly deep and large. Holy oarlocks, Batman, these deep ocean waves are nothing like even a stormy day in good old Long Island Sound.

Grabbing a deep breath, I now gave the order to release the boat-falls, dropping the boat into the water, followed by a command to start the engine, which an engineer did in quick order. So far everything was working to my best expectation, and my years of boat experience were slowly overcoming irrational fears. Now my eyes leaped from the bow of our boat back up to the ship as I readied for my preparatory order to release the boat painter.

A boat painter is a long rope, about three hundred feet in length, led from the bow of our little life boat, way up to a cleat near the bow of the mother ship. As the ship continued at about two knots through the water, this painter pulled us along, giving us headway so that the rudder in the small boat would steer her and would keep us alongside until such time that the boat engine was running smoothly, and we were ready to shear away. Once ready to begin our run, we would cast off this line, turning freely away to find and secure the buoy and the dummy. But releasing the painter took much more seamanship than just untying the line from the cleat and tossing it out into the seawater. Assuming that there was an experienced AB at the bow to handle this job, it did not enter my mind to verify his experience or ability to perform this most important task.

Things in the little bobbing boat were now happening very fast. We needed to get away from this massive gray steel wall—the side of the troop ship—before a wave slammed our little boat into her hull. With my eye on the big ship, I yelled my order forward to release the boat painter, followed by my hard push of the rudder tiller to port, steering the lifeboat away from the ship. In an instant disaster struck, and it struck hard in a way now permanently embedded deep in the cortex of my memory storage, that in all likelihood, will only ever be released by my death.

Due to the seaman's failure to have the painter coil released only at the last second and well away from our recovery boat, this rope now lay in the water just to the port side of the boat, a place about to be visited by our stern due to my quick turn to starboard. As it slid by beneath our stern, the painter rope suddenly entered an underwater space sometimes occupied by a spinning propeller blade. All forms of wishing, praying, and asking for good luck were of no use as one little blade, just one little bad-luck, poorly timed, ill-mannered prop blade decided to go rope hunting. And sure enough, a rope was found, a rope was grabbed, and a rope now looped over the blade to be instantly reeled in at about 2000 revolutions per minute. The ensuing contest between the spinning shaft of a powerful diesel engine testing the tensile strength of three-quarter-inch sisal rope resulted in a no-contest win for the rope. Our painter instantly wound into a compressed, resolute mass, jammed in between the prop and the shaft bearing, stopping the engine while proving itself the master of this event. The lifeboat now not only had no power, but as soon as we lost headway, the boat was violently yanked around end for end to where it was now being towed stern first by the painter, one end firmly secured to our prop shaft, the other end still firmly secured to the ship.

This left the boat at the mercy of the seas, and to confirm my worst fears, the waves began slamming the boat against the side of the troop ship. This was when all hell broke loose. Next came several hours of very risky manhandling of this multiple-ton lifeboat in a worsening ocean, as the crew led out a new painter, turned the boat around, and hooked it back into the boat-falls so that it could be hoisted back up to a stowed position, all the while ensuring that no arms or legs came between the lifeboat and the ship's hull, where they would be crushed as the two slammed together. It was a nasty, dangerous job, one that nobody up on the ship could help with other than to yell down well-intentioned but useless suggestions. Once we were re-connected and while being lifted back aboard from our miserably failed mission, I realized that this was, and I believe that it is even to this day, the most embarrassing day of my life.

In my lifeboat story I could now labor with all of the details of how it took four hours to fix this mess; of how the rope had to be sawed free of its death grip on the prop shaft; of how this new, high-tech, very expensive buoy and the man-overboard dummy were never seen again; of how the ship was now five hours behind its very tight schedule; of how many pages of log entries along with government lost property forms were required to be completed and signed; of how embarrassed the captain was at this disgraceful event, which was witnessed by half the English speaking maritime world, and how

The Faithful Sextant

he never again spoke to me. But it is all history now. That day was costly to my image and self-worth, but it was to be invaluable for the rest of my life. Very few of us have the opportunity to learn such an intense lesson; the only personal damage suffered being that of a severely bruised ego.

One of my fellow junior officers, only half in jest, suggested that if we needed to do another man-overboard drill, that I might once again be of use, this time to serve as the missing dummy!

As my mind comes back again to the reality of the typhoon, a death grip on the railing inside the wheelhouse of the *SS Exhibitor*, my memory again grinds through that horrible lesson, and I am reminded of just how dangerous lifeboat operations can become and how important readiness will be should it be necessary to launch tonight. The day of my man-overboard incident we had almost no wind and nice rolling two- to three-foot swells. Tonight we have gusting ninety- to one hundred thirty-knot winds and twenty-five to forty-five-foot and higher waves with a ship steeply rolling from side to side.

The more I think about our rickety lifeboats, the more I think about an alternative means of escape should it become necessary. Most of the Vietnam charter ships had been outfitted with new inflatable rafts stored in canisters resembling fiberglass fifty-five gallon oil drums. Two of these canisters were strapped down just behind the bridge wings, one on each side, very convenient for the captain and mate (that's me), who would supposedly be the last two off if we had to abandon ship. It is my understanding that these inflatable rafts had not yet received Coast Guard approval for general use, but maybe they offered a safe way to abandon ship. I had never seen one of these rafts used, much less unpacked from its container and launched; this might be the time to learn.

Here is the picture: the typhoon is just reaching its maximum intensity; it is almost 0300 in a pitch-black, screaming night; the ship is rolling violently as we find Third Officer Robert McEliece out behind the bridge wing, stooped over a new-fangled inflatable raft, flashlight in hand, trying to read the small print from a manufacturer's operating instructions label attached to the side of the raft canister in hopes of learning how to launch this thing to save his life. Did you get that! He's trying to read the damn operating INSTRUCTIONS from a label as the typhoon of the century rages! Are you fucking kidding me!

Holy shit! Is this any time to explore arcane fine print instructions about how to save your poor sorry ass during a killer storm on a sinking ship? You were trained at the finest maritime academy on the planet. What in the hell is going on here? Where has your mind been on all of those nice sunny afternoons when you could have studied this at leisure? I know more about the internal working of the high-pressure boiler and the steam turbines (which is near nothing) than I know about the use of this life raft. Why have we never had a drill to practice launching these things?

Little did any of us know just how totally useless these inflatable rafts really were in a howling storm.

On the night of the typhoon, as I return to the wheelhouse, Captain Winebrenner looks at me asking, "Where have you been?" I explain that I had been behind the bridge wing trying to read the instructions for launching one of the new inflatable rubber rafts. This sends the captain into a spirited laughing fit. "Mate," he says, "if you are planning on that as a way to get off this ship, I suggest that you just bend over right now, kiss your ass goodbye, and save yourself the trouble later." With a look of honest confidence he goes on, "There is a crew of men on this ship who I trust with my life, knowing that they will find a way to overcome every disaster this storm can throw at this old bucket of rust."

Just then the phone from the engine room rings again, and I can see from the expression on the captain's face that it is not good. In spite of the brave face shown by Captain Winebrenner, it is clear that there is a real possibility that none of us will live to see the Christmas of 1965. Water is still pouring into the engine room; it is only a short time before the boiler fires are extinguished, soon leaving us with no power on a cold, dark sinking ship at the mercy of five-story-high, angry walls of water. At the same time, unseen and just over the horizon, lies the rocky shore of Iwo Jima. calling to us with a siren song born of the memory of long-dead, heroic Marines.

For the first time I can smell the evil odor of fear creeping into the small wheelhouse, our home, our safe haven, the heart and brains of an aging wounded warrior, the command decision center of our only hope for salvation. A short list of items and actions over which none of us had any control is getting longer and longer. There is little or no time for introspection about fear that evening, but it is there: real fear, the real fear that one may have a very short time to live. This is a kind of fear that most people never experience until the day that a doctor looks squarely into their eyes and says, "There is nothing more we can do about your cancer. I suggest that you might want to put your affairs in order." Of the many kinds of fear, the kind that comes from a lifetime of the inevitability of death by old age is very different than the fear experienced in youth when faced by a situation that may have all the danger but lacks the marquee of inevitability.

Writers and philosophers oft times color these life-threatening, fear-laden events as a coin whose obverse is bravery. I have grappled with the concept of bravery for many years, forming a skeletal definition about this subject. All humans face fear of mortality, thus the mere act of trying to prevent personal mortality does not, in my eyes, reach the level of bravery, yet we see many a comment in obituaries about the bravery of the dearly deceased as he or she fought to extend life. Mortality from natural causes is not bravery; it is just the way life always ends.

Soldiers dying to save a fellow brother in arms are always called brave, but even this is suspect to me as war skews all human response. A person who faces the fear of going through organ transplant by donating a kidney so that another might live, rises to my nomination as a brave individual. In general terms, bravery in the face of imminent threat of life, where there is no coward's escape route, probably does not rise to my definition of bravery. Here is my personal short definition of bravery: If there is a coward's escape route, the coward will use it and the brave will not, simple as that. Bravery is action taken that could have been avoided; action taken where the outcome is anything but certain; action taken whose consequences might be disastrous to the actor even to the extent of his death. The typhoon that night on the *Exhibitor* was to reveal a man of bravery, a man of all these traits.

But thinking only of my emotions up in that wheelhouse on that fateful evening, I must go back to the stories of my childhood where fear was always just an emotion to be taken to a limit, lessons about adjusting the outcome to acceptable results that allowed me to put fear into a box of acceptability. My scuba diving accident, from which I never should have survived, was just an extreme example of a learned experience, pushing aside fear of mortality in favor of concentrating every human fiber to craft an acceptable outcome.

Fortune has allowed me to survive several of life's terror lessons, graduating with a trait that allows my survival instincts to drop into bunker mode when events begin to spin out of the usual experience patterns of control. Everything slows down. Time will begin to crawl. The brain goes into deep focus, surrounding events becoming a buzzing annoyance getting in the way of solving the problem. It then only seems natural to start making a plan that will change the forces of a desperate situation, making for an acceptable outcome. Thoughts of bad endings feed fear and are best replaced by action to change the end result. I do not believe that there is anything special in this trait;

it is just a symptom of the many experiences of my youth. It is most certainly not bravery, and as some philosophers have noted, might actually be a total lack of imagination of how bad spinning events can become. Most people have the good fortune to live lifetimes never experiencing truly life-threatening events, making this trait one that is nice to have but of little use in the humdrum of everyday events.

But in the reality of steel versus storm, as my dream-cast creation of terrifying images plays out in the movie called Bob's lifeboat launching disaster, the terror is interrupted by the ships clock striking seven bells. There are only thirty minutes left in this never-to-be-forgotten night watch, bringing me to consult with the captain about logbook entries documenting shipboard events. He tells me to enter the standard weather and steering data and leave him five blank lines to highlight all of the other mayhem of the last four hours. Holding on for dear life in the chartroom behind the bridge, where the logbook is kept, becomes a challenging exercise in one-handed writing. The second mate, a tall German named Gunther, also an Academy grad, pops in the chartroom and asks how it's going. He is here to relieve the watch and is looking tired and not at all happy about his next four hours. The second mate serves as the ship's navigation officer, always putting him on the four-to-eight watch cycle, ensuring that he will be on the bridge at sunrise and sunset, the only two times of the day that a navigator can see both the horizon and the stars, allowing for accurate angle measurement with a sextant.

"Gunther," I tell him, "the captain will fill you in on all the really bad news, but I have some good news for you. There will be no need to worry about a sextant star fix. The island of Iwo Jima is on radar bearing 032 at a distance of twenty-nine miles, and if we're lucky as hell and manage to stay afloat, you'll probably have it on radar all watch." My smarty mouth kicks in adding, "They tell me that Iwo Jima has not moved in a million years," (which is technically not true due to continental drift). Then I add, "You could, however, do all of us off-watch sleeping beauties a big favor and not hit that rocky bastard."

Gunther scowls at me before beginning to read the logbook. "Hey McEliece, I expected a busy watch from you. What's all this blank space in the log book about?" I once again inform him to speak to the captain, who has found a dark spot in the corner of the wheelhouse, where he is testing which will arrive first: his own total state of exhaustion or an abatement of this typhoon.

After a hushed conversation with Captain Winebrenner, Gunther formally relieves me of my duties as the Officer of the Watch, suddenly throwing me into an unexpected tailspin. What do I do now? It is 0400 in the morning, I am exhausted and need to sleep, but the engine room flooding has not been resolved. My ship, my home, my salvation is likely to roll over and sink before morning. Hitting the rack does not seem like a prudent course of action.

Climbing back into my shell, I sort through all of the mayhem of the last four hours, coming to the following conclusion. *What the hell, if we have to abandon ship in this storm, none of us is going to live anyway. Might as well get some sleep and see what happens.*

Back down in my cabin, I fall into my life-jacket-shaped cocoon, not bothering to remove clothes or shoes, knowing that if we do have to try to evacuate this rust bucket, there will be no time for locating shoes and tying laces. No sooner than I close my eyes, there is a sailor pounding on my door. "Hey mate, it's 0800. You gonna have some breakfast?"

Am I dreaming, or have I already died and it turns out that eternity in the afterlife for drowned sailors begins with the serving of bacon and eggs?

He pounds again, and I yell, "Okay!"

Climbing out of my cocoon fully dressed, I stumble down the still storm-racked stairs to the officer's salon, sleepily grabbing for my designated chair in the dining room. The table cloths have been soaked with water to keep plates and serving dishes from sliding off—a normal heavy weather routine—but on the whole, living conditions on the back side of the typhoon are nowhere as violent as they were several hours ago. Santiago, our Filipino mess man, hands me a menu saying, "Kitchen closes in five minutes. Will it be the same, mate?"

The usual small group of off-duty watch officers sit eating, but unlike a normal morning, talking or chitchat or laughing at stories and jokes has taken the day off; somber rules the roost. Having ordered my usual bacon and pancakes, my good buddy Bernie staggers into the room and slides into the bolted-down swivel chair opposite me. Bernie, the third assistant engineer, and my oft times wingman, looks as disheveled as I am sure I do. He also works the twelve to four watch, making him my counterpart in the engine room during my watch cycle.

"Bern, you look like shit!" I tell him. "What in the hell were you pipe monkeys doing downstairs last night, trying to install a swimming pool for crew recreation?"

Bernie stares back at me for several seconds and then turns to grab the mess man, quickly ordering food before the kitchen closes. Next he turns to stare at the first assistant engineer, a stare not quite normal, a stare made when words need to be spoken but the speaker knows not where to begin. I look over to see some pretty big bandages on the side of the First's head, an engineer's occupational hazard. After a minute of this, Bernie turns back to me, shakes his head and says, "Later, Bob."

Bernie and I finish our food in silence and, as usual, are the last two officers out of the dining room. As soon as the mess men clear the dishes from the salon, disappearing into the pantry, I look Bernie in the eye and ask, "Okay pal, just what the hell went on down there last night?"

Bernie then began a story I would never forget.

"Bob, this rust bucket was going down. Somewhere under the lowest level of the engine room floor gratings, on the port side, a large intake pipe that brings in raw seawater for what I think is the fire main system, finally gave way after one of those bone-jarring shipbreakers you guys were throwing at us. It began flooding raw seawater into the engine room. We tried to get suction from the bilge pumps in that area but all we got was vacuum lock; you remember how that piping is all full of crap the shipyard refused to remove. Pretty soon the water was over the first level of grates. I got the chief down there right away, but as you can imagine, he already had a full case of beer under his bloated belt and could do little more than hang on and swear. You guys upstairs were not making it easy to live down there, you know," he went on.

"Then the first assistant showed up with pipe drawings, and we began to search for bubbles coming up from the raw seawater inflow. The next thing I know, the First lifts up the steel access grating, takes off his shoes, and dives into the bilge water with just a channellock wrench and a flashlight."

As Bernie pauses in the telling of this chilling story, my memory of the violence of last night's storm fuels my imagination, thinking what it must have been like down in the engine room. Life on the darkened bridge of a ship creates its own small world, leading to the false belief that everyone else on the planet is living in some other, calmer, more normal universe. Nothing could be further from the truth. Every time I was thrown violently against the bulkhead in the wheelhouse, that same deep roll of the ship was happening in the engine room. In a way, these rough storms are worse down in this claustrophobic pipe torture chamber since the engine room crew has no view, as we did on the bridge, of the size or direction of the next incoming wave; they can only guess at what's going to hit next.

Trying to imagine what it would have been like down in the bilges, below the decks of the engine room, this picture comes to mind. Once thousands of gallons of seawater have entered into the bilges under the engine room flooring, this salt water has become a living, moving, liquid nightmare. Just as I was thrown against the bulkhead in the wheelhouse, so too would all this water have tried to rush as quickly as possible to the low side of the engine room. The instant that the First entered this frigid water, he would have been swept along with its every movement. Beneath the steel grates that form the floor of the engine room, the spaces are full of pipes, valves, sharp steel angle irons, and every other kind of unforgiving structure just waiting to break bones, shred skin, tear muscles, and puncture vital organs. As the mass of this water moved inexorably from side to side and from front to back with each movement of the ship, it would have seized this rag-doll of a human, dragging him along with no regard to these cruel objects sticking out to intercept warm flesh. Oh yes, and did I mention that this guy needs to breathe while this is happening? He would have to have known of the danger that this flood of water might have trapped him into a corner of the bilge, where there may have been no way for him to get his face above the water for a breath of air.

I look very sternly at Bernie and ask, "What the hell did he do?"

"He kept diving down, trying to find the broken pipe. Once he got swept over to another section of the engine room, but managed to lift up another grate and get some air. By now he was bleeding from several deep gashes." Bernie went on, "He then struggled back over to where we thought the pipe broke and dived in again. This time he did not come back up. We could see his light flashing around under the water, but then suddenly the light went out. Time ticked by for what seemed like an eternity as the ship rolled and pitched when that bloated sot of a bastard chief engineer starts yelling at me to do something. What the hell was I going to do, Bob?" Bernie cried. "One guy was down there probably already dead, and for me to follow him wasn't going to make any of this better."

Bernie is now looking at me with a pleading look in his eyes, desperately wanting me to know that he was no coward; there was nothing that could be done.

"Then suddenly the First's head popped up, banging against the flooring grates," Bernie continued, "We grabbed his arms, pulling him up onto the grating as he gasped for air. He was shaking like a leaf, his right hand, though covered in oil and blood, still had a death grip on his pair of channellocks, his chest heaved and his head was covered with a mixture of blood and dirty bilge oil, making him look like a dead body washed up from the sewers of Brooklyn."

"As the near-dead first assistant coughed and spit up blood, the chief ordered an oiler to immediately get at least two blankets, while he grabbed a phone to call the captain on the bridge, asking for medical help. Then between coughs, the First looked at the chief and told him that it was okay, he had found the thru-hull valve and had it mostly shut."

"Holy shit," is all I can mutter.

Bernie then begins to tell me that much is still wrong in the engine room but that they had the flooding under control. Later that morning as I was sleeping, the captain and the chief engineer agreed that the ship was in no condition to make it to Saigon. We had no fire main—no way to fight a fire—and that was only the first of a long list of problems. Accordingly, the captain woke the radio officer, ordering him to send a message back to Military Sea Transportation Service (MSTS) asking for approval to limp into the nearest port for repair. A couple of hours later a DIVERTORD was received from the CO of the MSTS, sending us to Yokohama, Japan for immediate repairs.

"Bob, we're going to be in Yokohama not Saigon for Christmas," Bernie squeals. "Yo, I'm gonna have a Yokohama mama in my stocking!"

As Bernie switches back to his normal happy-go-lucky self, I am anything but joyful. The full impact of what the first assistant, a middle-aged maritime engineer, did for the crew of this doomed ship is just sinking in. He saved the ship all by himself. He also saved the lives of all fifty-two of us on board. Last night, no one was going to get off that ship into small boats and live through it. Had that thru-hull pipe continued to flood the engine room, the steam plant would have drowned out in about forty-five minutes, followed by total loss of power. If it had not been cargo breaking loose and tearing the ship up as she wallowed broadside, probably broaching, then in several hours the flooding from this pipe itself would have sent her to the bottom. To this day I have never been able to dream up a way we could have lived through an "abandon ship," though I have replayed the experience many times. This night of horrors has invaded my dreams on many more than one occasion.

Thinking of the first assistant, my mind goes back to my definition of bravery. Was he a hero?

The author Wallace Stegner, one of the most gifted craftsmen of the English language, tells a story in his book *Wolf Willow* about cowhands caught in an early winter blizzard while moving cattle down from high summer grazing pastures. One of the young cowhands stayed with an old-timer, even at the risk of freezing to death, and ended up saving his life. Stegner writes, "It was a step in the making of a cowhand when he learned that what would pass for heroics in a softer world was only <u>chores</u> around here."

That's it. That explains what was going through the mind of the first assistant engineer the night he saved all of us from a cold, wet, salty grave. Special excellence? Yes, maybe in a softer world, but not in the world of a boneyard ship headed for Vietnam. Here it was just chores!

Does that take away from the courage and determination, not to mention raw strength, that this officer displayed down in the bowels of the *Exhibitor* during that typhoon? Of course not! Many of those onboard that night, such as the drunken, overweight, gout-stricken chief engineer, did not have the physical strength and stamina for such a feat, but a greater number would have simply been too scared and would have instead chosen to let fate determine their outcome: the ultimate coward's path to ruination.

For a long time I tried to come to grips with where my good friend Bernie fit into this picture of heroics. Finally giving up, deciding that it was not my place to judge how any of us would have reacted unless we had been there; unless we had the flashlight; unless we had a death grip on a pair of greasy handled channellocks; unless we knew that if we did not go fix it, no one else could or would!

Years and years of life experiences have allowed time to play its dirty worst on the storage pathways of my mind, and try as I might, I cannot remember the name of this heroic maritime engineering officer, though I can see his face as vividly as yesterday. Name or not, there is no question for me that this man will always sit at the head of my table for dinner with brave men, for supper with heroes.

She shall be my jailer
Who sets me free
From shackles frailer
Than the wind-spun sea.

She shall be my teacher
Who cries "Be brave,"
To a weeping creature
In a glass-walled wave.

But she shall be my lover
Whose mocking despair
Dives headlong to smother
In the weeds of my hair.

Elinor Wylie
"Drowned Woman" from
Black Armour: Breastplate

Keiko

It was not until many years later that I was able to learn the name of our storm. The American Weather Service had named her "Typhoon Faye," in the days before western Pacific typhoons garnered local language names. Faye had been born as a westbound tropical depression in Micronesia, becoming a long-lived "super" typhoon. Faye traversed a near perfect parabolic path around the Pacific. As this storm neared the Philippines, her intensity increased to a category four, registering winds up to 150 mph, just shy of the most powerful typhoon on record. The storm then bent to the north towards Japan and again to the east in the direction of Alaska. Faye had spared virtually every populated landmass, thus it was that she gathered little attention, or as the forecasters love to say, she "passed safely out to sea." Safely, that is, except for those poor bastards who were "out to sea." I do not know if Faye was a category 1, 2, 3, or 4 typhoon as she passed over us, as the *Exhibitor* had no way to register wind speeds of these magnitudes, but I do know that we had been beaten, pounded, left for dead, and we were damn fortunate to still be afloat and alive.

By the beginning of my noon watch the next day, the typhoon had roared well past us, the seas had moderated somewhat, and we had set a course almost due north for the entrance to Tokyo Bay, where a shipyard in Yokohama awaited.

The Faithful Sextant

While serving as a cadet/midshipman with my classmate Bill Cratty on a States Line ship, the *SS Hawaii* in 1962, it had been surprising to see how many damaged World War II fortifications had been left in Tokyo Bay by the Japanese. Now in 1965 it seemed that not much clearing had been accomplished, as if the Japanese thought that enemy ships might still appear at any minute on the horizon.

The Imperial Nipponese Army and Navy of WWII had created a series of forts, strategically sunken ships, man-made obstructions, minefields, and gun emplacements designed to complement the natural small islands found in this huge bay. The result was a nightmare of winding channels forcing a ship to zigzag between these obstructions in such a way as to insure the slow movement of any enemy between lines of fire from shore guns and submarine nets. And block it they had.

We had, by law, stopped to pick up a Japanese pilot, experienced in the ways of these treacherous waters, to help us safely navigate north to Yokohama. In spite of his manifest experience, it was possible to see a look of concern on his brow as we snaked our way to Yokohama.

This, my fifth visit to Japan, came almost exactly twenty years following the utter and complete destruction of Japanese cities by the Allied forces of World War II. My great-grandfather Frank Devereux had witnessed the utter and complete destruction of Atlanta by the Union Army almost exactly one hundred years before 1965, and I can assure you, from stories he told, that twenty years after Sherman's burning of Atlanta, Southerners had no clear vision of the road to recovery. Yokohama, in a similar manner, was by no means ready to hang out the "ready for business-we have recovered" sign.

With Christmas just days away, the *SS Exhibitor* pulled alongside an outfitting pier in a shipyard repair facility in the port of Yokohama. At once a swarm of Japanese workers invaded our archaic engine room, excitedly jabbering with each other over the best way to fix its classic steam engine. The Christmas holiday was not a widely accepted fixture in their culture; repair of our ship would be just another workweek with no intervening days off. It was refreshing to note, even though I spoke none of their language, a sense of pride in their ability to find a way to get this steam plant back to tip top shape. This was a very different feeling than the one we had seen earlier in Long Beach, where the mechanics took one callous look at this outmoded steam plant and declared that it was beyond repair. This was another thing I liked about the Japanese.

Several hours later the yard-engineering foreman (likely chosen because he spoke broken English) met with the captain and the chief engineer to detail what work was needed and how long it would take. Negotiating for some time, they finally laid out a schedule. For once my friend Bernie was spot-on: we were going to spend Christmas in Yokohama and then some. We might not get out of the shipyard for a week to ten days.

Just like our experience in Balboa, there would be no cargo operations occupying the deck officers, just some survey work assessing damage to the cargo, as the little men in white suits scurried around our engine room making repairs. Our evenings would be free.

Walking around Yokohama in 1965 it was possible to notice positive changes since my last visit three years earlier, noting many areas where reconstruction had erased all scars. Losers of modern wars, including our own Civil War, suffer most grievously and will continue to do so as we invent better means of destruction. History books award the winning side the halo of "righteous cause" while the loser dons the mantle of...well, of "loser."

In my previous visit I noted that in addition to mending the destruction of infrastructure, the Japanese people had, for the most part, mended their hatred of the Yankees. My own baby face helped insure that the Japanese I met viewed me as too young to have participated in the destruction of their country, resulting in my being treated as an okay foreign visitor. There were many things to like about Japan; the industriousness of the whole population was a sight to behold. Every citizen seemed to have a purpose, as if some imaginary list of chores simply must be checked off before the day was done. Cleanliness was also a national obsession. The neighborhood might be in need of mechanical repairs, but while waiting for this to happen, someone was seen sweeping, polishing, or scrubbing what was there.

Some things in their country could be very foreign and less than nice. Many public bathrooms still used a hole in the floor, where either the man or woman squatted (sometimes both sexes using the same room at the same time). It is very hard for a westerner to get the hang of this squatting thing. Later trips to Japan found all of these facilities being replaced by modern toilets, so that to now find the old squat hole requires a trip out into the countryside.

The first evening was spent with Bernie as we went cruising the sailor bars, along with several of the other ship's officers. With a look of boredom on his face, Bern tapped me on shoulder, suggesting that the two of us split for a joint he knew from previous trips to Yokohama; the red light district of China Town beckoned. Picture this; the boys in Japan are headed to China Town for fun. Oh, the irony of it all. Novice western travelers view all Asians as look-alikes; in truth the differences are profound, especially in China Town.

The main street in Yokohama's Chinatown looks much like one found in any other large city with a developed Chinese community, except this one, in catering to a large population of worldly sailors, mainly featured bars and girls. Bernie's joint, the one having his mark carved into the wall in the *benjo* (bathroom), a word not used by cultured ladies in Japan, was dimly lit and quiet. Half way through our first drink, Bernie had already hooked up, fled out the back door with his girl, and left me surrounded by ladies hovering like birds of prey circling carrion on the African veldt. Knowing that Bernie might not be back for hours, or at all, and really not being interested in the ladies *de la nuit* fawning over me, I drank up and headed out to the street to find something to eat. My journey took me well away from China Town to the business section of Yokohama, to the part of town featuring pleasant shops and restaurants.

The Japanese make it easy to select a nice meal in a local restaurant without benefit of speaking or reading their language. Most restaurants highlight their menu by featuring a display of plastic meals in the window. Calling a waiter to the sidewalk window and pointing to your entrée choice gets a meal ordered with no discussion necessary.

Having picked out a mid-scale, moderately busy establishment, I entered looking for an inconspicuous corner where my blond hair and blue eyes might not attract constant stares. Selecting a small table alone, I was soon feasting on a wonderful shrimp tempura dish, when, nearing the end of the meal, a young Japanese girl approached me. She appeared to be about seventeen or eighteen years of age. With a great deal of blushing and shyness, she asked if I was an American. Swallowing my last bite of tempura, I gave her back my deepest smile, replying, "Yes I am," then pausing without breaking my smile or eye contact, I asked, "Are you Japanese?" She did not expect such silly retort, causing her to begin giggling and blushing.

In the past while riding the trains in Japan, I had experienced young students shyly asking for permission to practice their study of American English by engaging in short conversations. Still trying to hold my most sincere smile as my comely intruder fidgeted, I guessed that this might explain a young lady breaking all codes of modesty by speaking to a single man in a restaurant in the evening.

Trying my best to put this shy, raven-haired lotus flower at ease, I looked her in the eye and asked very slowly, "Would you like to practice your English?" This boldness left her speechless, but after a few seconds, she nodded yes. I then motioned her to sit down. Suddenly the stakes in this conversation escalated; speaking to a strange man at night had been bold, but sitting down with him was another matter altogether. She was being asked to cross the Rubicon of modesty.

Seeing her panic as she glanced towards the door, looking for an escape route from her little social checkmate, my senses told me to quickly take the lead by standing and moving around the table to pull out a chair. With a bowed head, a furrowed brow, and a pleading look, I once again asked her very softly if she would please sit with me. She did. The first move in this little game of chess went to the ship's officer.

Once seated, I waved the waiter over to our table. Since Japanese waiters in mid-level restaurants rarely spoke English in post-war Japan, it was necessary that she become our interpreter. I turned to her, talking slowly while using my best English, asking her to order two cups of evening tea along with an assortment of sweet rolls. As the waiter patiently watched, looking from one young person to the other, mentally wagering on the tense outcome, she stuttered, trying to tell me that this was not possible as she was not hungry and besides…At which point I interrupted her and said very clearly, "Here is what we would say in America. We would say, 'Yes, thank you very much; I would love some tea and rolls,'" again giving the most confident and caring look in my arsenal of looks. With more blushing accompanied by a roll of the eyes by the waiter, her desire to be "American" won out and she gave him instructions in Japanese for our dessert and tea. The second strategic chess move also went to the young ship's officer.

Subsequent to a few minutes of awkward looks and questions, she told me that her name was "Susie" and that she was a student enrolled at university in Yokohama. It was easy to guess that her name was probably not Susie, but the wildly popular 1960 movie *The World of Susie Wong*, starring William Holden and Nancy Kwan, had been every bit the rage in Japan that it had been in America, leading many Asian teenage girls to adopt the name Susie.

I introduced myself as Robert with the short name of Bob, slowly beginning a pleasant conversation as she worked through her knowledge of English. She had many questions about life in America, wanting to know what it was like to live as a star of a Hollywood movie. But for every question of hers about America, I asked her a sincere question about Japanese life. She did not want to talk much about Japan but answered politely, seeming to appreciate my interest. Our conversation became more animated by the minute as time flew until, with a quick glance, it was obvious that the restaurant was ready to close. The owner was standing at the door with the waiter quietly pacing nearby; they were not having near as much fun as we were. The bill had been on the table for some time, and thankfully, I had remembered to exchange American dollars for Japanese yen, avoiding the gritty monetary faux pas of having to do a currency exchange in a small restaurant. I wanted to tip the waiter for his patience but remembered at the last minute that tipping, except in big American hotels, was not done in Japan.

Leaving the restaurant it was apparent that neither of us wanted the evening to end. My heart was racing; I simply could not let this attractive young lady walk out of my typhoon-ravaged life. There had been no previous life experiences with girls covering the drama unfolding at that minute between Bob and Susie. Many things this was not: It was not a pickup, not a blind date, not a date of any kind that had fit in my book of my life; this was new ground and where it went would likely be determined by what I did and said in the next minutes. Thoughts were racing through my mind when a stanza of the lyrics to Gilbert & Sullivan's wonderful play *Iolanthe* came to mind.

> *While the sun shines, make your hay-*
> *Where a will is, there is a way-*
> *Beard the lion in his lair-*
> *None but the brave deserve the fair!*

I looked deep into those onyx eyes and said, "I must know more about Yokohama. I must know more about Japan. I must know more about you, Susie. Will you show me?"

She stared back at me, her flawless alabaster face framing eyes now wide open in the dim light as if I were looking at a Japanese anime cartoon character. "Yes Robert, of course."

The night did not end in front of that restaurant. In honesty, it has become impossible to remember where we went next. Perhaps a late night coffee house, perhaps a low-key nightclub, perhaps a bar, or just perhaps we strolled through the city talking and wondering how different our backgrounds were and yet how alike were our goals and ambitions. We now found ourselves plunging into a most intense human bond, where translation of our so-different languages was surmounted by electricity, each almost knowing what the other was saying without the tedium of translation. This brought joyous laughter that can only be shared by the young who have not learned the cynicism of bad experience, where all new things seem to offer untold promise. Well into our laughing and touching as the city quietly closed for the evening and with no warning, she turned to me wearing a pixie smile, asking, "Robert" with a sudden shy pause, "Have you ever slept on a futon?" And that is how the real story began!

From our first conversation in the restaurant, I explained that as a ship's officer, my pay was high, even by American standards, and that spending money generously as I saw fit was the reward for hard and sometimes dangerous work. Clearly understanding this perk, Susie led us farther into the heart of Yokohama, taking us directly into the lobby of a new, first class, post-war Japanese hotel. She looked at me with apprehensive eyes. "Is this okay?"

An enthusiastic yes from me sent her to the front desk, where a brisk conversation in Japanese left me uneasy. The law in those days in most places in the United States required couples checking into hotels to be married to each other, some even asking for proof. I had no idea what the law or culture in Japan said on this subject. Susie was a model of self-assurance, the desk clerk glanced up at me twice with squinty eyes as he nodded yes to her questions, and in a minute he called over a bellboy and handed him a key. Now I would learn culture.

The room to which the bellboy led us was not a hotel room by any American standard. Inside the door, just to the left, began a bathing area occupying over half of the room's square footage, in the style of a Hawaiian spa. Inlaid lava rock covered the walls, the fixtures hidden behind strange controls, the effect creating the feeling of entering a grotto. A sink with mirror was missing, there was no toilet; all normal bathroom needs were handled by cleverly installed running water ducts. There were lots of generous towels along with many varieties of scrub brushes combined with strange bamboo poles.

In place of a bed, the room had a large, fluffy futon. There was no television. There was not one thing you would find standard in a Holiday Inn, such as plastic drinking glasses hermetically sealed in Saran wrap. The whole thing was magic, and now before me stood a beautiful, young, alabaster-skinned guide who was going to show me how the upper tier of folks in Japan lived.

I stared in amazement as Susie looked up at me, murmuring in a soft voice while gently tugging at my sleeve, "Robert-san, we must now take a Japanese bath." I must indeed have had a bewildered look, leading Suzie to softly add, "I will show you how."

She reached over, sliding off my coat, placing it in a hidden wardrobe while motioning for me in pantomime to begin taking off the remainder of my clothes as she disappeared into the bathing grotto.

Once my clothes had been removed, I stood patiently in the middle of the room like a little boy holding his breath on Christmas morning waiting for permission to come down stairs for the opening of presents.

Shortly I heard, "Robert-san," leading me to venture into the bathing grotto where I saw her naked, bent over the bathing pool, testing the water. Approaching the pool, I stuck my foot into the steaming water. Susie immediately blurted out, "No, no!" and motioned for me to sit on a small wooden stool. Wearing only a twinkling smile and carrying a large wooden bucket of very warm water, she poured it over my head, soaking my entire naked body. In one swift motion with a bar of very coarse soap and rough bristle brush; she began a vigorous scrubbing of my hair, back, chest, legs, and feet. A large, soft soapy sponge for use on delicate areas such as the face and groin came after the brush, followed by another rinse from the bucket. This process was repeated again until it felt as if my upper epidermis had washed down the drain in the middle of the floor. The diminutive size of this petit girl combined with her so very feminine and coquettish façade gave no hint of the strength in her hands and arms.

A full twenty minutes of this routine cleansed the grime accumulated from months of life on a post-war, rust bucket of a ship, washing it away down the drain in the center of the grotto. Though not scrubbed by the brush or the sponge, I could also feel the stain of fearful memories of wartime ships breaking in two, of little men in black pajamas trying to kill us, and of many of life's unfair judgments, both past and future, also sliding down the drain. The scrubbing was followed by several more buckets of steaming rinse water. Now she smiled and pointed to the soaking pool.

There were no gentle steps leading into this chest high pool. Trying to figure how to get in, she whispered, "Very hot!" For a second I remembered the frigid ocean water near Iwo Jima and thought, *What the hell, how bad can it be?*

Whoaaaa! Was it hot! As the steaming water came up to my chest, I grimaced and then smiled, refusing to let her know that Americans are wimps. Her giggle told me that she already knew otherwise.

She began scrubbing her own slender body in the same process as used on mine. She still looked to be at least eighteen, but Japanese girls are so petite that naked they almost look pre-adolescent. Very little body hair graced her petite form, her breasts were tiny, and there were virtually no folds of skin on her porcelain body. She quickly and quietly scrubbed everywhere in a practiced routine, without wetting her face or hair, concurrent to sending coquettish looks of false modesty my way. Her wordless smile warmed my inner soul several degrees above the already steaming pool, and then she slid gracefully into the other end.

After a generous parboiling, she helped me out of the pool, throwing a large cotton terry towel over my shoulders before the next phase of rubbing, patting, and poking. No hidden crevice or flap of skin was overlooked. My imagination went into overdrive. Past experiences in erotic surroundings such as this toweling off by an Athenian Goddess would have severely tested what little self-control remained in my hormone-flooded cortex. None of that was going on. My mind was in a state of tranquility, creating a truce between my brain and my testosterone. Could this actually be the intimacy thing I had heard mature women talk about?

The thorough toweling of both of us completed, Susie then looked up at me to say, "Now I will show you the Japanese futon."

My mind had always seen this futon thing as just another way of sacking out in a sleeping bag on the floor, something I had experienced many times as a kid. Slipping naked into the futon, it struck me that this did not feel like a sleeping bag. Then she slid in and curled up very close to me. Nothing like this had ever happened in a Boy Scout tent or on sleepover at a friend's house.

After a minute of very tender togetherness, she put her face close to mine whispering, "My name is not Susie. I am Keiko." There was a long pause as she watched a deep grin spread from one side of my face to other and I said, "Keiko, your name should be beautiful! How do you say beautiful in Japanese?"

At this Keiko deeply blushed and replied, "Oh, the informal way is to say *kirey* but a more formal word is *utsuksuhii*." Looking deeply into her eyes, I stumbled through, "*Anata wa totemo utsukushii desu*," loosely translating into "You are so beautiful."

Then the tenderest of lessons one can hope to experience led sweetly into the mysterious world of the futon. Emotional reverence and intimacy found only in the tight beauty of two very youthful bodies proceeded with no need for translation. That evening sleep became the casualty of the kind of bonding reserved for those discovering the beauty of being young, of being vibrant, of being able to explore every little corner of a lovely person from a culture so new and so surprisingly fun. Giggling, it turned out, is the same in any language. Touching and moaning, it turned out, is also no different.

Dawn, that pitiless revealer of the true face of what had seemed so mystical and beautiful the night before, did not join us until late. The winter solstice had just slipped by, leaving the weather cloudy and bleak. Many a time the arrival of daylight, followed shortly by the arrival of reality, had left me wondering just what a mess I had created the night before. The arrival of dawn in this exotic hotel room framed by my current romantic surroundings by far exceeded all previous hopeful expectations. All parts of my soul were warm and at peace with the world. We found ourselves just returning from Xanadu, a most unique magical mystery tour. Neither wanted it to end.

As the hour approached when my workday back on the ship would begin, I asked Keiko what the day held for her. She told me that she had two classes at university just after the noontime. Suddenly we were nearing the shore at which most one-night affairs flounder on the rocks of societal realities. I wanted to see more of her, but this had to fit into the daily routine of a ship's officer. Then there was Keiko. I had no idea what else her day held, what job she might have, what education classes, what friends and family, and (ugh) what male relationships. Most importantly, I had absolutely no inkling about Japanese societal edicts affecting the continuation of our newly discovered romantic friendship.

Looking over at Keiko, I found her once again staring with those huge "anime" eyes, waiting for me to take the lead. She too must have been going through a mental triathlon; who was this man, and what could I expect next. Confirming what I had believed from when we met in the restaurant, her concerned look and body language seemed to say that all of this was new.

Speaking slowly, I explained that our evening had been exquisite (a word unlikely to translate into Japanese), that my ship would be in Japan for many more days, that I did not want this to be goodbye. Heck, is there even a word in Japanese for goodbye or is it like Hawaiian where aloha means hello and goodbye? This difficult land mine-infused conversation stretched her schoolgirl English, but her looks told me that somewhere in the translation lay affection and agreement.

Hopping up to my feet to gather on my pants, I returned to kneel next to her on the futon where with care, using pantomime, I tried to explain with the numbers on my watch, that I had to work but would meet her back in the room at five o'clock. Impulsively, I then reached into my pocket and pulled out fifty thousand Japanese yen in the form of five, ten thousand yen notes, which I folded into her hand and asked her to reserve the room for four more nights. Keiko was shocked; this was a lot of money in post-war Japan. Recapturing her poise after several looks down at the money and back up at me, she nodded yes, as I finished dressing.

I slowly walked to the door as she sat still and upright on the futon with a surprised and slightly confused look on her face, when suddenly she threw the money on the futon, leaped up, ran over to me, and threw her arms around my neck, and her legs around my waist. That little move almost cost me a day's pay!

Down at street side in front of the hotel, it was a rush to my romance-addled senses to find the city of Yokohama in the full rhythm of a workday. The hotel doorman found a cab whose driver did not speak English, dispatching us as if he knew I was in good hands. I knew the name of the shipyard and held up four fingers to indicate which pier number we occupied. The driver may not have spoken English, but he immediately understood by my dress and looks that I was an American but not one of the occupying servicemen and certainly not one of the very rare tourists, reducing the obvious choices down to a maritime sailor. This told him that we needed to head to the docks, so off we went into the morning smog.

Cab rides with non-speaking cabbies are a great time for introspection. First, I always find viewing a large foreign city as it awakens to its workday to be fascinating. Just what is it that each one of those little ants rushing around will be doing today to justify his or her place in this society so foreign to me? After a minute of this rambling thought, my mind quickly snapped back to the subject of the day: Keiko. It was at that moment when the dam holding back the waters of reality broke.

I, this man of the world, had just grievously broken one of my top rules of foreign culture survival. Never, never ever pay for any service or goods up front. I had just handed Keiko what was in Japan in those days, a very large sum of money. She was not a prostitute so just exactly what was it that was being bought? Even my sleep-starved brain could understand that my action was a purchase of some form of future loyalty. However, past experience had established that in spite of promised fealty, the ease of moving on with a stranger's money was too large a temptation for many of those just met in foreign lands. These bygone experiences had exacted a grievous toll to my expectation regarding the ability to trust my fellow man. From past lessons I held this do-not-repeat mandate very close to my chest.

I remembered Montevideo in 1962, when I had left a photograph and money with an artist who promised a nice oil paint portrait in the likeness of the photo. The samples of his work were excellent, and I believed his promise that a portrait would arrive at my home address within a month. The money and the photo were never seen again. Later in my seagoing career, there had been prepaid promises of cab rides, dinner reservations, packing and shipping of mementos etc., promises costing money that were broken faithlessly, costing me worst yet, self-esteem and trust in others. My line in the sand on this subject was clear and deep, and it had just been scraped away as if I was some rube who had just fallen off the turnip truck. How was it going to feel this afternoon when upon returning to the hotel there was no room reservation at the hotel desk, no Keiko, and no 50,000 Yen? Damn it, what is wrong with me. I remember well that ubiquitous little plaque which states, you have to keep repeating life's lessons until you get them right.

My thought at that minute was to tell the cabbie to turn around, taking me back to the hotel immediately. Fortunately, judgment grasped the failed logic of this action. First, if I had been scammed, the scammer would be long gone with no telltale traces, and secondly, if it was not a scam, there would only be humiliation shown by a lack of trust or of character. There I was, hooked on the horns of an old-lesson-learned dilemma while being firmly hoisted on my own petard. I hate it when I am forced to preview a nasty outcome of a flawed plan put in place by none other than my own imagination living deeply in the land of wishful thinking. At about this time in my gloomy outlook, the cabbie turned in though the shipyard gate, where immediately before me floated the creature of my recent angst, my gray dowager the *Lady SS Exhibitor*. Oh pitiless dawn, but that your freshly minted rays could assure me that my dilemma could have a happy ending and, oh yes, while you are at it, make this ugly duckling of a ship turn into a nice white swan.

Having paid the cabbie, as I trudged up the wet, chilly pier, it came to me that the apparition of my typhoon tormentor, a relic of better days dressed in her out-of-style lines framed by rusty rivets, was certainly a way to get my mind off of Keiko. Leaning forward to begin the climb up the steep gangway, my shoes began to stick to the steps, nasty lay-up goo now having been tracked all the way from the bridge wings to the gangway; meanwhile an assault began on my nose by the odor of paint chemicals trying their best to keep the salt water from destroying the old steel of her soul. Perhaps I should have been kissing her hull for bringing me through the typhoon to the safety of this shipyard, but on another level I intuit that it was the living breathing men of her crew who deserved that credit.

At the top of the gangway, two malingering crewmembers were all smiles at the pleasure of welcoming an officer aboard after what they believed to have been an all-nighter ashore. "Hey mate, did you leave some for us?" came the first one, and from the other, "You did remember to pay her didn't you? This rust bucket is jinxed as it is. We sure don't need no more bad weather 'cause someone don't pay."

Long ago hard learned lessons made me ignore sailors whose worldly interests seldom expand beyond cheap booze and women for hire. Technically, I supervised these men and although another book could be written about that relationship, it would never do to have them gabbing about my personal life.

Checking my watch, there was just enough time before breakfast food cut-off to slip into the salon, pleading for a quick bite. Entering the officer's dining room, it was apparent that almost every officer was seated as shipyard operations reverted the crew from watch standing to day work. My obvious attempt to sneak in dressed in liberty clothes, while everyone else was dressed in workday khakis or boiler suits was a sure prescription to take a ration of shit. Bernie looked up, then began pointing and laughing. Damn I wish there had been time to slip into the cabin for a change of clothes.

Bernie immediately began badgering me to spit out the details of my nightly adventure. A quick glance around the room revealed most of the other officers with ears cocked our way so that they too could enjoy the story. Now it was my turn to tell Bernie that we would discuss this later. At about that time the captain walked by our table, looking down to say, "Nice of you to join us today, mate. Check with the chief mate when you finish eating. We need to get this ship back in working order."

What a long morning it was. All of us knew there would be damage within our cargo holds from the typhoon, now was the time to document and, if possible, repair the damage. Working through the ships agent in Yokohama, a maritime carpentry company had been hired to provide men to replace damaged shoring and bracing within the cargo holds once the officers had drawn up plans.

The chief mate had split the deck crew into thirds with one third reporting to me. He gave me the responsibility to report back to him on the state of damage in the aft two hatches, number 4 and 5. This meant crawling down hatch ladders, through two decks, and into the lower hold. Once in the black, cold, and clammy bottom of the ship, we would need to climb through a junkyard nightmare of stowed cargo, over trucks, around trailers, squeezing between wood crates, all the while making notes as to where and what would be needed to secure things before we headed back out to sea. It came to me that falling asleep on my feet might be one benefit of a morning of strenuous manual labor. On the other hand, climbing down those slippery, vertical ladders into the dark of the hold was deathly risky in my sleep-deprived condition. Oh, how I longed to just find a nice corner behind a stow of boxes where I could curl up for a short nap. This, however, was out of the question as we used a strict buddy system in these dangerous jobs, meaning that I would have been missed in a matter of minutes.

Several hours later a plan was ready of the work required for hatches 4 and 5. This would be handed off to the ship's carpenter, who, along with the bosun, would supervise the shoring-up process that afternoon. I then politely pleaded with the chief mate to take the rest of the afternoon off. He noted that I looked terrible and that I should get some sleep. Every man on that ship had been through a rough week, it would take some slack time for us to recover. Off to the faithful bunk was my next port of call.

About three hours later I arose, showered, and changed back into nightlife clothes. A little after four o'clock, I slipped my head into the radio shack, where to no surprise, I found the afternoon cocktail group already one and a half sheets to the wind. Bernie immediately pounced, wanting to know where we were going tonight.

"Bern, there will be no 'we' tonight," I sadly informed him. "Wow," he said. "So you hooked up with a steady in one of the bars, huh?"

With some careful explanation, I began to spin a tangled lie, telling him that I had run into a classmate from another ship and that we had made plans to get together. There was just no way to tell the truth when the truth might involve me returning early to the ship with my tail between my legs, after once again flunking the lesson of fleeting loyalty.

Having pieced together this perfectly cogent explanation, I looked optimistically around the room, finding not one single believer in the crowd. What…was it the lack of conviction in this semi-plausible account?

No, that wasn't it. These men knew me well, and guys like me do not meet another guy and stay out all night, returning back to the ship at the crack of dawn with eye rings giving my face the look of a great gray owl, only to turn immediately around, heading back to ask for more.

Oh what the hell did I care what they thought. It was time for me to hit the beach and find a cab.

Foreign cities are so wonderful; there always seems to be a cab conveniently waiting whenever and wherever (except behind enemy lines, but that story comes later). The cabbie quickly found the hotel, leaving me standing in the lobby with my heartrate almost as high as it had been during the typhoon. Grabbing the house phone, I dialed the room we had occupied the night before. A young female voice answered, "*Mohsh mohsh.*" I replied "*Konnichiwa, Keiko?*" She then said in English, "Is that you, Robert?"

My mouth was so dry and my heart beating so fast that I was almost unable to reply. Riding up the elevator it came to me that the problem with past lessons is that they have no built-in allowance for future variables. So what's a man to do? Go through life making the same mistake over and over hoping for a new variation or just always say no? Indeed, what a dull life that would be. To quote Mr. Gilbert and Mr. Sullivan, "None but the brave deserve the fair!"

The hugging scene at the hotel room door between the little Japanese pixie and the young American ship's officer could have been scripted out of the last scenes from the mushiest of Hollywood movies.

What a special and different Christmas the one of 1965 turned out to be. It was spent with a wonderful non-Christian girl in a foreign land of no snow, no nativity scenes, yet surrounded by friendly people whose language was not understood and culture still foreign. Still, in a way, it symbolized the faith and tradition of the best of Christmases. Together we spent five or maybe it was six days, including four whole days that were taken as days off from shipboard duties, leading us to places known only to locals and into experiences that would never have happened without her knowledge. It was a unique opportunity to experience newfound warmth in her city and with her people. We were not tourists; we were pilgrims experiencing the love and youth of life. We were newborns finding all old things suddenly changed and novel. We were the ones at whom others secretly stared with smiling envy.

There was a train trip to a little village where we visited a small grotto on the water for some of the best seafood ever tasted. We rode the bullet train to Kyoto to visit the magnificent Shinto shrines. We took another train to Tokyo where Keiko bypassed the obligatory tourist trip to the Ginza, instead taking us to Akihabara.

Akihabara is the young man's vision of what Santa's workshop should look like: magnificent modern buildings, one after another, all overflowing with shops touting the latest electronic gadgets dreamed up by budding young Japanese electrical engineers. On display was a very recent invention that played music on a small laser disc (a CD), a music-changing technology not seen back in the United States for several years. It was audiophile heaven. Keiko could by now read me like a book. Perhaps it was the foreignness of it all or maybe the newness or even the emotional release at having lived through the typhoon, but whatever pixy dust was in the air, it was seriously messing with both my head and my heartstrings.

The young American girls I had been dating back home had a certain sing-song mantra that went something like this, "Me, me, me, me." Keiko effortlessly made it all seem to revolve around Robert-san. She was the product of a well-entrenched culture that taught young girls to think of other's needs before thinking of their own.

This cultural man/woman relationship in Japan of Keiko's generation was, however, very much different than that of their mothers. The post-war girls of Japan had already come a very long way. Much had changed in their world. After the complete and total destruction of Japan and their abject domination by the new western cultures of their occupiers, Keiko would never be a traditional Japanese Mama-san! She was an educated woman who was born at the calamitous end of the war. The university and the new birth control pill shaped her world.

Keiko had no agenda that I could read. My impression of our relationship was that she was having the time of her life in a new environment that her own parents would not have understood and might not have accepted.

As we shopped and toured, I had asked her for help with a needed purchase. For some time the duties as a navigating deck officer had required the ownership of my own navigation instrument, a sextant. Past voyages, where I had been forced to rely on the beat-up, ill-calibrated, old instrument provided as ship's equipment, needed to end. All good career deck officers have their own sextants, a vital instrument that they guard and care for as if it was the queen's own jewelry. I had yet to purchase a sextant of my own and now it was time.

The German Company Carl Plath had set the gold standard for sextants. These fine sextants were expensive, as if the gold standard instrument was itself forged of fine gold. A Plath sextant was a big investment, even for a well-paid ship's officer. As Germany had recovered from WWII, some of her exquisite engineering companies, such as Plath, had survived mostly intact. Once the occupying forces allowed the companies to reinstate production, they were to become leaders in the recovery. The industries of Japan had seemed to struggle more with this recovery, but one lesson the young Japanese engineers had learned very well: find the best engineered machines and tools made in developed economies, copy them with small improvements, and produce this copy a whole lot cheaper than the other guys. In an effort to help Japan recover, the US and other countries often turned a blind eye to this bending of international patent laws. I had done my homework, deciding, after talking to many other officers, that a new, high-end, Japanese Tamaya sextant would be as good as a Plath, at half the cost.

The buying and selling of marine navigation instruments was a subject foreign to Keiko. Nevertheless, in no time her university-trained mind had directed us to a very modern, top-quality instrument store serving the Japanese maritime in Yokohama, where her ability to translate English proved pivotal in negotiating this important purchase. I was able to select a fine Tamaya, one that went on to serve me well for years, now holding a place of honor on my personal bookshelf of nautical books. Fifty years later, the world considers Plath and Tamaya to still be the gold standard in sextants; they never grow old. Modern GPS is fantastic, but give me my Tamaya and a good clock and I can always tell you where I am anywhere in the world!

The price of the new Tamaya was just under 120,000 yen, a transaction for which I was prepared to pay in cash, again, being armed with a large wad of five and ten thousand yen notes. For Keiko, this transaction would today be akin to walking into an exotic auto dealership in a large city to purchase a new red Ferrari by spilling out one hundred dollar bills on the salesman's desk.

She had never seen so much money. It looked as if the clerk had never seen that much money either; he had to call the manager. This was an unusual transaction for everybody involved. Evidently, this kind of purchase was normally done though a business invoice.

We walked out of the store with my new sextant in its very own wooden box like two kids having just held up the candy store. Keiko kept looking at the box and back up at me and smiling.

Shortly afterwards she really dropped a bombshell on me. She wanted me to come to have dinner with her family that evening. This unexpected invitation rocked me for a few seconds, leaving Keiko with a look of disappointment on her face.

Right then a little voice in the back of my head was shouting, "Very little upside to this invitation, perhaps lots of downside, at best a very awkward evening." Another voice was telling me that the safe move would be to counter her invitation by upping the ante and inviting her to a really expensive restaurant in Yokohama, thereby avoiding the question of familial awkwardness. One look into her pleading eyes led me to paste on my largest and most sincere smile. "Yes, I would love to have dinner at your house." This brought a huge smile to her face. It was sort of surprising that she had waited until the last minute to ask me, as she must have know about this for at least a day or so. Perhaps she thought that asking at the last minute would bring with it less chance of rejection.

We returned to the hotel to clean up before dinner at her house. After the ritual hot bath and dressing for dinner, I steered Keiko to a small table at the elegant rubbed-wood and carved-stone lobby bar; this evening was most certainly going to require added distilled fortitude. Keiko ordered hot saké so I followed suit. I would have preferred a Beefeater martini but I bowed to saké, for about the same reason that tourists and showoffs request chop sticks in American Asian restaurants. A few minutes later, while looking at the patrons in the bar, it was clear that the Japanese businessmen dressed in fashionable suits and ties were all drinking manhattans and martinis. Once again one of my foreign culture rules had been broken. "Trying to look and act like locals is fruitless. Be yourself, order what you want, never be a jerk about demanding things done like they are done at home, and keep a smile on your face." Note to self: Stick to your own rules.

Finding a cab outside the hotel, Keiko issued directions to her family home, sending the cab driver winding through early evening traffic into a part of the city that had suffered grievously from American bombing. After the war, basic wooden housing had been re-established as soon as American ships arrived, bringing wood from the forests of the Northwest. The American firebombing had damn near wiped out anything made of wood in the cities of Honshu Island, leading to a shortage of wood, a severity that even required the Japanese to search for substitute materials for chopsticks.

A concerned look on her face as the cab pulled into a small alley, Keiko nodded to me that this was where she lived. It then occurred to me that she was every bit as nervous about this evening as was I. It was going to strain all of my manners and social skills in what was sure to be an alien setting to make this a successful evening for her as well as her family.

We ducked into a short doorway, through a hall, and into a row of residences formed mostly by moving shoji doors. Keiko signaled that we should remove our shoes, putting on slippers left conveniently at the doorsill. She then slipped through a door, speaking to a woman who came to the door, bowing deeply and, in very broken English, asked me to come in. Keiko introduced her as Mother.

The Faithful Sextant

There were four other women, two about the same age as her mother, two who looked to be about thirty, a very old gentleman, and a boy of about ten. Keiko introduced the two older women as aunts, the middle-aged women as cousins, and the boy as a cousin. She waited until I had bowed to the aunts, said hello to the cousins, and then she introduced me to her grandfather, the old man in the corner. He did not bow. I bowed to him and he nodded back, saying nothing. This I took for his ascent that my being there was accepted, but that I would not be feted as in the parable of the prodigal son.

Trying to find a parallel to this setting left me feeling like an actor in an old Kentucky story, where I was Bob McCoy showing up for dinner at the Hatfields' with Keiko Hatfield as my dinner date. How nice, the Hatfields and McCoys for a sit down dinner.

The women hurriedly busied themselves with the preparation of dinner after leading me to a cushion on the floor. Looking around the room, it came to me that there were no middle-aged men. Keiko had told me nothing about her family, and now it was left to me to try to construct a story. First, I realized that Keiko had to be at least twenty-one years old and that her father had died in the war. Her uncles had died. Her male cousins had died. This extended family was held together as best possible by the aging grandfather, who had been too old to fight. He was the emblematic man of the house.

These were very simple, hardworking folks whose lives had found stratification near the bottom of history's barrel of shit choices. They were proud of what they had, yet Americans surely would have viewed their possessions and housing as abject poverty. They deeply missed the men of the family lost to the war but were determined not to let this tragedy destroy them. To me a summation might be the great line uttered by Lara to Dr. Zhivago, from the movie of the same name, in explanation of the terrors of the Russian Revolution, "What a horrible time in history to have been born."

❀

Sitting alone for a few minutes, my mind strolled back to a time in early 1962 when I was a nineteen-year-old cadet during my year of training at sea. Our ship, the *Neva West,* had docked in Bremen, Germany, working cargo for two days, when a German friend of our ship's captain suggested a blind date with a young girl who was a friend of his family. The other cadet, being engaged, was not interested, so I agreed to meet this young *fraulein* for lunch. Her name was Barbara Nemier. She had a good command of English, and with my Teutonic heritage, together we looked like any other young German couple, both of us fascinated to learn of our first year college experience. The weather was nice for a northern European winter day, we enjoyed each other's company, and so we agreed to meet again the next day for tea followed by a movie.

I met Barbara at her mother's apartment the next day to have afternoon tea. The apartment was nicely furnished, in a good building, what you might expect of a widow living on a well-funded pension. Before we sat down for tea, Barbara showed me one or two family antiques but skipped over the collection on the fireplace mantle, what appeared to be a small shrine to the German Wehrmacht. There were pictures of men in German uniforms that, once I asked, Barbara explained to me were her father, a grandfather, and a mixture of uncles and cousins. Included with these pictures were combat medals and campaign ribbons. Barbara explained that she was too young to remember her father as he had died early in the war on the Eastern Front.

Staring at the pictures, it was hard to imagine the feelings had our roles been reversed, had my country lost the war, had I to explain a picture of my deceased father to a young girl whose own father might have killed him. Barbara and her mother quickly changed the subject back to questions about life in the ultra-rich United States as seen in Hollywood movies, to which I shared distracted nods of agreement. Meanwhile, my mind still struggled with visions of hand-to-hand combat in the snow of the Eastern Front during a Russian winter.

The Faithful Sextant

The visit with Barbara in Bremen was brief, a blind date with none of the intimacy now shared in Japan, yet while the end of war details in Bremen differed greatly from those in Yokohama, haunting parallels were everywhere. My own mother's family in Granville County, North Carolina must have gone through much the same thing in the winter of 1866.

Bringing myself back to sitting on the floor in the small room at Keiko's house, I remembered to put a smile on my face and tried not to look over at Grandfather. The meal served was traditional Japanese with rice, some sort of green vegetables that tasted like leeks, and a fish soup served in small slurping bowls. The meal tasted good and at the same time, knowing the ingredients were freshly caught or picked, made me happy that this was a far better dinner than the fat and sugar loaded slop and moldy, weevil-infested breads served from the galley of the *Exhibitor*.

The cousins and aunts laughed and giggled along with Keiko through most of the meal. Her mother was solemn and Grandfather ate sparingly while staring straight ahead, never making eye contact with me. Unlike the story in Bremen, here there was no display of war pictures, medals, ribbons, or mementos—family keepsakes likely to bring up the subject of the missing male members. I asked no questions.

The dinner was pleasant, made more so when Grandfather rose, bowing to the women of the room before making his exit, again making no eye contact with the guest. The women continued to bustle around until the socially correct time for the two of us to leave came around. Fortunately, in the previous days, I had found time to do some shopping, purchasing several items that could serve as nice gifts for use in Japan or to be carried home if gifting became inappropriate. With a promising idea for gifting, I had found a small shop in Tokyo that made and sold items crafted of solid gold, an appealing idea since Americans were still not allowed to own gold (from 1934 to 1975).

In Japan gold was made into jewelry and many other small mementos that could serve as a storehouse of value protected from post-war inflation. Staying away from jewelry with its huge markup, I had instead bought two items of differing sizes, all in nearly pure 24kt gold. Should there be no reason to use these amulets as gifts, I knew there would be no trouble sneaking them back into my country as US customs spent little effort chasing down rusty, old merchant ships arriving back stateside from war zones where they often found dockage at hard to reach piers in shabby port areas. The US government set rate of thirty-five dollars per troy ounce for gold in those days was way below the market rate, but black markets exist in the US just like everywhere else, and besides, before we got back home, we were going to Vietnam, the capital of black markets. Years earlier I had augmented a meager cadet salary of one hundred and eleven dollars and fifteen cents per month (half of an ensigns pay) by dealing in currency, carry trade, cigarettes, and gold between port cities in Asia, the start of my lifelong love and obsession with markets, both free and black.

One of the purchases at the gold store had been a fancy gold spoon worth perhaps 30,000 yen. The hotel concierge had surreptitiously wrapped this spoon in gift paper prior to our leaving for dinner. Keiko was allowed to peek in the wrapping, with the understanding that it was just a small memento purchased in San Francisco to be given to thank her mother for dinner. It was very necessary to keep this gift concealed. Accepting a gift of this value would have brought a serious loss of face for her mother, as she would not have had a gift of equal value for me. My plan was to be long gone with Keiko before her mother opened the package to find the 24kt gold marking on the back of the spoon.

It is easy to love gold; it is so fungible. (An explanation of this marvelous word follows in the Vietnam story). The utility value of the spoon was negligible, but it could always be converted to commodity value and sold if times became more difficult than they already were. Giving gifts is such a basic human reward system that mostly benefits the giver.

The escape plan worked as Keiko and I quickly found a cab, transporting us back into the heart of the city before Mom opened the gift.

As my idyllic Japanese fantasy drifted into the coming New Year, a ticking clock kept bringing me back to the reality of why I found myself here in the first place. Preview pictures flashed of a rusty hulk loaded with olive drab war machines, daily challenges of grit, sweat, and ingenuity to make it work, and a still far-off, sweltering war zone. Then, much quicker than I wanted, the previews ended. The main feature began. The ship had been repaired…the sailing board, announcing to the crew our official departure time, had been posted.

Saying farewell to Keiko was couched in my mind with the possibility that I might return to Yokohama, a delusion again from deep in the land of wishful dreaming, which even my storm-rattled, romance-addled brain knew had no chance in hell. Nevertheless, my imagination fed at the trough of a rumor that some merchant ships serving on military charter had indeed been assigned to shuttle between Japan and Vietnam. I knew that there was no chance of ever seeing Keiko again, but how can one know for sure? Speeding off into tomorrow, how do any of us know for sure where the next course line plotted on the chart of our future will take us? While it was uncertain what came next in Vietnam, it was clear that the memory of my Christmas spent with Keiko in Japan would stay forever, and it did.

Our last night together had to have been memorable, but again the sands of time have erased the minor events. There were just too many emotions crowding out details that I cannot remember what we ate or what we did. I do remember that sometime late in the last evening, back at the hotel, I asked her to open a gift that had been purchased at the same time as the one for her mother. This gift was a large, solid gold heart to be worn on a chain, engraved in Japanese printing in the form called *onnade* or women's hand, the symbols meaning *utsuksuhii*.

After opening the gift, Keiko stared at the gold heart, looking up at me several times. She was speechless. She knew very well that this was no trinket bought in San Francisco, its weight and luster murmured valuable gift. She was biting her lower lip, while looking up at me with a furrowed brow and huge eyes, where a tear formed near the edge. This biting the lower lip thing that girls do has for me a way of transforming strong intentions into silly putty. In spite of her cultural face-saving position that she should not accept this expensive gift, one look up into my fierce blue eyes told her that no amount of argument, denial, or compromise was going to see this gift retracted. It was also obvious that social face-saving mores aside, she very much wanted to keep it.

Fortunately, this awkward moment had help on the way; Keiko had also brought a gift. Though there would be a sharp contrast in market value between our gifts, we were well into the understanding that monetary value could be trumped by symbolism, and she had brought the perfect trump card.

She smiled deeply while holding the gold heart close to her chest, suddenly jumping up to run to the other side of the room where she had hidden a small bag. Returning to my side with a look of excited expectation, she handed me her gift wrapped in filmy Japanese paper. Carefully discarding the wrapping paper, there appeared a hand-carved wooden horse about twelve inches long, covered in many coats of black lacquer, with hand-lettered Japanese *kanji* on the side of the horse retelling an ancient story.

This horse had been carved very much in the style of the Greek Trojan horse, leading me to ask Keiko if this was from Greek mythology. She replied, "Oh no, Robert-san. This is the magical horse of a Samurai warrior. The *kanji* tells a story of a very brave warrior, of the strength and agility of his horse, and of their many feats of daring, courage, and heroism. The Samurai believed that their life and the life of their horse were intertwined as one. The boldness of the horse is conveyed into the boldness of the warrior, and the boldness of the warrior is sent back to the horse." As she stared steadily, a tear forming, she went on, "I know you are a strong and courageous warrior, and this horse will remind you that you are not alone. It is a very strong token and will keep you safe where you are going."

I kept that Samurai horse for a long time. The mythological magic held by this horse, gifted by a special young girl, I attributed to pulling my sorry ass out of serious danger on more than one occasion. It was, in fact, going to need to start exercising its magic to keep me well and alive much sooner than either of us might have expected.

Also coming much sooner than expected was the wakeup call from the front desk. This time my leaving did bring tears, there could be no plan for tomorrow, no letter writing, no phone calls.

I had asked Keiko not to come down to the ship to wave goodbye. We were leaving very early the next morning with the turning of the tide. It would serve no purpose to have her staring up at me with tears in her eyes in the half-light of a gray, wet dawn in the land of the rising sun. When the time came, I went alone through dark, misty, deserted streets with no thought about anything but the most special time I had ever spent in a foreign country. The love and beauty I found as a result of the chance meeting with Keiko took me to a new place of understanding, of hope and expectation, of joy at the wonder of how youth and love bind all humans.

The War Zone

Early in the morning, once the shipyard workers and their tools had been removed, we cast off lines, heading out into the gloom of Tokyo Bay. After a quick twenty-five minutes on the bridge during undocking, I immediately returned to my lonely bunk, sleeping fitfully as the ship weaved its way south though the labyrinth of defensive forts. As I lay tossing, reviewing the events of the last week, it was understandable that these fond memories would rob the sandman of some quality sleep. In another several weeks I would purposely bring these heartwarming memories back to life in an effort to block out the ugliness of my new real world: life in the war zone of Vietnam.

Just before noon, I returned to my assigned watch on the bridge as the ship turned southwest into the Pacific, laying a course just skirting the Okinawa islands. That evening we celebrated New Year's Eve with a bigger-than-life drunk fest in the radio shack and later in the captain's office. To a man, we toasted the hope that 1966 would find a better year for the *SS Exhibitor* and her crew.

Daily duties of navigating the ship in these busy shipping lanes between Japan, Okinawa, Taiwan, and the Philippines kept the mind active, relieving the thoughts of typhoons, Japanese baths, and a certain blonde girl back in New York who had not been heard from now in over seven weeks and who still occupied the top spot on my dance card. As we entered the South China Sea, it seemed that every sunset came with a yellowish haze as a result of dust blown eastward from the Chinese mainland. Even though the calendar reminded us that the month was January, mid-winter in the North, the weather became sunnier and warmer by the day.

Soon Gunther, the second mate, broke out the charts of Vietnam so that we could begin drawing a mythical pencil line around the country. This pencil line was to demark the US military definition of the Vietnam "War Zone." Our union contract rules required that our base pay would double starting on the day we first crossed over this line into the zone. Gunther and I ran our vessel track line up to the edge of the war zone, calculating our estimated arrival at this critical line. According to our calculations, we would enter the demarcation line of the war zone at about 3:00 a.m., meaning from that day forward our pay would double. It was only a few minutes following this calculation that the "what if" imagination began.

Missing our entrance into this zone by three hours, and thereby missing another whole day on double pay, seemed a terrible waste. If we were able to be there even a few minutes before midnight, we would receive an extra full day of bonus pay. This was the kind of thinking that came to men who have too much time spent on boring four-hour watches, combined with deceptive skills finely honed while locked up in a four-year service academy.

It came to us that by moving our track to the north and increasing our speed by a knot or two it would put us over the line before eight bells struck, gaining that extra day of bonus pay. Gunther looked at me and moaned. "Bob, you know well that there is no way this old rust bucket could manage even a fraction of a knot more than our current speed, and additionally, it is unlikely the captain would approve a course change." My larcenous mind poured over this dilemma for a few minutes until it came to me. Excitedly, I cried, "Gunther, the whole answer lies in sloppy navigation. We have over two days before we get to the line, so let's assume bad weather forces us to DR (dead reckoning), leaving us north of our track and faster than usual. We make a log entry as to crossing the line just before midnight and correct our actual position with an 0800 sextant shot the next morning."

"Yeah okay, but what is the captain going to say about all this sloppy navigating?" Gunther replied.

To which I answered, "I bet he will call it very creative."

Thus it was that the old worn out *SS Exhibitor* was able to report two days of speeds well in excess of any she had been able to achieve since her days as a new shining pup just out of her construction, as some unknown current—not discovered until she was well into the war zone—had mysteriously pushed her faster and to the south of her assumed DR track. An official entry was made in the logbook showing our arrival in the war zone just before midnight, and thus it was that this rusty old ship and her anxious crew found themselves sailing the waters of a country at war one day earlier than expected.

The crew was predictably very happy that we began drawing double pay a day early. As for the captain, his only comment was a long "Hmmm" given with a smile on his face. He was the captain after all, making tacit approval of fraudulent logbook entries punishable misconduct.

The ship now experienced warm days and calm seas as we sailed under full steam, heading towards the strangely shaped coast of Vietnam and to the mouth of the Saigon River system. It is uncertain what those little midget Japanese shipyard workers had done in Yokohama, but the *Exhibitor* was performing like a champ. During my afternoon watch the next day, perhaps one hour into the watch, all shipboard activity had found a quiet corner for siesta. Relishing the quiet, I was in what I called my wheelhouse reverie. This somnolent numbness, aided by a mind wandering to any subject except running a ship, is created on drowsy, early afternoons where no ships or land are anywhere in your eyesight, where the sun is warm, the ship has a smooth tender roll, the helm is on auto pilot, and all other crewmembers are asleep or having coffee. This lazy, hazy setting gives the sensation of being the only human in attendance on a moving island of steel, of existing only in this wondrous moment, of being the master of all that I can see.

Suddenly my trance was shattered by a cacophony of blaring horns coming from directly behind our ship, as if there was a giant 18-wheel semi-truck coming from behind, screaming for us to move over.

Almost jumping out of my skin, I ran out to the bridge wing, looked astern, where to my amazement I saw a US Navy destroyer escort (DE) plowing through the waves, coming right up our wake as if to slice us in half. This sleek ship then bent over as she changed course to pass us close alongside to port. At the same time this was happening, a Navy crewman on the signal bridge was working the destroyer's flashing signal light like a nervous baseball manager chewing gum in the bottom of the ninth. Once again the Navy ship sounded her steam horn at the same time that an officer ran out on the bridge wing with a voice hailing horn. Out of the corner of my eye I noticed my captain and chief mate coming up the outside stairs of my ship, three at a time. Concurrently, the Navy officer began yelling into his bullhorn, "What ship are you? Why don't you answer your VHF? Stop your ship immediately!"

Captain Winebrenner yelled at me, "What the hell is going on?"

I explained that this irritable naval vessel wanted to know who we were, demanding at the same time that we stop our ship. He grabbed the phone, called the engine room, and asked the watch officer to slow the ship to ten rpm (revolutions per minute), doing this carefully so as not to put any strain on the boilers.

"Captain," I then said, "it seems that the Navy thinks we have a working VHF. They are wetting their little neatly pressed white pants that we are not answering their call. What the hell. Do you suppose they think we are the enemy?"

Seeing the flashing light on the destroyer still chewing away in Navy gibberish, the captain asked me to break out our flashing light. He then gave an order to the chief mate, telling him to send a man back to the stern flagpole to raise our American flag. Merchant ships rarely fly a flag of their country, except in port, as winds at sea will shred them in a matter of days.

With our signal light now plugged in and operating, at the captain's order I began sending our call sign, our official number, and words to the effect that we were a United States ship under charter to the Military Sea Transportation Service. The Navy petty officer working the signal light was, of course, frustrated that I did everything in plain language without using the prescribed Navy format. I then told the Navy that we did not have VHF and that they would need to contact us at our guard frequency on our main ship's radio. Having ordered my best able bodied seaman to steer the ship, the captain dropped down to the radio room to receive and send messages to the Navy ship.

Now that both ships had slowed to about five knots, my entire attention focused on handling our ship so that we did not inadvertently collide with the destroyer, who now lay about the width of a football field off our port side. So here we were in this tense stand-down, just me and the AB on our bridge. Meanwhile, over on the Navy ship there were about two dozen officers and crew running around in their small wheelhouse and above on the signal bridge as they looked up regulations in notebooks, broke out signal flags, and sent a steady stream of flashing light messages. I had no idea in hell what they wanted from us, but an evil thought slipped into my mind that since the *SS Exhibitor* was probably twice the tonnage of the DE, a little game of "chicken" might be fun. Oh yeah, but on second thought, they had two dual gun mounts on the bow; maybe not!

A few minutes later, a huddle of senior officers on the bridge of the Navy DE formed around a young sailor who had a message from their radio room, most likely sent half way around the globe and back all to span the meager few yards between our two ships. Now they knew who we were: just another struggling American ship trying to fight the same war as they were. The captain of the destroyer then had one of his officers look up the details of the supposed offense we had committed and messaged this back to us.

In his best James Cagney acting role, the Navy captain, probably a freshly minted commander, having proven what a sorry lot of undisciplined, uninformed sailors these merchant mariners really were, smugly smiled to himself and turned over op-con of the bridge to his command duty officer and his sixteen assistants and headed down for a cup of congratulatory coffee in his wardroom.

As for me, I turned to Captain Winebrenner, who was by now back on the bridge wing, and asked him, "Should I hoist the foxtrot-uniform code flags or just send him back F-U by flashing light?"

The captain smiled, replying, "There is probably no good reason to piss off the Navy today. Get us back on course and speed, and oh yeah, have your ordinary seaman take down the American flag on the stern. Those damn things cost money!"

There it was in a nutshell: "Those damn things cost money." This entire incident all wrapped up and explained by the essentials: we represented a committed group of career mariners dedicated to getting our job done in the most expeditious and cost-effective manner, whereas the Navy destroyer had been given a job guided by the vaguest of goals, fuzziest of objectives, and with almost no regard for cost efficiencies. They, however, did have snappy uniforms.

Now is a good time to review with the reader the seeming incongruity of my intense dislike for the pompous arrogance and glacial unmoving reverence for tradition found from the top to the bottom of the United States Navy, played off against my own thirty-one-year career served in that same Navy.

Over and over in this memoir the reader will find collisions between the revered motto of my alma mater, *Acta non Verba* or "Deeds not words" and events occurring during my long climb through the bureaucracy endemic in the naval rank structure. Some of the bumps came because I did not always fit the frat house/Officer Candidate School (OCS) model.

One Saturday morning, mid-way in my Navy career, after morning muster and inspection at a reserve weekend drill, a run-of-the-mill officer who outranked me by a lousy half stripe, did not think that I, as a lieutenant commander, knew the proper Navy way of saluting. He had me stand all alone on the parade grounds, after other officers and enlisted men had been dismissed from morning flag raising (colors), while he humiliated me by demanding that I practice his instructions on the proper way to render a Navy salute.

What made this particularly galling was that he had become an officer after graduation from some mundane college by going through OCS indoctrination: twelve short weeks to learn everything about ships. On the other hand, I had completed a four-year United States Service Academy, an institution requiring salutes to everything, everyone, every day, including the squirrels picking up acorns. Four long years of shining shoes, polishing brass, perfecting the wearing of the uniform, manual at-arms drilling, parades, inspections, demerits, and all the other horse shit that comes with making it through one of the five outstanding service academies, and now this ninety-day wonder from an upgraded community college had the balls to publically insult me in front of the other officers and enlisted men. I was most proud that I walked away from this incident, forgetting about the whole thing in a few minutes—a trait they also teach at those fine academies.

The saluting instruction type of insult happened more than once, but somehow along the way, certain senior officers saw that just perhaps, if we ever really had to mobilize, I would be the kind of leader needed to get a job done. I got promoted to captain and was selected as a commanding officer; my ninety-day wonder fellow officer was awarded neither.

Much later, as a commanding officer, it became my duty to send men and women off to combat in the Middle East, one of whom was wounded by a Scud missile. These members knew and appreciated that my command style from top to bottom stressed that it was more important to know how to set and achieve valid objectives than to always have the "snappiest" uniform. Near the end of my Navy career, when I could personally influence some changes to this archaic Lord Nelson attitude, this became one of the most rewarding experiences of my life, and I grew to love the Navy for giving me this opportunity.

Vũng Tàu

From a small spring over 17,000 feet high up on the plateau of Tibet flows icy water from the snows of the north face of the Himalayan Range, becoming the source of a river. This grows in volume as it flows past tributaries, gathering their waters until it forms a potent torrent. The sometimes-violent rush of silt-laden water then passes through the countries of China, Burma, Laos, Thailand, and Cambodia before entering Vietnam, where it flows into the South China Sea. This mightiest of rivers is the Mekong; it is the twelfth longest in the world. Where the Mekong meets the South China Sea it forms one of the great river deltas on earth, rivaling that of the Mississippi. In a curious trick of geography, another river system has its much smaller delta a scant fifteen miles north of the northernmost tentacle of the huge Mekong Delta. Included in the delta is the Sài Gòn River.

  The huge river delta system of the Mekong/Saigon, forming most of the geography of the entire southern tip of Vietnam, is brought to an abrupt halt by a curling outcropping of limestone and bedrock laid down as a dike, almost as if an archaic god of geology held up his hand, saying enough of these mangrove swamps. The Vietnamese named this demarcation peninsula Vũng Tàu.

  The high solid ground formed by Vũng Tàu has historically served as a playground for the wealthy merchants and aristocrats of Saigon and, in particular, the French colonists. Bathers and sun worshipers were enticed by the pristine, white sandy beaches on the South China Sea side of the peninsula, leading to the growth of a resort with spas and social clubs. The development of this resort made huge strides during the French Colonial days as a way to help convince weather weary Parisians that there were some advantages to living in this far flung colony. Following the French defeat at Dièn Biên Phũ and the wind-down of French colonial power, most of the French citizens, lacking a permanent financial stake in the colony, fled back to the Gallic homeland, leaving the resort in the hands of well-to-do people of the Indochina.

Having never seen an upper-class person of Asian ethnic heritage purposefully expose their body to direct sunlight, as favored by the sun worshipping young girls of North America or Northern Europe, the end of French colonization brought with it an evacuation of the bathing beauties from the beaches of Vũng Tàu, but the clubs and spas still managed a good business.

The western or inshore side of the Vũng Tàu peninsula forms a large bay offering a very sheltered anchorage of about five miles in diameter. It was in this bay that American Army logistics planners chose to locate a floating war material warehouse. This floating war material storage took the form of one hundred or more merchant ships hanging on anchors awaiting fuzzy decisions about how and when to mesh their cargos into the war effort. The overarching result of a policy maker's decision to expand this war faster than logistics could manage made for a mess in the Port of Saigon. Now, planners had to treat this fleet of ships at anchor as one giant warehouse, selecting ships one at a time to proceed up river to the port based on the need for their cargo.

After sending a radio message to the military sealift office announcing our ETA, we were advised to look for a pilot boat off the southern point of Vũng Tàu. At mid-morning the next day we slowed near the Vũng Tàu point where a civilian harbor pilot approached in a small US Navy Mike 6 landing craft. He boarded our ship and proceeded to guide us to almost the middle of what was the largest collection of merchant ships I had ever witnessed. What a sight it was! Scattered all over the bright polish of the roadstead, these ships at anchor floated in perfect stillness under a bright, hazy tropical sun, opaque and bloated like strange and monumental structures left to swing and rust by sailors in an eternal slumber.

Unaware, we had just found our new home in a purgatory of silent, steamy tropical airs and boredom fueled by no information, no action, no written plan, and most all, by no mail. Our very first question to the US Army pilot had been, "Where's our mail?"

He had brought an envelope full of official documents for the captain, but no personal mail for any of the crewmen. He had promised to check on our mail, but several days later no mail had arrived. It had now been over two months since any of us had heard from loved ones.

There was no mail for us. No mail came during our stay in Saigon. No mail was waiting when we arrived back in the United States. Our mail was finally delivered when we once again arrived in Saigon on the next voyage. The letters were now crusty. They asked why we were ignoring requests. Many letters were so out of date that the loved one had now moved on to someone else. The *why* of this mess-up was simple: no one cared. On the military "give a shit" scale, we rated right up with latrine duty done by a drafted, war-protesting hippie.

Ship arrivals at anchorages or berthing in ports are events that normally find a number of new folks scurrying around the ship to make it ready for its next evolution. Nothing could be further from the case at our anchorage off Vũng Tàu. We became enveloped in silence as each crewmember gathered his thoughts about what came next. Oh yes, the chief mate and the first assistant engineer could always find small jobs to fill the open time of idle hands. Cargo lights needed to be hung over the side so that we could spot potential sappers sneaking alongside at night to blow a hole in our ship. Valves needed to be cleaned and repacked. Rust somewhere always needed to be chipped and painted. But very quickly even these two paragons of busy work ran out of reasonable tasks. Deck and engine room watches were still observed, but mostly the two watch officers, one for the deck and one for the engine room, could be found sitting outside under a canvas awning reliving sea stories with other officers. The captain's only rule for these watch officers was that they wear some sort of shoes—even though shower clogs later became acceptable—and that the consumption of the dearly beloved, cold Budweiser be performed either before or after the actual hours each watch officer was scheduled to be the officer on duty.

Boredom immediately set in. Just how many hours can one spend reading Zane Gray's *Riders of the Purple Sage*? The only change in the scenery occurred with the semi-diurnal change of the tide from ebb to flood. Every time the water molecules of the South China Sea began their twice-daily chase to follow the gravity of the moon, all of the ships in the bay would begin their slow motion dance of swinging around as if there was a barn dance caller singing out to each one to do-si-do with your partner. This swing would be brought up short by the ship's anchor chain just like a cowboy dancer grabbing his partner as she came swinging by. All ships would now rotate to the call of the dance master such that the fleet turned to stem the incoming tidal flood, just waiting for the next ebb, becoming "painted ships upon a painted ocean" for another six hours.

The fleet of ships represented just about anything and everything that would float and carry military cargo through some sort of charter agreement with the Pentagon. Included in this fleet at anchor were two old World War II Liberty ships. Of the two thousand seven hundred and ten liberty ships built for WWII, never once had I ever seen one actively engaged in cargo trade; they had all been torpedoed or sunk in storms or turned into razor blades. It was shocking to recall that these ghostly relics of the "Great War," were newer than the *SS Exhibitor*.

The water from the South China Sea in which we were anchored was crystal clear as the muddy effluent from the Saigon and the Nha Be Rivers flowed south of us. The afternoon of our arrival, several of the crew approached the captain, asking if it would be okay to swim alongside the ship using our gangway as a swim platform. He gave his assent if we agreed to form a swim group with lifeguards and lookouts just in case a shark came near. Recreational swim day was set for early afternoon the next day. That evening, the thread to this poorly woven plan unraveled.

Darkness near the Equator arrives with surprising speed as if some nether-world unseen hand yanks the window shade closed. As the sunlight of our first day at anchorage came to a sudden end, the on duty mate made his rounds, checking anchor bearings and turning on the large cargo lights hung over the side of the ship. The evening cocktail party had moved outside on the boat deck where the usual suspects sat around in deck chairs recounting well-worn stories. The deck chairs had cleverly been bought in Japan by one of our entrepreneurial fellow officers, to be resold to us at a huge profit margin, an early sign of black marketeering. Our cocktails were well along when suddenly one of the guys near the railing shouted out, "Get over here and look at this!"

As a group, his shout brought us quickly to the rail where, looking over the side of the ship into the water below, we witnessed a twisting and wriggling tangle of sea snakes brought up from the depths by the lure of our powerful cargo lights. As we stared in silence at this writhing group of six to eight foot snakes, one of the guys stated with authority, "You know, they are venomous." So it was that our only hope of physical activity came unwound, leaving the hanging question, "Say, do have any more of those Zane Gray books?"

Several days later two of the sailors in the crew dreamed up an outlet to express their discontent at our boring though well paid steamship imprisonment. It is possible that their discontent may have been heightened by the captain's rule allowing officers to drink alcohol but prohibited non-officer crewmembers from this recreational pleasure. Thus it was that these two malcontents simultaneously came down with a well-rehearsed illness of some obscure ailment, having symptoms strong enough to require that they be taken off the ship and sent to the hospital in Vũng Tàu.

The action by these two merchant seamen requires a digression into the workings of the psyche of men who go to sea on merchant ships. Most of these career sailors make a study of short cuts, malingering, lawyering, loop-holing, and in general, a lifestyle insuring that no extra energy is used to accomplish the minimum to do a job. This world view includes watchfulness to insure that no other crewmember receive some extra favor or benefit due to be shared by all: the equalitarian lifestyle so favored by wanna-be socialists. It is unclear if there is a genetic trait that leads these men to go to sea or whether it is a learned response coming as a result of long days of almost no human contact interspersed with short periods of very hard and sometimes dangerous work. In olden times of sailing ships, burly, sometimes sadistic, "bucko" mates would simply bash heads of errant or misbehaving sailors, bringing order back into the "fo'c'sle" crewmembers. Once maritime unions were firmly established in the early 20th century, these sailors found their expression of a seagoing lifestyle as a manifestation of the many clauses and nuances of the hard won union contract, a document they studied and revered more closely than the Bible.

Thus it was that these two malingerers, union contract books firmly in hand, demanded that they be taken ashore for medical treatment. They had told other jealous fo'c'sle mates that they would bring back good stories about the bars and nightlife in Vũng Tàu. The Army was called and a Mike 6 boat was sent out with a corpsman to escort these two to a military facility for treatment. The two deal-pullers had no idea what lay ahead for them.

The best-laid plans of these shirkers had two serious flaws. First, the Army has a long history of malingering soldiers; this is

The Faithful Sextant

why they invented sergeants. And second, these two were not even soldiers; they were lowly merchant mariners, civilians who, in the eyes of the sergeants, very likely had chosen going to sea as a way to avoid the draft.

However, the most serious flaw in this *Ferris Bueller's Day Off* plan, not taken into account by our two maritime dealers, was their failure to understand that there was a real war going on nearby. The shooting had become serious by 1966, leaving lots of young boys eviscerated in the meat grinder of this nasty conflict. Coming back from the ever-shifting front lines were young men in body bags and more young men with serious wounds to be patched up as best as possible before flying them back to Army hospitals in Japan and then on to the States. Others, lightly wounded or suffering from battle fatigue, were removed from their unit to recover at places like the facilities at Vũng Tàu. The doctors, nurses, and corpsmen had seen it all. There would be no tricking them into a nice bed, some pretty nurses, three good meals, and a pass to check out the nightlife in town. Their immediate reaction was to make examples of these two miscreants in such a way as to craft a story to circulate in the union halls, stopping any future shenanigans of this nature.

The Army sergeants put the hammer down on these two. They did not allow them to return to the ship for three days while they were assigned every rectal exam indignity, every available form of vaccination shot, and every toilet cleaning detail designed to inflict the most pain and humiliation possible. A pass out the front gate for barhopping was out of the question; these men were sick. Once our two unfortunate sailors had been thoroughly re-educated by grizzled non-coms, they were released to the Army supply guys for transport back to the ship. Never were two deck hands ever so happy to see the rust and grunge of our lady, Miss *Exhibitor*. And did they have a sad story to tell.

Several days later we got our first chance to see the war in action. The now usual afternoon on deck/under tarp, siesta group had its hot tropical silence broken by a flight of four US Navy A-1 Skyraider fighter aircraft. Enemy action had been spotted in the swampy delta near our anchorage, and these pilots were out to churn the mud. As the flight of four aircraft circled above the target, they peeled off one by one to drop a bomb or strafe with the four 20mm M2 cannons. Binoculars helped us identify individual aircraft numbers, leading to a claim of ownership of one aircraft by each of the four of us watching. This in turn immediately led to a betting pool, where a bet would be won by picking the pilot who would dive the lowest before climbing back out to join the waiting group as another peeled off for an attack. What great fun. We ordered another round of cold beer from the watch officer (who could not drink) and began serious scoring and handicapping. The strafing continued until the pilots had eliminated all of their ordnance, sending the four propeller-driven aircraft scurrying back out to sea to find an assigned carrier, drop a tailhook onto a waiting wire, and head down to the wardroom for an evening meal.

The Douglas A-1 Skyraider made its first flight in March of 1945 and was delivered to the Navy in December of 1946. Thus it was to become one of the last great piston-powered, propeller-driven aircraft of the WWII era. As such, it was also the epitome of propeller technology in a fighter/attack aircraft. It would never have the speed of a jet fighter or the bomb carrying capacity of a jet bomber, but there were things it could do and do them well. Perhaps its best quality can be summed up in the word "loiter." This aircraft could carry a lot of different stuff, and it could hang around potential ground targets for long periods of time before delivering a variety of rockets, bombs, and cannon shells onto an enemy with surprising effectiveness. The slow-moving Skyraider was the perfect ground support aircraft for a war where the enemy essentially had no air force acting as a deterrent.

The slowing effect of external drag was never a big consideration in the design of the Skyraider, leading to its being equipped with seven hard points or racks on each wing and one on the centerline of the fuselage; fifteen racks in all. These racks were multi-functional, holding just about any kind of bomb, rocket, wing tank, or gun pod that might be needed for an assigned mission. Showing off this plane's versatility, in October of 1965—just before our ship arrived in the war zone—a Navy pilot, Commander Stoddard, took the multi-functionality of the wing racks on the Skyraider to new limits of absurdity. He ordered his maintenance crew to fabricate a special mount that was attached to a regular white ceramic toilet. This "john" was then loaded up on the outboard rack on his starboard wing where it accompanied him on his next mission to be unceremoniously dropped on some Viet Cong position. This became known as the "John Bomb"; all had a big laugh.

This toilet-bombing incident certainly showed the flexibility of the A-1 Skyraider but let's take a look at the bigger picture for a minute. What the hell was a United States Navy commander doing fucking around with a stunt like this! The gentle reader might say, "Lighten up, McEliece; it was just a prank: good for morale."

Let me give this prank context. Suppose for a minute that a wing commander in the Second World War had approached a B-17 pilot telling him to load one or more toilets into his bomb bay for the next evenings bombing run over Berlin. You know, "Just a little joke to show old Adolph just how little we think of him." If this pilot had been on his twenty-fourth mission, just before completing the needed twenty-five for reassignment, he would not have laughed. He might just have gone berserk, beating the crap out of the wing commander, releasing tension and emotion built up from nightly near suicide missions. The Allied soldier or airman had a deep loathing for the Germans, having seen many of his friends splattered and killed by the enemy. Each pilot knew that he shortened the odds of ever again seeing his wife and family each time outboard engine number one fired up to begin another daily mission over enemy held territory. There was no joking around about this. There was nothing funny at all. This young pilot's only constant thought was, *What can we do to live though this next mission? What little edge, what little token of luck, what little superstition will work just one more time to bring us safely home? Pull a prank on Hitler…are you nuts? We just want to kill that bastard. Kill him. Kill him. Do you understand? Humor, you say…we have no time for humor. This is life or this is death.*

Commander Stoddard was a long way from the emotion felt by the pilots flying over wartime Germany. A very long way. Our whole outlook on this trumped-up political force of wills and farce of intent between a corrupt government in South Vietnam opposing a small group of zealots in North Vietnam was far removed from the horrors of the Second World War. If, however, we tried hard enough, if we experienced enough death, dismemberment, and destruction, if well-trained soldiers armed with modern weapons designed and fabricated in China or the Soviet Union came into the war, then likely it would be possible to craft the necessary hatred and loathing to turn this conflict into a real war. Pranks done for morale would then not be thinkable. Also, though at that time in the conflict unlikely, had Commander Stoddard been shot down during his toilet mission, to serve perhaps ten years as a POW in North Vietnam, he wouldn't have found the stunt laughable.

So it was that we sailors of the military's logistics service had our first taste of folks trying to kill each other in Vietnam, and disingenuous or not, note that we also thought that this thing was a big joke. Bloody war experiences—that leveler of reality—would soon change that thinking. Could we call this a combat education leading to a PHD, Practitioner of Hate and Death?

So just who were these little guys in black pajamas that everyone was trying to kill, and why were they so angry? During the French colonial days these revolutionaries were known as Viet Minh. Their goal had been the removal of French colonialists. After the departure of the French and the subsequent takeover of corrupt, semidemocratic governments of the southern partition, these determined revolutionaries had taken up the banner of communism. They then became known as Viet Cong. With the later arrival of Americans, the GIs referred to them as Cong or mostly just "Charlie."

A small library of books has been written about the decline of the French Colonial Empire, the partitioning of Vietnam, the trail to communism led by Ho Chi Minh, and finally the American involvement. A good place to start for those interested is a book titled: *Valley of Death* by Pulitzer Prize winning author Ted Morgan, or perhaps the starkest of all, Bernard Fall's masterpiece, *Hell In A Very Small Place*. The Defense Department lists the first American death due to our involvement in Vietnam as coming in mid-1956, almost exactly two years after the French suffered their colony-ending defeat at Dièn Biên Phũ.

Following World War II, American policy makers (think brothers Alan and John Foster Dulles) had acquired a morbid distaste for communism. The leaders of North Vietnam (think Ho Chi Minh) had accepted the communism policy model, thereby chilling our leaders with the thought that this new government could spread all throughout Southeast Asia. American involvement began to ramp up after the Gulf of Tonkin incident in the summer of 1964, which let congress give President Johnson all the authority he needed to declare war and send troops. For us it was now eighteen months after that declaration; the fat was in the fire.

Our life of sweltering tedium finally came to a halt at noon one day, almost a month later, when a small boat pulled up to our gangway with an Army rep who informed us that we would be heading upriver with the next morning's incoming tide. He also told us that before the river pilot arrived, we would receive an armed guard.

Early the next morning eight soldiers, led by a sergeant, boarded early with various weapons. Heavy-duty .50 caliber machine guns were mounted on the bow and stern, handled by a two-man crew, while two individual soldiers took up positions on the mid-ships walkways on either side of the ship, armed with 7.62mm M-60 machine guns. The soldier taking position on the starboard side sat directly under the porthole to my stateroom. Before my watch began, as we started upriver, I leaned against the rail to talk with him about life in the Army. He told me the ship guard duty was a much sought-after assignment in his regiment, that the food on ships was better than that in camp, and that the likelihood of being shot at would be smaller than out in the jungles walking patrols. This young man looked to be about eighteen years old. He was very interested in our lifestyle on the ship, and he seemed amazed that anyone would come over to this hellhole without having been strong-armed by a bunch of old women on a local draft board. I did not mention to him that my pay was likely more than ten times what he made in any similar period of time.

Viewing the tangled river delta surrounding the capital city of Saigon was like looking at the root structure of a mangrove tree, that ubiquitous flora found on the banks of these same twisting rivers. The mouth of the Sài Gòn River does not flow into the sea, it flows into another river, and there are two ways to get to it from the South China Sea; a longer broader river named the Nha Be or a shorter more direct channel named Sông Lòng Tàu or the Lòng Tàu River.

As with most low country, swampy river deltas, the main channel of any of these rivers snakes its way inland as if the water could not decide from minute to minute whether to go right or left. Rivers with bends always scour out the outside of the bend and deposit silt on the inside of the bend, meaning that our path looking for the deepest part of the channel required taking the longest possible transit. Shortcutting though the inside of the bend was a sure formula for going aground. The Viet Cong owned the swamp; this was no place to get stuck in the mud, becoming a large stationary target or LST, an acronym borrowed from the guys who operated the old WWII landing craft. No one wanted to become a stationary target.

Our Vietnamese pilot elected to take us up the Lòng Tàu River, a shorter but narrower river, a river ideal for Viet Cong mines and ambushes.

A favored river tactic of the Viet Cong used homemade contact mines. These deadly mines were buried into the mud on both sides of a narrow point in the river and then connected to a wire strung across the river from bank to bank. Hidden under the mud, the wire hung such that its catenary lay unexposed just under the surface of the muddy river. A ship passing between these two mines would inadvertently hook the submerged wire, pulling the two contact mines out of the mud and into the side of the ship, a very low tech and yet frightfully effective way to sink a ship. A human trigger or presence was not required. Several ships had been so severely damaged by this homemade, improvised explosive device that they had floundered in the river, blocking traffic in both directions until the ship could be refloated and salvaged. To put a stop to this tactic, the Army had procured small mine-sweeping boats to run ahead of us on each side of our ship, finding and cutting these underwater cables.

The topography of this part of the Saigon River delta was low laying mud flats covered with swamp grass and dispersed copses of mangrove trees. The lack of vegetation provided no cover for an ambush, especially in light of the ability of our armed guard to radio back for air cover from the afore mentioned deadly "Skyraiders" or their evil twin, the deadly Huey Cobra gunship. No one seemed worried about an armed attack; however, I noted that the river pilot and other crewmembers, myself included, did not lounge around leaning on the ship's rails once we got into the river proper. Intuition told us that a Cong sniper would just love to try a long distance kill shot from some hidden spider hole, testing one of those fancy Soviet Sniper rifles carried down the Ho Chi Minh Trail from China. That same intuition told us to keep a steel bulkhead between our body and any open field of fire. We had now entered the land of "not quite safe."

Some hours following our transit up the Lòng Tàu, just past

where it joined back to the Nha Be estuary, we came to the point where the Sài Gòn River flowed into the Nha Be. This was a very strange river mouth. It required almost a 180-degree turn to the left, seeming as if we forgot something and needed to retrace steps. Here too the riverbanks now became populated.

First, there were fishing villages, followed by piers and wharves supporting industrial ventures. In a sudden night for day reversal, we rounded a bend, finding ourselves amid a cacophony of motion involving commercial vessels of every type, from small coastwise freighters to tankers and even WWII "Baby" flattop aircraft carriers pressed into service, supplying helicopters and aircraft parts. Navigation in the river became very stressful now as there were large ships anchored in the middle of the river discharging cargo on both sides to barges secured alongside. As my wide-eyed, gaping mouth surveyed this port operation, I noted that most of the large ships carried American flags from their sterns. We were passing though the largest assemblage of American merchant ships I had ever witnessed in any one port.

Our transit up the Saigon River was going to take place during my afternoon bridge watch, allowing me the opportunity to absorb the full impact of American policy on this small, post-colonial country. Moving farther upriver it became clear to me that our Vietnamese river pilot was an educated man with a first-rate command of the English language. Ship traffic in the busy Port of Saigon soon forced us to slow to a stop, awaiting a clear channel, presenting me the opportunity to engage this man in deeper conversation. Previous experiences with third world pilots had set a very low bar, so it was with some amazement that I found this man to be not only erudite but also well informed of current world events. As our conversation became more animated, I tried to keep my questions focused on the war without asking awkward-to-answer questions. This Vietnamese professional freely shared his views of the conflict between the two parts of his country, expressing the opinion that with help from our coalition, Vietnam could be separated very much like Korea. He, however, seemed very concerned that our country may not have the stomach for an extended war. Further, he was very concerned about the future prospects for his family in the coming years.

As we neared the large loop in the river where we would need to turn around before tying up to a wharf, he became too busy to continue our conversation. Then, like all pilots worldwide, the second that the ship was secured alongside the quay (and please, pronounce this term *key* like old-time English mariners), the pilot shook the captain's hand and bolted for the gangway to be the first ashore. I very much wanted our conversation to continue, but all port arrivals bring a hubbub as if the army ants have returned to the nest. I will always remember our conversation that sultry day as we passed through the chocolate muddy waters of a war-torn land, often wondering what happened to him and his family when the curtain on his world fell in 1975.

Sài Gòn

So this was it! This was Saigon.

First impressions are so sticky.

I stood by the rail up on the third deck, silently observant, listening as the small men ran around on the quayside apron babbling their sing-song Vietnamese language, American military standing nearby as if frozen in the heat—a case study of indifference. Taking it all in with curiosity, the noise coming from every direction, the sun never moving, the smell of a million sweltering people, the war—an idea without destiny—I could discern no inkling of a master plan.

It was the end of January. Back home in New York people were freezing their butts off as they dug cars out of snowdrifts; here it was hot, but it was more than just hot. With mountains to the north and west and the South China Sea too far away for ocean breezes, Saigon sat squarely in the middle of a giant sump. It was a kettle; we were the little clams about to be turned into Bouillabaisse.

The sprawling city lay emitting every kind of foul odor on the land side of our ship's berth. On the river side, the far bank was occupied by a few fishing shanties with the low swamp land stretching uninterrupted to the north and west until it met the central highlands. In this swamp the weather never changed, the air barely moved. Effluent drifted into the sultry air or was poured into the river as untold numbers of humans toiled through the day, cooking, eating, and shitting. All of this mix in the kettle was then turned up past simmer.

The Vietnamese had, of course, adapted. I cannot ever remember seeing a longshoreman manhandling cargo in the bottom of a 120-degree cargo hold drenched in sweat. Humans must perspire to cool our bodies, but I just never remember seeing them sweat. As for this huge, muddy, brown river/open sewer running next our ship, everyday saw fishermen casting those circular purse nets, bringing in a catch of fish for the home kitchen or the market. I made an immediate mental note to self: Avoid the local fish. My later failure to remember this dictate was to cost me dearly on our next trip to Saigon.

A picture also arose in my mind from the imagination of Joseph Conrad's *Heart of Darkness*. The trip up the river in Africa, native drums beating to a background of rusting, tin-roofed cargo sheds alongside the muddy sweltering river, created a second strong impression. Years later, the inventive mind of Francis Ford Coppola was to write and direct *Apocalypse Now* set in my Vietnam War but whose plot line came directly out of Conrad's *Heart of Darkness*. It matters not whether one follows Marlowe up the African river to find the insane Mr. Kurtz who has gone native or one sees Captain Willard go up a river in Vietnam to find the also insane, also gone-native Colonel Kurtz; the settings of both stories are tropical jungles where no allegiance could be trusted.

It felt as if, had either Kurtz stepped out of one of those rusting cargo sheds, perhaps no one would have noticed.

The French designed much of central Saigon with wide boulevards and low buildings, a vision of Paris in the Orient. They instead created Asian urban sprawl. A city that cannot grow upwards to the sky can only grow sideways to the horizon. All of this was done without public transportation infrastructure, giving birth to an expanding population of the nastiest, noisiest, and smelliest forms of human transport: the motor scooter, the 50cc motorbike, and the moped. The Japanese and Italians gratefully provided these two-wheeled, two-stroke, non-muffled, buzzing mad hornets at prices insuring that every mother's son had one between his legs. Petite Vietnamese mademoiselles were frequently seen riding sidesaddle over the rear wheel of these darting two wheelers as their flowing *áo dài* gowns—the traditional very feminine dress—fluttered in the wind.

The French created wide boulevards, lining them in Parisian style, with stately shade trees. Honda built two-stroke motorbikes with a cheap design, insuring a steady spew of partially burned hydrocarbons, which when multiplied by hundreds of thousands of units, became a blue haze of pollution, soon killing those lovely French shade trees. The trees died, leaving behind barren monuments of wood trunks, suggesting eternal winter in spite of 90-degree heat.

The berth selected for the *Exhibitor* was a mystery to me, as we had been assigned what might have been the number one primo spot to tie up in all of the Port of Saigon. Many of the merchant ships bringing war material to Saigon were old and ugly, but none could have been older or in any way uglier than our ship, and yet the military selected a spot for us that was the envy of hundreds of other ships. Between our cargo apron and Trình Minh Thê—the main port city street—laid an old, exclusive, French Colonial mansion housing the offices of the Military Sea Transportation Service, our Navy contracting organization. The port was fenced in by a tangle of razor wire, and the gate to our area guarded by .50 caliber machine guns in a heavily sandbagged checkpoint. Located nearby, just in front of the old French mansion, Ham Nghi Blvd—the widest of all the boulevards—was found only a couple of blocks from the guardhouse to our berthing area. From there the heart of the city was within walking distance.

Many ships were tied up miles upstream or downstream. Worse yet, there were quite a few ships that never tied up but were instead anchored in the middle of the river, working cargo into barges on both sides of the ship. Crewmembers on these ships desiring a trip

The Faithful Sextant

to town had to rely on small bumboats to get them back and forth. Just prior to our arrival, based on a tip, two Viet Cong infiltrators had been caught leaving one of these bumboats, secretly carrying a supply of C-4 with the intent of blowing up one of these anchored ships, thereby blocking the river for months. One of them was an older woman with the C-4 wrapped under her loose flowing dress. Charlie was everywhere!

What luck! We could walk to town. Out the gate, turn right on Trình Minh Thê (now Nguyen St.), cross over a little canal and there we were at Ham Nghi Blvd, right in the heart of Saigon. The US Embassy was located nearby, as well as an exclusive floating restaurant. Seemingly, fortune had smiled upon us; still, there was this nagging question roaming in the back of my mind: if this is such a good spot, what's with the .50 caliber machine gun at the gate? Oh, we had so much to learn!

Indeed, about fifty yards directly behind our ship, floating in the river and tied up to the shore, was the famous My Cahn Floating Restaurant. This was an upscale Vietnamese restaurant catering to wealthy, local patrons as well as American contractors and US soldiers. Right after our arrival in Saigon, an American sergeant told us the following story about this upscale restaurant.

A scant six months before our arrival, the Viet Cong had placed two Claymore mines near the restaurant. One was set in the riverbank, carefully aimed horizontally across the main open seating area; there were no walls needed due to the climate. A second mine was set to go off two minutes later near the entrance to the restaurant, designed to kill first responders. Almost fifty people, including a bunch of American contractors and several soldiers, were killed and peripheral shrapnel wounded another eighty.

What a wonderful paragon of death: the Claymore mine. Appropriately named after the medieval, Scottish, two-handed sword, this was one of the most effective new ideas gaining infamy in the Vietnam War, a weapon of death seemingly from James Bond and the diabolical labs of "Q."

The Faithful Sextant

The Claymore is more than just a mine, it is a shaped charge meant to be aimed. Constructed in a plastic box, a layer of C-4 explosive located behind 700 steel balls set in an epoxy, backed up by a steel plate, the Claymore is deadly. Once detonated, the steel balls can only come out the front of the box, spreading in a 60-degree pattern like a shotgun. The killing range is out to the length of a football field. GIs hunkered down in an overnight position in the jungle often protected perimeters by setting out Claymore mines. Using a trip wire for activation, the Claymore sprays everything in a pattern in front of the charge, a very indiscriminate killer and maimer. In war it has been said that a bullet fired from a rifle at the enemy has a very personal connotation, as if to say, "Here, this is from me to you; it has your name on it." The Claymore, on the other hand, is so very much more impersonal, as if the message sent says, "To whom it might concern!"

The placement of this weapon was critical, the Claymore box had to be aimed correctly as noted by the raised lettering found on the blast side of the box: "FRONT—TOWARD ENEMY." This is one of the reasons the Army requires recruits to be literate.

The sergeant telling this story about the My Cahn Restaurant had been in country for most of a tour. His retelling was not in a bragging voice, it was not in a storytelling tone, or in a serviceman's "can you believe this shit" sense of wonder. It was told in a sort of matter-of-fact manner of a high school teacher explaining the Pythagorean Theorem. Nevertheless, and in spite of having heard the story of the My Cahn attack, and showing great disrespect for the deadliness of Claymore mines, take a guess where Bernie and I decided to have our first lunch ashore? You guessed it! At the My Cahn Restaurant. We just had to see what was going on.

There was much for us to learn, stuff that battle-hardened veterans had learned, often the hard way. Stuff such as "situational awareness." If the Cong blew a place up once because it is full of folks they hate, would they come back and blow it up again? You bet! This had nothing to do with lightening striking twice in the same place or any other childhood homilies.

To stay alive in a place where people you do not know have the desire, have the opportunity, and have the capability to kill or hurt you, one simply must stay aware at all times of the nature of every little thing going on around you. How secure is this joint? Why has that guy circled the parking lot three times on his motorbike, glancing over his shoulder? Would this be a good place for Charlie to make a statement? If it did not feel right, it probably wasn't right, summed up in the acronym DNFR: Does Not Feel Right. With the beginnings of experience and wisdom, Bernie and I had made a pact that if either of us, for any reason, lip synched DNFR, we both agreed it would be time to quickly move on, or in local GI vernacular, to "di-di" out of there.

On our second day in the Port of Saigon, several of our deck crewmen passed throughout the ship installing hand grenade screens. These screens were a heavy-duty mesh fitted into a circular solid metal ring designed to fit securely into the opening of each porthole in the cabin of the ship. The job of these screens was to prevent some nasty Viet Cong terrorist from walking by and tossing a live hand grenade into a crewmember's room.

Aside from the chilling thought, *Crap, you mean this hand grenade in the room thing actually happens*, the immediate problem was heat. Our cabins were hot, really hot. The ancient *Exhibitor* had been built long before the advent of air conditioning. My cabin was effectively a six-sided steel box, a single little porthole for a window, a steel door facing into the interior passageway, and no air circulation. The door to the room had to remain locked while we slept since longshoremen and other workers sometimes used the passageway outside the door, and since we had already established that no one knew Charlie from anyone else! My eventual failure to keep my door locked while sleeping would cause me anguish on the next trip.

It is said that everyone's ceiling is someone else's floor, a truism for the boxy nature of my tiny cabin as the other side of the steel plate of my ceiling was an upper deck. The maritime industry's ever-popular answer to rust, a mixture of fish oil and lampblack, covered the deck above my head with a heat-absorbing black coating. As the sun beat down on this black deck, the cabin below became an oven. This latest addition, the hand grenade screen, meant that no air could come from the outside into the room, adding one more level of cooking temperature. Hanging a thermometer in the cabin, I discovered that nighttime temperatures in my sleeping area never went below 95 degrees and daytime temps were unknown as the thermometer was calibrated only to 120 degrees. It maxed out at 120 degrees every day at about noon.

Sleep was impossible. Between the noise level of a ship discharging cargo twenty-four hours a day and a sleeping cabin, usually hotter inside than the internal temperature of the human body, the ship's crew quickly became walking zombies. At least one deck officer was required to be on duty at all times during cargo operations, meaning that we had to revert to some sort of watch rotation. The captain, who remained aloof from cargo operations, agreed that any sort of flexible schedule was fine as long as a deck officer was always on duty to supervise discharge. The three deck officers standing watch, that is the second mate, third mate (that's me), and the junior third mate (also called fourth mate), all agreed that we would take shifts sixteen hours long, followed by a full twenty-four hours off. Our plans for the twenty-four hours off included a trip downtown to book an air-conditioned hotel room, where we might get ten to twelve hours of restful sleep. The sixteen-hour shift out on the deck and down in the hatches of the ship was brutal, but no one was going to sleep in that environment anyway. The plan for a frosty hotel room was good, excepting one small snag: GIs on R & R.

❖

We kept changing hotels, looking for a quiet one, but it was a fruitless task. The appetite for a nice bed held by soldiers returning from wartime action took up the slack in hotel rooms vacated by fearful tourists and businessmen. As we continued exploring accommodations, one memory stands as an example of bizarre life in the zone.

It was early evening. Bernie and I had just arrived downtown after our long shifts. As we entered the lobby of a nice hotel, looking for an air-conditioned room for the night, a ruckus broke out right in front of us at the front lobby desk.

Flexing his six and half foot frame, a very large American non-com had reached over the front desk, grabbing the Vietnamese hotel agent by the collar as he yelled in his face. The GI, probably three times the weight of the diminutive hotel clerk, was dressed only in a pair of flip-flops and white boxer undershorts, nothing else. As we stood behind him, the huge American let go of the small Vietnamese, took a step back, and pointed down to the front of his boxer shorts. There, for everyone to see, stood a large bulge, something one would suppose housed an erect sex organ. He then yelled, "Boy, where's that girl you promised? Ya'll don't expect me to sleep with 'this thing' all night do you?" as he again pointed down at the bulge.

"Yes sir, yes sir...she be right up," quivered the small Vietnamese. As the large American squinted his alcohol-fueled eyes at Bernie and me, he turned and headed down the hall to the stairs, yelling over his shoulder to the desk clerk, "Don't you make me come down here again, y'hear."

I shrugged my shoulders, and we checked in as the young man behind the counter finished a phone call to some pimp, pleading his case for help with a lady *de la nuit*. As we completed checking-in, a young, petite Vietnamese girl came running into the lobby, where she began a quick tense conversation with the previously threatened desk clerk. He pointed her down the hall with room number instructions as she scurried off to find the large sergeant. This girl could not have been over fourteen years old and could not have weighed more than ninety pounds. The desk clerk smiled at us and turned to disappear into the back room.

Built in an old box style so that the rooms on each floor surrounded a large open area in the center of the box, this hotel was both modern and old European. Stairs to the upper floors circled around an open atrium making for a modern feeling of openness. GIs on R & R partying around this central atrium on each floor found it a convenient way to yell from one floor to the next, smoke from cigarettes and joints wafting upwards, and an occasional empty beer can falling downwards. It seemed that they had the complete hotel booked. Whiskey and marijuana were held in abundance. Bragging about war stories was the main topic of conversation, with notable tension shown over the sharing of girls who slipped from room to room.

Walking up through the floors, no one took notice of us. No bags in hand, dressed in sloppy American clothes; we looked just like everyone else. Finding our rooms, Bernie and I agreed that sleep would be difficult, so we best join the party. We had brought a couple of bottles of vodka, helping us fit right into the middle of the group. We were eventually noticed when one of the GIs asked what unit we were with, and what part of the country we had come in from. He was amazed to find out that that we were civilian sailors. Asking our names, he introduced us around the room while inviting us to help ourselves to the food and drinks. He did warn us that helping ourselves to the girls might be a problem, which was fine with us as this had never been on our menu. Rumors of "Super Clap" may have just been urban legend, but I was not for testing the verity of this legend.

Being surrounded by these young men coming back from patrols into enemy territory was a real eye opener. Listening to their stories as we shared drinks, one impression became clear; serving as the point man for a squad or platoon walking down a jungle trail was well beyond the normal human capacity for fear. Getting ambushed by the enemy was bad enough, but the real terror came from booby traps. As we listened, the apparitions of their nightmares ranged from cleverly concealed pit holes hiding sharpened bamboo spikes covered in human feces to the deadly, almost invisible trip wire activating a stolen Claymore mine aimed right at your face. The guy walking point found the traps and trips first. The grunts who had been in country for the better part of a tour had seen these things or lost a buddy to one. There were no FNGs (f***ing new guys) in the R&R group; the new guys simply had not built up enough time to earn the days off. Everyone we talked to had a story.

One story two guys told, to the nodded agreement of others, was not easy to forget. This was a story about ambushers, or in their words, "bushers."

Setting up a nightly encampment for a recon team behind razor wire and Claymores had become a problem. As the enemy became more and more North Vietnamese Army regulars, they had managed to infiltrate these perimeters, causing death and destruction in the camps. The "old man" had had enough; he asked for young volunteers to teach these sappers a lesson. He wanted men to sneak out of the perimeter and ambush the enemy.

Sure enough, guys volunteered. These were not your average draftees counting days backwards, these were guys thirsting for blood, these were the bushers. Just before nightfall, in teams of two, they would strip off all flashy metal, just taking a bayonet or Ka-Bar knife, some twine to tie between themselves so they would not get separated, and silent close-in tools like a blackjack knife or a bicycle chain wrapped in black tape.

Silently sliding under the razor wire after dark, the two-man teams would slip between their own Claymore trips and disappear into the jungle to find a spot to hide. Enemy patrols passing near would lose a man or two—their throats being silently cut and their bodies, sometimes missing an ear, left as a message to be found by comrades. Our guys would then wait until morning when they could creep back in through our wire. Sometimes the two-man team did not show the next morning, never to be seen again—part of the long list of MIAs. The troops inside the wire thought the bushers were rat-shit crazy. The guys telling this story got real wide-eyed, telling about details on the other side of the wire at night.

Over and over, one theme stood out with all of these guys. To a man, they could quote the exact number of days, hours, and minutes left before boarding the big silver bird at Tan Son Nhut for the trip home. The exact day that each of them had arrived in country, a clock began ticking counting 365 days run backwards, until it reached zero, when orders would send them to another duty station—not in Vietnam; this usually meant going home. The senior guys who were approaching this 365 day mark, when asked to head out on a recon patrol, had the usual response ready, "Jack you, Mac! I have only fifteen days and a wake up."

Under no conditions was he doing anything risky with just days left; to the point that direct orders were ignored even under threat of the brig followed by a court-martial. Sort of like the Uncle Remus fable of Br'er Rabbit and the tar baby, when Br'er Rabbit pleads with Br'er Fox not to thow him in the briar patch, the "short" soldier thought, *What are you going to do as punishment, send me back to the States?*

Data discovered long after the War revealed that 997 soldiers were killed on their very first day in Vietnam and 1,448 soldiers were killed on their very last day in Vietnam. As I have stated elsewhere, in war there is no lucky. There is no unlucky. Combat demands its casualties. Whether this happens on the first day of a tour or the last day, dead is dead and there is no calendar for dead. Nor is there one for luck!

This theme by all of the GIs we met illuminated one more glaring problem unique to this nasty little war. Their fathers, who had fought the Nazis in Europe, knew that the only ticket home came as soon as they were able to storm the Reich chancellery to capture Hitler. For the soldiers in the Pacific, they pretty much knew that they could not go home until every Jap with a weapon who wanted to fight was dead. There was no twelve-month calendar event. There was also no R & R for most of them. The WWII soldier had a well-defined goal, and nothing nice was going to happen until it became a deed.

Most folks I met in Vietnam had no idea why the United States was there; no one had a clearly defined goal of what had to happen to bring it to an end. The lower-ranking GIs viewed the whole thing as a giant clusterfuck. They did not want to give their lives or a body part for some ill-defined goal of a politician. They would, however, give their life to save their platoon buddy if caught in a firefight. Their ranks were full of shirkers, slackers, troublemakers, and substance abusers. These same ranks were also full of heroes and warriors. Often they were the same guy.

The Rex Hotel

> *Avoid the reeking herd,*
> *Shun the polluted flock,*
> *Live like that stoic bird,*
> *The eagle of the rock.*

Elinor Wylie
"Nets to Catch the Wind"

Our search for a quiet hotel in Saigon finally led to the Rex. Built by a French businessman when the French renewed interest in colonies after the First World War, the five-story Rex Hotel was designed very much in the Parisian style. Most striking of its traditional French features was the large, outdoor, rooftop bar, decorated fashionably in Indochinese period furnishings, sitting over the hub of central Saigon and featuring a view well out beyond the city suburbs. The Rex had been extensively remodeled in 1960, just in time to begin receiving large numbers of American military advisors as early as 1961. Soon, the Rex became not only housing for US military advisors but served as a gathering point for journalists covering the war as well. As more and more senior military officers, along with influential members of the press, found a temporary home at the Rex, the higher military brass declared that the Rex Hotel was, in effect, an Officers Club; off limits to the marauding GIs on R&R. This was a thinly veiled attempt to keep the frontline grunts from spewing their version of how the war was going to the press corps. To further this control over the media, the upper brass scheduled a daily afternoon press conference at the rooftop bar, where designated military public relations officers spoke in measured terms of the events of the day to war journalists. Members of the media soon began calling these briefings the "Five O'Clock Follies." Further insuring good relations with the media, happy hour prices were in effect for all present. Alcoholic drinks were ten cents, beer was a nickel. Booze had become so cheap that offering to buy a round of drinks brought no cachet.

Discovering its quiet grace, the Rex became our first choice for a restful night and a relaxing and cheap place to drink. The drinkers in the bar were of a different class and mostly older than the grunts in the other hotels. To be sure, these gentlemen (ladies were rare) were by no means nicer than the NCO seen pounding on the hotel desk demanding a girl. Reading about the exploits of John Paul Vann, who became the senior US government representative in charge of American military affairs with his multiple wives (two in Vietnam, one with kids back home) in the book *A Bright Shining Lie*, proves this point. They were, however, quieter.

Life at the rooftop bar of the Rex was good, even though we were probably breaking situational awareness rules by hanging out in a place full of high value Viet Cong terrorist targets. We still had a lot to learn.

Hot, sultry nights viewed from the rooftop bar at the Rex brought a conflict of emotions. The beer was cold, the martinis were dry, the service was elegant, and the clientele was cultured, but there was the big But…but there was a war going on just behind the potted plants, on the other side of the railing. Looking over this railing, out and away from the city, found a steady show of hostilities. Star parachute flares were a constant reminder of what was going on. Once launched, the heat from the white phosphorus in the flare would make a steady flow of hot air under the parachute, allowing the canopy to rise, sort of like a hot air balloon. By adjusting the amount of heat and the size of the canopy, these flares could stay aloft for about a quarter of an hour, lighting up large swaths of the countryside. As soon as one flare exhausted its fuel, another was launched. Sometimes there would be small arms fire in areas beneath the flares, followed by more intense fire from a helicopter or from larger guns.

This wonder chemical—white phosphorus—had many uses. Packed into an artillery shell, it made a huge impression when it detonated, spraying white-hot, burning chemical in all directions. Pouring water on a lump of burning WP (white phosphorus) only made it burn more intensely, as the chemical reaction from the burning WP was so hot that it could break water into its component parts of hydrogen and oxygen—both of which are explosive. A tiny bit of burning WP landing on a soldier's uniform would burn all the way through to the bone. The boys in the field had a nickname for WP; they called it "Willie Peter." Once, while watching a white phosphorus display at night from the deck of the *Exhibitor*, a huge black soldier standing nearby nonchalantly noted, "Willie Peter make yuh believer." He mouthed this piece of poetry in such a way that his huge lips made no visible movement.

One night while watching the follies from the rooftop bar at the Rex, "Spooky" put on a show for us. Spooky was the call sign given to a squadron of old piston engine C-47 (commercial DC-3) cargo aircraft, outfitted with General Electric Gatling gun-style mini-guns that could fire up to one hundred rounds per second. This new concept of installing electric guns on old, slow-moving platforms had met with great success. Watching from a distance at night was surreal.

The tactic used by the pilot was to put the aircraft into a perfect spiraling turn such that the mini-gun, firing from an open side door, maintained a constant aim at one single point on the ground like a dancer doing a pirouette. The mini-guns were firing a tracer bullet every fifth round, giving the effect of a river of fire falling from the gun ship to a single point on the ground. As intense as this stream of lighted bullets was, it was shocking to remember that spaced in between each of the lighted tracer bullets were four unlit rounds. These flying monsters of death were putting a real crimp on Charlie's larger operations. The American grunts on the ground loved this new idea. They had nicknamed the old C-47, "Puff the Magic Dragon," from the Peter, Paul, and Mary song.

Life down on the streets of Saigon tried to ignore the challenge brought by civil strife and the invasion of foreign armies. One afternoon brought me into a barbershop where I found a row of fifteen barber chairs; all of which had been manufactured in Toledo, Ohio. The local Vietnamese barbers, both men and women, were very busy, singing or whistling as they worked. In spite of a steady stream of customers flowing in and out, I got a shampoo and one of the best haircuts ever with efficiency and with a smile on the face of every employee in the place. Life in the barbershop went on as if nothing had or was going to change. I became an instant hero when I paid with a crisp new American one hundred dollar bill and accepted change after a very large tip, in local dông. This payment showed off the fungibility of the American "C" note. Examples, in my opinion, of the three most fungible commodities are the good old Ben Franklin American hundred dollar bill, a South African solid gold Krugerrand coin, and pussy.

Now before my gentle readers go wobbly over the above vulgarity, I present an appalling historical event proving the validity of the above proposition. Subsequent to the utter destruction of the city of Berlin, Germany by the Soviet army in May of 1945, the citizens found themselves facing daily life with virtually nothing of value with which to buy daily needs. Society's basics had reached a point where the trading of sexual favors for food or a scuttle of coal was the only trade left. Indeed, one fungible commodity for another.

Bringing us to the subject of currency.

South Vietnam had its own currency, the Dong, a ridiculous

sounding name to Americans, spawning a lifetime of tedious puns, jokes, and word plays. Inflation and its twin sister, the black market, had been extant in Vietnam prior to the arrival of Americans. The tidal wave of money, in the form of a strong currency such as the dollar, became incendiary to the black market. The economies of small developing nations will not withstand the use of two currencies where one is the strongest in the world and the other is more than suspect.

As the number of US military advisors and contractors grew exponentially, so did the American greenbacks they brought into the country. The explosive growth of Saigon's black market forced their government to plead for help from the Americans. Our military had faced this dilemma before and knew the answer: They issued their own money, known as military script. All American Servicemen and where possible, contractors, were paid in this unique currency. Mariners such as me avoided this stuff like the plague.

So why were greenbacks in such demand?

The Dong, as the sad joke went, wasn't good for much except sticking in a hole. It had no purchasing power in foreign markets. The Viet Cong was an ad hoc army made up of poor people and ideologues from the south of Vietnam. They had no factories. All of their war material had to be stolen or bought from North Vietnam or farther north from China and Russia. Problem was, no one up there was dumb enough to accept the flimsy currency of the south, therefore guns, bullets, and war material had to be bought in a strong currency: in other words, the dollar. Charlie could not just walk into a bank in Saigon with a basket of Dong and ask to convert it to dollars as this would have led to the collapse of the Dong, not to mention the immediate arrest of the Viet Cong courier. The corrupt South Vietnamese government was having none of that. Meanwhile, the US military had turned off their spigot; military script was worthless in the North. So where could Charlie get dollars?

The black market became the source.

Maritime unions had fought to keep their members paid in dollars, with the one hundred dollar bill as currency of choice. Captains on commercial vessels kept a safe in their office stuffed with hundred dollar bills that the ship's purser would parcel out to crewmembers in the form of allotments against monies owed to them by the steamship company. Playing with currency exchange rates became a source of new income to us, albeit one which carried with it some danger here in the world of "not quite safe."

Prior to President Nixon's decision in the early 1970s to abrogate the Bretton Woods agreements, allowing world currencies to float, the accepted practice of central banks had been to establish set currency exchange rates. The Vietnamese government attempted to establish a set rate for their currency, which meant that if we walked into a bank in Saigon with a handful of American dollars, we could exchange these bills for a set amount of Dong. No one in their right mind did that.

Meanwhile, out on the street, everything was for sale, everything floated. Using a one dollar bill was worth about a 10 percent discount to the advertised price, a ten dollar bill could command a 20 percent discount, and the much adored face of Ben Franklin on the one hundred might even see a 40 percent to 50 percent discount. These values were discounts to purchasing a product sold informally on the street, a transaction opined by all not to be a true currency exchange, which was illegal.

Doing the true currency exchange of your cash in a back alley was also possible but carried a much greater risk of the transaction suddenly flipping into a gun-barrel-enforced zero exchange rate, also known as a robbery, including the final risk of spent cartridges as the ultimate way to seal the deal.

Another currency holding a position on the playing field of currency exchange was the MPC (military payment certificate or script), held by soldiers and secretly by many citizens. It seemed that everyone holding MPC wanted to exchange it for dollars, but no merchant sailor I knew wanted the risk of holding this funny money. GIs would give handfuls of MPC to Vietnamese girlfriends or to shop keepers willing to accept this currency in order to make a sale, in hopes of quickly dumping it by using it to pay off debts to American GIs, who could then use it at the base. About once every six months or so, the US military bases would lock all GIs inside for two days while reissuing new MPC currency for old bills held by the GIs, making all old bills worthless, thus wiping out certain local citizens who had accepted the risk of squirreling away this money, often leading to riots at the front gate of the base.

Americans raised in the long-term, stable economy of the good old USA rarely think about or have ever experienced a black market. If the idea is brought up, it brings visions of back alleys in a Kasbah of darkest Morocco. Oh, this is so far from reality, though often black markets do indeed find a home in such back alleys. Earthy economists understand that the black market is the "real" market. Black markets are where the true human nature of demand meets the real world of supply. I have always said, "Show me a product or service that people really want, which is for some reason not readily available, and I will show you the makings for a black market." Prostitution is the truest and perhaps oldest example of a black market, although perhaps not the most noble.

A small-time example of the black market saw an eighty-year-old Vietnamese grandmother selling a bottle of Johnny Walker Scotch from her little hooch on a side street in Saigon. She would never have considered herself to be an international "Black Marketer." She was simply trying to find a way to afford a bag of rice, allowing her to feed her widowed daughter and orphaned granddaughter, all of them victims of a world not of their making.

Not all of our days found us off duty in the world of the Vietnamese. Life on the streets of Saigon or in the Rex Bar had to be earned; it was the reward (such as rewards go) for having worked the sixteen-hour double shift back on the steamy decks of the *SS*

Exhibitor. Cargo unloading operations went on twenty-four hours a day with short breaks as longshoreman crews rotated.

Saigon has been an active seaport for centuries, meaning that it has had an active labor force doing longshoreman work of loading and unloading ships. Nothing, however, could have prepared this labor force for the steep escalation in jobs, resulting from the sudden demand for war materials following the invasion of American armies. Longshoremen, even those working without union representation, are well paid relative to other manual labor, making it easy to find willing workers from the countryside of southern Vietnam. Finding willing wage earners is different from finding skilled workers, as we were soon to discover.

The historic training process for longshoremen often found youngsters apprenticed to fathers or uncles who taught the son the tricks of moving heavy blocks of cargo without breaking your back or having a swinging load in a confined cargo hold crush an arm or leg. The flood of new jobs on the waterfront in Saigon had left no time for niceties such as apprenticeship, leaving many young Vietnamese farmhands to learn on the job.

Under normal conditions, the most important responsibility for the deck officer during cargo loading/discharge operations is to see to it that the longshoreman crew does not damage the ship. Additionally, the steamship company assures the shipper that cargo will be delivered in good order, which gives the deck officer the added responsibility to insure proper stowage and removal of the cargo. In Saigon our jobs took on a third responsibility: the safety of the longshoremen. Not only did many of these young men not know how to safely and efficiently work cargo, it became clear that many of them were working way more than eight-hour days. Finding them asleep in corners or walking around in a daze became the norm. Officer of the Deck McEliece solved this problem by going to the French wooden block program.

Stowing cargo on old, break-bulk cargo ships uses a lot of wood.

The Faithful Sextant

The many different sizes and shapes of stuff that gets stowed in the bowels of a ship requires lots of carpentry such as blocking and bracing or just good old filler. As this cargo is broken out of the stow below decks, scraps of wood are everywhere. Many of these scraps on our ship came in the form of blocks of wood that fit conveniently into the palm of my hand, serving as a perfect missile to be thrown at a slacking longshoreman. At the same time as my well-aimed missile, I would yell in French, *"Regardez-Vous or Faire L'Attention."*

Why yell in French? Well, the French had been the boss man in Indochina a whole lot longer than the Americans, and on a primal level these small men in black pajamas responded to urgent orders much quicker *en Français.* As I began to notice the positive effects of my commands in French, I went back in memory and brought up some French curse words. *Zut alors* worked even better to get some attention. There was no intention on my part to hit a guy in the head with a block of wood; my job was to help protect his life and those of the men working around him. A workspace where tons of dangerous stuff is moving around and over your head is no place for groggy workers.

Tedium soon became the norm as hour after hour I performed these long shifts; the dreariness becoming more exaggerated in the evening hours of round the clock unloading. Some shipboard routine was observed such as three meals a day, served at routine meal hours, attracting Navy and civilian contractors looking for a free meal featuring an American-style menu. After the evening meal in the ship's salon, crewmembers and shore-side staff quickly found their way off the ship, often leaving Bernie down in the engine room and myself up on deck as the only ship's crew representatives aboard. This singleness of representation offered a degree of solitude as the duty watch stretched on, but it also left very little flexibility should a predicament or emergency suddenly play into the evening routine. One evening was to test my ability to keep a grip on poise during a crisis.

Two weeks into our unloading cycle found me as the officer of the deck, wearing dirty, cotton khaki pants, a short sleeved khaki shirt with salt rings around the armpits from days of wetting followed by drying of perspiration, and a well-used officer's cap—my sign of authority, featuring a dark streak of grease across its Frisbee-like top where a wire cargo unloading cable (called a runner) had nearly decapitated me in an earlier life. The evening's sweltering air, heavily loaded with moisture from the nearby cesspool Saigon River, made movement a chore—a penance for enjoying twenty-four hours of an air-conditioned hotel room.

I had climbed up two decks to the secret fan room, where the officer's beer refrigerator was housed, grabbing a cold Coke previously stashed, when I suddenly noticed that the usual whining noise from the cargo winches had stopped, to be replaced by that certain high-pitched sing-song whine of distress from several young Annamite longshoremen. My highly sensitive "Oh shit" meter ,acquired from several years of deck experience, sent me flying down the outside ladders, knowing that this change in tempo was likely bad news. Nothing, however, had prepared me for what I was about to find. The sight coming into view on the aft main deck next to the onshore side of number four hatch confirmed my worst fears. Several longshoremen stood around a young man who lay sprawled on the filthy deck as a pool of dark fluid spread quickly around his waist. My first hint of panic came as I noticed his leg distorted at a most inhuman angle, while nearby three stevedore bosses wildly gestured and chattered.

I grabbed the one boss known to speak English, asking just what the hell was going on.

"He try jump over wire…no make it," cried the small boss man.

One of the young, new-hire longshoreman had tried to step over the relaxed, onshore, wire cargo runner just as the winch operator had given full throttle to the winch drum, immediately reeling in the runner as the lift began to rise from the hatch below. The man on the winch never saw the worker stepping over the slack cargo runner wire, the second wire in the historic yard and fall, a soon to be archaic system left over from the days of pulling cargo out of the hatch on a sailing vessel using ropes attached to the sail spars. As this skilled choreography of winches and wires speedily proceeds, the wire found lying slack on the onshore deck, the wire responsible to pull the cargo lift over to the boom hanging above the pier, often becomes taught in a matter of seconds. In this case the onshore wire snapped tight right between the longshoreman's legs, almost cutting off one leg while tossing him about fifteen feet in the air. The swiftly moving cable running between his legs severed his femoral artery. Twitching violently, he bled to death on our deck as we watched.

There was nothing we could have done. The artery had been severed so far up in his hip area that a tourniquet wouldn't have been effective. Perhaps a trained surgeon standing by could have pinched off the artery, but we all knew that no such resource existed on the deck of this highly dangerous workspace. The remaining Vietnamese longshoremen stood around jabbering in low whispers for some time after their fellow worker was removed.

Meanwhile, I had just started into the first of the five stages of human trauma: denial, anger, bargaining, depression, and acceptance. Denial went by real fast; there wasn't much doubt about what had happened. Anger set in real quick.

Yeah, I know, what could I have done…but still, here it was again, I was in charge when someone lost his life to a safety issue. I grabbed the stevedore bosses and made them gather the longshoremen around me. I went around in silence and looked each one in the eye before making them follow me over to a slack wire cargo runner lying on the deck. I then began yelling, in French when I could remember the word, telling them that they must always STEP ON the cargo runner, never, never step OVER the runner.

After a few minutes of fuming and ranting, I slipped into bargaining mode. Walking over to a slack, wire cargo runner that lay on the deck, I purposely placed my right foot squarely on top of the wire as I called one of the stevedore bosses over to my side. I then demanded that he grab the wire some ten feet away from me and pull on the wire as if the winch were reeling in the wire out from the hatch. He gave a little tug, and I yelled at him to pull as hard as he could, which he did, sending me over backwards on my ass. The young longshoremen looked aghast that their boss had just knocked over the ship's officer, but the graphic visual had been received; a bruise on the butt was better than a severed femoral artery.

I yelled over and over "Pied, pied…step on it, step on it." After a few minutes, I turned in disgust and revulsion and walked away to my room where I took two long swigs from a bottle of gin and spent fifteen minutes sitting and shaking, eventually slapping water on my face to get the redness from my eyes.

Struggling up to the bridge, it was then necessary to begin the log entry noting the times, names, and circumstances; certainly this was going to cause a whole lot of paperwork. Then as I calmed down, it came to me. Just like the D-8 Cat tractor that went over the side in the typhoon, this young man's death was going to receive no investigation, there would be no forms to sign, no rites to attend…his name would simply have a line drawn though it on the manifest of workers for that evening's shift, just like the Army sergeant had done with the missing million-dollar bulldozer. Just one more mistake in a world gone crazy with mistakes.

Now our lady of angst, the Miss *Exhibitor*, along with the old man from the shipyard in the lifeboat, would once again log the death of a worker. Both men had died in service to this aging vessel, herself pulled from the grave to once again serve the people of the country who had so proudly built her. Once again, her third officer was the man in charge when this tragedy took place.

It has been said to me that ships are dangerous workplaces, even more so in a war zone, and that these events should be closed out as occupational hazards. However, if this is true, then why is it that even to this day I remember the vision, the smell, the noise, and the taste of these two deaths as if they happened yesterday? The "acceptance" part of life's five stages of trauma takes a long time; sometimes it never happens.

Steel decks covered in fish oil/lampblack coating are indeed black, however, the large pool of blood left by this young man soon dried on the deck, leaving an even darker mark next to number four hatch for many months to come. The discharge of war material would continue; life and death in the war zone would also continue.

New experiences would also continue. Two days later my next sixteen-hour duty rotation was to bring yet another new, potentially deadly occurrence; on that evening we were to experience a fire fight with live ammo.

There was no room in warehouses or transit sheds to store the flood of cargo coming off our ships, nor could it be hauled immediately to battlefronts. As a result this stuff just piled up on the aprons surrounding the quays, higher and higher. The Viet Cong could not help but notice this mountain of shiny goods made in America. Accordingly, just like the little rats they were, darkness found them sneaking into this mound of goods to pry loose anything they might find to be handy. The Army did not appreciate this inventory shrinkage, so MPs were called in to guard this depot of war material. Just before midnight of the aforementioned deck watch, small arms fire broke out between the MPs and some of these little Viet Cong vermin.

There is nothing in a war zone to get your attention like live weapons firing nearby. I decided the best course of action was to kiss the nasty fish-oil-soaked deck right behind a hatch coaming until things got sorted out. In the next half hour or so I learned a couple of lessons.

The first thing that I noticed was the difference in sound made by an American M16 and the Russian designed AK47. The AK47 uses a 7.62mm round whereas the M16 uses a smaller but longer 5.56mm NATO round. These differences give these two assault rifles a very different sound, one sometimes helpful in telling friend from foe; allowing that your foe has not stolen one of your rifles and is using it on you. The next thing I noticed came as a shock that once again Hollywood and real-life bear little resemblance. Gunfights in the movies need to have lots of sound effects to keep the audience involved, such as loud bangs coming from the weapons along with pings and cracks and screeches as the bullets ricochet near the actors. It isn't like that!

Most small arms weapons make surprisingly little firing noise if you are away from them in open areas. So often we hear a witness to a street shooting saying that they though the sound was a car backfiring (Seriously! When was the last time you heard a car backfire?) because Hollywood sets our expectation for a loud sound. As for ricochets bouncing around, that is fantasy needed to convince the audience that lead is flying near the intended victim. Bullets do make noise; they create a spooky whisper, not pings and cracks.

Bullets, when they are coming from a high-powered cartridge, move faster than the speed of sound. Coming at you, they are breaking the sound barrier, creating their own little sonic boom. This is not like a supersonic jet going over; a bullet disturbs a very small section of air, but it does cause a unique sound, similar to the ripping in half of a piece of paper. Of course, if you have heard the ripping, then the round has missed. The bullet will be well out in front of the small shock wave. Cliché tells us that no one ever hears the bullet that kills him!

After a period of time a military police soldier came up our gangway to tell us that all of the excitement had ended. I began walking around the ship, yelling at stevedore bosses to get the men back to work when I noticed two or three crewmembers with flashlights climbing around the outside of the ship inspecting every inch for bullet holes. This brought a smile to my face as I remembered that our union contract stipulated that if our ship were ever to be struck by any enemy missile, including bullets, while in the war zone, each crewmember would receive a onetime bonus of $500 (about $5,000 in 2015 dollars).

Here came the irony again: crewmembers exposing themselves to continued fire from assault rifles as they grubbed for money, incented by a clause in a union contract. Just because the military policeman says the shooting is over does not mean that it is over. It is only over when they guy holding the AK47 says it is over. Most unfortunately, it seemed that none of the finely engineered lead speeding around faster than the speed of sound managed to be diverted or stopped by some part of our ship, putting to rest the frequency of those aforementioned ricochets. Ah, what the hell, no extra $500 on payday, but at least none of us had stopped any of this lead with our soft, fleshy body parts.

Life continued in this routine of long periods of duty on the deck of the ship interspersed with days off in the Rex Hotel, until we began to see places in the holds of the ship where the flooring at the bottom of the lower hold was visible. We were getting near the end of our stay in Saigon. To celebrate our last night out, Bernie and I went out to dinner followed by an evening of barhopping.

Saigon was a huge city with all of the evening frills designed to entertain the troops, businessmen, soldiers of fortune, and all kinds of other pleasure seekers, in other words, guys just like Bernie and me. But, there was a war going on. Charlie was everywhere, so the United States Army had set a curfew for all outlying districts surrounding the central core of Saigon. At that time if you were staying at the Rex, you could carouse all night downtown, arriving back at the hotel at dawn if you so desired, all of this provided one stayed in the downtown core. If, however, you needed to get to an outlying district, you had better be there before the midnight curfew because the MPs were going to shut the streets down at the edge of the central core. We were

The Faithful Sextant

not soldiers, but the military police curfew still directly impacted us because our ship was located outside the city limits. Knowing that we needed to sleep on the ship that evening in order to be ready to sail the next morning meant that we had to be back aboard before Cinderella's carriage became a pumpkin.

Most of the city of Saigon moved to the rhythm of the military curfew. Every evening just before midnight the streets took on the air of a Chinese (oops, Vietnamese) fire drill. The two of us had little concern about getting back to the ship, even allowing that we had anesthetized millions of brain cells with 33 Beer and Suntory liquor. Stumbling out of a bar, about forty-five minutes before curfew, a sight appeared in the street that was to lead us to make an impetuous decision, a decision that would have life-threatening consequences.

Standing at the side of a large boulevard in the still-sweltering heat, a trishaw came bouncing down the boulevard bearing a sight that our alcohol-fueled minds found uproarious. Seated in the front of this little bicycle-driven carriage was a larger-than-life, black US Army sergeant in full uniform. He must have been at least six foot six, stretched out over the whole seat, head tilted back, a grin from ear to ear, a can of beer in his hand, and an oversize stogie cigar stuck in his mouth—a long trail of cigar smoke following him and the tiny Vietnamese driver down the street. Bernie and I were laughing our asses off at the incongruity of this sight, which was funny only to two guys in our condition, when Bernie turned to me crying, "That son of a bitch is on top of the world. We can't let some no-account non-commissioned live life better than us. Bob, we gotta have one of those things to go home in tonight." Booze and good times had just erased all of our situational awareness.

Shortly after the wheel came into general use, man put an axel between two wheels, added a seat over the axel, and two long poles such that the whole thing could be pulled by a human; thus was born the rickshaw. As the modern bicycle found its way into Asia, industrious entrepreneurs in Singapore married the rickshaw to the bicycle, creating a human-powered, passenger-carrying tricycle called the trishaw or pedicab.

GIs called these bicycle contraptions pedicabs, but I prefer to use the name trishaw in deference to Graham Greene's classic book *The Quiet American* about life in Saigon during the French Colonial War of 1953. The trishaw of Saigon was a bicycle frame modified into a tricycle with a cushioned seat for two adults carried over the frame of the front wheel. The trishaw driver rides on a seat behind the passengers while guiding the front wheels with a rounded handlebar, vigorously pumping the pedals as his life depended on keeping enough speed to avoid being run over by the buzz saw of motor bikes, Vespas, and French Citroens.

The streets of Saigon, particularly just before curfew, were a dog-eat-dog jungle, and the trishaw was at the bottom of the food chain. The drivers of these vehicles were always young, wiry men; this was no job for the timid, the overweight, or the old. This career did not come with a retirement plan!

Bernie and I had no trouble waving down a trishaw, hopping into the seat next to each other, then turning around, trying to make the non-English-speaking driver understand where we were going. The kids who worked the streets of Saigon always wanted to please. In their Pidgin English, they nodded yes to everything, whether they understood or not. Several times we repeated the instructions to get us to Trình Minh Thê, where we would find the gate to our quay in the port area. How could this young man not know Trình Minh Street, it went through the busiest part of the older port in Cholon. As I was to learn later, even the trishaw drivers knew better than to go into Cholon at night; besides, he had already decided that we were GIs and needed to go to the air base at Tan Son Nhut, all other English spoken directions becoming a buzzing annoyance.

Our cabbie peddler was now nodding enthusiastically that he

understood. Everything was "numbah one," meaning they understood it to be the best (where "numbah ten" was the worst). So off we went into the night with the driver assuming that we were American soldiers needing to get to base barracks and we assuming in our alcohol-sodden bliss that we were headed to the Port of Saigon. Neither of these thoughts was correct.

Pedaling powerfully through traffic, our young muscular engine of three-wheeled locomotion whistled as he dived in and out of traffic while Bernie launched into a threadbare tale of a previous maritime port-life conquest. Only paying half attention to Bernie's well-worn tale, I started to notice that the streets were becoming dark and quiet. Having made the trip from the ship to the center of the city and back on many occasions over the past several weeks, these dark streets did not ring of familiarity. Our usual route down Ham Nghi Blvd to the bridge and into the waterfront would have found us on wide boulevards and busy, well-lit streets.

As my attention became diverted from Bernie's story, I suddenly began to think, *I wonder if this guy, in whose hands our young lives now ride and who I cannot see because he is behind a curtain behind us, just might have Viet Cong leanings?* As this thought is gelling, we made two more turns into a silent, rundown neighborhood, making me finally turn around, pull the curtain aside, where I see the driver looking anxiously from side to side. This was quite enough. Situational awareness finally overrode the pleasure centers of my brain, causing me to stop Bernie mid-story and to stop the driver mid-street.

"Bernie, this guy has no freakin' idea where we are or where we are going," I blurt out. The driver then anxiously begins rattling off Vietnamese before we demand that he be quiet, while we raise our voices wanting to know where we are. This heated discussion between two parties suffering from no common language, was going nowhere.

At last the driver came up with a word he knew in English, "Police, Police" he cried as he pointed down the street. We figured that we might be safer with the police; perhaps one of them might speak some English, so we told him to drive on. It turned out that the police station was not just down the street. We continued to harangue the driver, he continued his demonic pedaling, and all of us continued into the heart of darkness.

Some minutes later we rounded a corner to see a small, lighted shed occupied by two of the local "White Mice" (Saigon city police who wore all white uniforms). I hopped out followed by Bernie, making a straight line to the two policemen, as if we were on the corner of Main and Elm in Anytown, USA. Oh, but Dorothy, we were sure as hell not in Kansas anymore! These two midget-sized beat cops were not happy to see us. Americans out after curfew in this neighborhood meant trouble. Like sweet rotting fruit, these policemen knew that two wealthy Americans would attract flies, flies in the form of Viet Cong cadre or more likely, a gang of "cowboys." The White Mice just wanted a quiet evening without shootings or trouble. Additionally, neither of the cops spoke a word of English other than to say, "You numbah ten GI."

Standing at the door to the police hut, trying to use some form of pidgin language, I notice a movement out of the corner of my eye. It was our trishaw driver bolting down the street. Assuming he was sufficiently scared to take off without making any motion to get paid—never mind a tip, then all the more reason that we too should be concerned about our safety. It was obvious that neither of these two small-time civil servants had any interest in helping us when Bernie shouted, "Bob, let's get the hell outta here."

At that second the two of us took off running back the way we had come. About three blocks later we drew up to the limits of our endurance. We were now much winded and quite sober. As we stopped for a breath, Bernie looked at me with big eyes pleading, "We are so fucked aren't we?"

I replied with a nod, while lip-synching "DNFR," sending him into a roar of laughter. "Okay, you frickin' master of understatement, let's get going. This place has to be crawling with cowboys," he insisted.

So what was this "cowboy" thing?

By 1966 the Vietnam War had been fuming long enough to leave behind a population of innocent victims—the orphans of war carnage. Many of the orphaned children could not remain in burned-out villages, leaving a desperate option to send them off to relatives living in the city, relatives who accepted the duty but were already overwhelmed by the stress of the war. Without parental restraints, these war waifs forged a life of necessity, a life with other expendables of their own kind, a life in the streets.

There was no authority wielding control over these street kids. The expanding war now vacuumed up the supply of able young men, leaving the city police force (the White Mice) to accept slim pickings, becoming a shell of law enforcement and a shill of graft, just the perfect formula for a little anarchy.

The youngsters of the street soon formed gangs and figured out how to get by day by day. With a nod to the American idea of lawlessness, lawless gangs of urchins came to be known as cowboys.

They found petty crimes were overlooked and serious crime was overbooked, as long as they avoided being cast as Viet Cong, their mayhem was shoved aside for later, even in some cases when it became murder committed in the act of robbery. Everyday civilian crime committed in an active war zone became cast in a new color. It is not a priority to worry about an inebriated soldier who has his wallet stolen in an alley when an hour later three Viet Cong terrorists might throw a satchel of C-4 into a crowded disco killing eighteen patrons. Dead GIs were the problem for the American military, dead civilian sailors were the problem for...and here it became beyond strange. No one, and I mean absolutely no one, wanted any responsibility for the legal status of the merchant mariner. Apocryphal or not, a story made the rounds that a merchant sailor had stabbed a shipmate to death in an alley in Saigon, never to face any kind to tribunal or justice. The story went on that he returned to the US where he went on with normal life.

We were on our own and we knew it!

The lower class neighborhood now surrounding us was eerily quiet, the kind of quiet allowing an already spooked brain to hear ominous sounds in every alley. This was no place to go knocking on a door to call a taxi. Every day the war brought new killing, wounding, or maiming, much of it tragic mistakes. In the world of unintended consequences, many of those tragedies turned average, apolitical citizens into Viet Cong sympathizers. There could be no knowing if the person answering a knock on the door might be a loyalist or a freshly minted ideologue, one who had begun to see Americans as invaders and Communists as maybe a not-so-bad alternative.

The two of us out-of-bounds boys continued as fast as we could in the general direction we believed the trishaw driver had followed. As we made a right hand turn onto a slightly larger street, all of the sudden a man stepped out from a shadowy gate, pushing a short-barrel, twelve-gauge riot shotgun into my chest. I stopped, my heart stopped, my eyes focused on the business end of the gun, as Bernie ran into my back, whereupon the gun holder in a deep Southern American accent demanded, "Y'all, hold it right there."

I looked up to see a large man in military camouflage, a flak jacket covering his torso almost up to where a dark helmet covered his head. Suddenly another guy appeared from behind the gate, also wearing a flak jacket; he was armed with a grenade launcher.

"What ya got there, John?" the second one asked.

"Well Billy, it looks like we got ourselves a couple of little lost pukes out after curfew."

As the second one shoved tight into my face, with bad breath and a black gooey chaw of tobacco, he spit out, "Well I be damned. Looks like we found a little, blond, lost bunny rabbit. You two have ID cards?"

Right at this minute I am thanking the Lord for my snow-white blond hair. I have now noticed military police badges on these two, letting me know that they are American soldiers, but the real test is what they think we are; after all, they are the ones holding the big weapons. We might be some sort of trouble for these two MPs, but no one had ever seen a Viet Cong with blond hair, putting them at ease that we were not there to kill them.

Bernie and I showed them our merchant mariner ID cards, in retrospect a much better move than showing them our military ID cards. We outranked these two privates, who were most likely draftees and who most likely had drawn this duty as a real shit detail—working a duty station all night in a dangerous neighborhood. This was no time to be pulling rank. What we needed were friends, and these guys were in a position to save us from a dangerous situation.

Now knowing that we were Americans, the two MPs lightened up and wanted to know just how we ended up on their street. We gave them the short version of our dilemma, telling them that we needed to be back on our ship for an early morning departure. After a few minutes of sorting out details, one of the MPs radioed back to his HQ for permission to take us back to our ship using the Jeep they stashed in an alley behind their checkpoint.

Permission was granted, giving one of the MPs a chance to give us a ride, breaking the tedious boredom of his long evening to come. We rode in a military police Jeep full of radios and extra weapons, an offer I would not have exchanged for a Hollywood-movie-mogul-owned, twenty-five foot limousine stocked with booze and babes. Almost exactly two years later, the now famous Tet offensive was to show just how dangerous the streets of Saigon could become in a matter of minutes. The Saigon part of this offensive was paid in serious blood by the American Military Police. There was never any way of knowing when or where this thing could blow up, not to mention the nightly terror dealt by the kids—the lawless cowboys.

As he drove us back to the ship in the duty Jeep, Private First Class Billy Whatever made a serious point of busting our balls. By then he had figured out that we were not deck hands or cooks, giving him the opportunity to do a little flush of his "ain't my life unfair" load from the toilet of his mind down onto a couple of guys who were in charge of something. In his life, Pvt. Billy had never been in charge of anything, making this an opportunity not to be missed.

Arriving by MP Jeep to the front gate had the additional advantage of getting us past another group of itchy trigger-finger guys, who this time were armed with .50 caliber machine guns. Out after curfew was not okay with these guys either, letting them in on their share of "B" busting before we headed across the quay apron. My last parting wish was that there be no Viet Cong sneaking around our cargo tonight. Both Bernie and I had seen enough; it was time to get back to sea, back to our element.

Departure

The pounding on my stateroom door was not harmonic to the throbbing of blood vessels somewhere near the top of my skull. "Hey mate, it's time to get up for undocking…C'mon, I gotta get back to work."

Time now to light a small mental candle in celebration of living through the previous evening, drink a gallon of water, and get this aging hulk of a ship out of Saigon and back to the open ocean.

As with most departures, I groggily found a spot on the bridge where I could stay out of the tangle of the captain and the pilot, while keeping track of the timing of events in the log book and a small pad called the "bell book." Oh sure, I was totally immersed in the professionalism needed to move this island of steel away from its temporary bonding to the work day world of the port, but the required intensity level was low, this was very routine, we were empty. Soon enough, the junior third mate relieved me on the bridge; I collected my one hour of overtime for a few minutes worked, and beat a path back to the altar of my sanity—the warm embrace of the bunk in my cabin. Just before flopping onto the mattress, I ripped the hand grenade screen from my one lonely porthole, hoping that the movement of the ship downriver might force some air into my cabin as respite from its still-sweltering temperature.

In what seemed to be a very short time, the same ordinary

seaman was once again pounding on my door to awaken me for a shower, a bite of lunch, and the beginning of my routine 12-4 sea watch on the bridge.

By the time I arrived back topside to relieve the junior third mate, the ship had steamed down the Saigon River beyond most of the human habitation. The weather was hot with a thin haze in the still-tepid air, promising a gentle, uneventful trip down to the pilot station at Vũng Tàu and on into the South China Sea. I grabbed a cup of coffee, chatted with the captain for a minute, and turned to ask a question of the pilot. Unlike the arrival pilot, this one spoke barebones English; he was not going to give me any kind of interpretation of politics in Southeast Asia.

About twenty minutes into my watch, as the ship began to turn through a sharp bend in the river, a strong rumble of thunder was heard from the starboard side of the ship. This first rumble was quickly followed by a more intense deep-throated roar, which seemed to be getting closer. I looked out across the swampy delta to a hazy sky that had no visible clouds, ruling out weather related thunder, when I noticed huge clouds of smoke and dust combined with bright flashes coming a couple miles away in the delta. Both the captain and I exclaimed, "What the hell is that?" as the pilot pointed to the sky and in broken English said, "B-52s."

I looked up and saw nothing. I grabbed a pair of binoculars, turned them skyward, and still saw nothing. There was no sound of aircraft or contrails to warn or give any sign that doomsday was minutes away. The sound of high explosive bomb detonation was now nonstop, rattling the doors between the pilothouse and the bridge wing as the noise came closer and closer. Meanwhile, down on the main deck at the bow of the ship, this airborne assault had the attention of our Army guard unit, causing them to point skyward while calling for instructions on their radios. From the looks of it, the Air Force had not deemed it necessary to let our Army group in on the plans for this bombing mission.

If this bombing run continued in its current direction there would be no place for our little ship to hide. A hung-up bomb followed by a delayed release, a not-so-unusual event, would have spelled big trouble. That afternoon I had brought my camera up to the bridge in hopes of catching a photo of local fishermen, so I grabbed it thinking, "What the hell, nowhere to hide. Might as well get a picture of what it looks like under a B-52 drop."

Later, when I was able to sort through the events of that afternoon, it came to me just how easy it would have been for this to turn into a life-changing event. In the days of our visit to Vietnam, no global satellite navigation system existed; many of these big aircraft navigated much as we did: by sextant. What they mostly relied on for bombing accuracy was good old clear skies and good eyes. The navigator found landmarks as they lined up for a run on the bombing target while the bombardier glued his eyes to an upgraded version of the Norden bombsight from WWII. It was easy to imagine that the *SS Exhibitor* might have looked to the bombardier to be a raft of floating excrement drifting down the muddy Saigon River. Nothing here to worry about if a few bombs slopped over.

An oft-used bombing strategy, as reported later by journalist and author Neil Sheehan, involved a flight of six B-52s dropping 750 pound bombs within a box about five-eighths of a mile wide by two miles long, virtually eliminating all but microbial life within this box, the same effect as a small tactical nuclear weapon. Sounds awesome when put in the light of a morning briefing, but my skeptical mind knows about the accuracy of these "dumb" bombs falling from a bomb bay attached to an aircraft that sort of knows where it is and sort of knows how fast the wind is blowing over the target. Whenever I hear an Air Force general crowing about "precision bombing," it comes to me that he must be referring to his own morning bowel movement; everything else is fantasy.

The pictures I took that afternoon will not be in this book. The only thing that showed on the developed film were clouds of smoke against a hazy, flat swamp background. Also impossible to recreate was the deep amplitude of sound combined with intensity of the shock wave. It felt as some force had determined to move organs within our bodies. For me there was no comprehension of how a human could survive anywhere near ground zero of this attack. Some days we gave Charlie what must have seemed to be his Catholic missionary's description of hell, some days we probably did no more than churn the mud, killing all unfortunate local flora and fauna.

As suddenly as the cacophony of noise had started, it ended. Looking around at the men on the bridge, the Army escort on the bow and a bosun's work party, it seemed that everyone, except me, nervously pulled out a cigarette and lit up in spite of no-smoking rules. Never having taken up the nasty habit of smoking, as rebellion to my chain-smoking, North-Carolina-bred parents, I dug deep in a pocket for a stick of Doublemint, jamming it between my teeth, punished by jaws working off nervous energy. *Just let us get down to Vũng Tàu without more excitement,* my mind was thinking. *This perceived voyage of interesting adventure and excitement has not turned out to be anything like I thought. In fact, just like over 250,000 American GIs already knew, the whole thing sucks.*

Just at the end of my watch, we made it to Vũng Tàu where an Army Mike boat picked up the pilot as well as the armed guard detachment, leaving us free to set a great circle course for San Francisco. Arriving back at my cabin, where I began to prepare myself for the resumption of officer cocktail hour, I fell into a funk of depression. This larger-than-life episode in hostile Saigon was not what I had expected. This malaise generated by life on the streets of Saigon heightened when memories slid back to my love interest in New York: Joani. It had been months without any form of communication, something youthful, exuberant, attractive girls tolerate poorly. I had decided to ask her to marry me, but the question remained whether she would still be waiting. Attractive offers soon find attractive girls, a thought further fueling my malaise.

Several days before our departure, I had found a street vendor selling liquor. With help from my old friend Uncle Ben's face on a "C" note, I was able to secure four half-gallon bottles of Beefeater gin at a very attractive price. The gin had most certainly come to Vietnam on a ship just like mine, to be stolen by a Viet-rat, sold by a desperate black marketer, with the proceeds headed north to buy weapons and ammunition for "Chuck." What a fucked-up system. Oh, well…a couple of Beefeater martinis up in the radio shack for happy hour will help leave all of this misery in our wake, a line of foaming water soon to stretch from Vũng Tàu to the Golden Gate Bridge.

Crossing to Home

Out of sight of land, navigating on the ocean in a 1966 world of paper charts, ship's officers put away the expensive coastline charts in favor of a large sheet of paper printed only with a grid. In a Mercator Chart world, the grid for latitude was preprinted, the grid for longitude was blank, letting the navigator make his own chart, but except for the lines of the grid, it was just white paper. The first day of the ocean passage, a dot was drawn on the left side of the paper for the correct ship latitude, then the longitude line was numbered at the top of the sheet as appropriate, and the ship's course was drawn as a solid line on a blank page. As we shot sun lines and star fixes with our sextants, these LOPs (lines of position) were drawn in to locate the ship on the plain grid-lined sheet. Progressing to the east day by day, at our meager fifteen knots, a day or so later the position of the ship hit the right side of the page; all of the old lines and longitude numbers were erased, the dot was moved back to the left margin of the paper, and the entire process was restarted. It felt a little like looking at the statement for your thirty-year home mortgage; you knew that you were paying off some principal, but it seemed as if progress was painfully slow, like plodding across the enormous blank sheet of the Pacific Ocean.

Then about ten days later, entering the chartroom behind the wheelhouse at the start of my afternoon watch, I see laid out, on the large chart table, a colorful chart of the coast of California; now we could see our destination, now we were making progress, now we knew that we would be passing under the Golden Gate Bridge tomorrow. Now we were home.

The next day, the *Exhibitor* made her way under both big San Francisco bridges, just past China Basin, to an old, dilapidated pier in the rundown Mission Bay section of the city of San Francisco. Here we would end the voyage, pay off the crew, sign on the new crew, and wait for the Pentagon to tell us where to go next. In most cases the crew signed off Articles and turned right around to sign back on for the next voyage. This is what I planned to do.

But not so fast! Not all of this crew was rolling over, they had seen enough. The adventure in the typhoon had done permanent damage to their warm feelings about all the extra pay seen in the "war bonus."

But for me, the huge amount of money we got at payoff made my decision easy. I was in for at least another voyage. A huge setback came when I learned that my friend and wingman, Bernie, decided he wanted out of that engine room, and he wanted off the aging *SS Exhibitor*. What he had seen down in that shop of horrors on that never-to-be-forgotten evening, where it looked for certain that we were all doomed to perish in a watery grave, pushed Bernie over the edge. The first assistant engineer, the hero who had helped save all of our lives, was also signing off.

I grabbed Bernie the afternoon of our arrival, demanding that we hit the shows in North Beach for one last farewell party, but he had sadly replied, "Bob, I cannot take even one more night on this ship." He had booked a seat on a redeye flight that very evening, flying back to New York. We were never to see one another again.

The first night in San Fran, in spite of having no wingman, I went over to Union Street for food, North Beach for drinks and girl shows, and then to the Buena Vista for Irish coffee. This evening of homecoming was a welcome relief from Saigon. The second night out on the town was okay. After that, boredom set in. I was bored and lonely and the ship just sat there doing nothing. We sat and we sat. We were to sit at China Basin for eleven days before the military found a cargo for us. Wait a minute, you say, they are giving you a room, they make your bed and scrub your sink, they feed you three times a day—all for free, as they pay you a handsome salary...and you are complaining! Well, it was something else. Something occupying my waking thoughts, something for which I had no answer.

It started immediately after our arrival with a phone call to New York to you can guess who! Following "Hello"—the first words out of her mouth—without pausing for a breath, were "What time does your flight arrive at JFK? I'll pick you up."

"Uh, well uh, I uh…

"I won't be flying home. I am making another trip.

"You understand don't you?"

No, she did not understand, not one bit. She had not heard from me in four months, no letters, no postcards, no phone calls…nothing. She did not know if I was dead or wounded or alive. Adding to the bill of family angst, Joani's own beloved older brother, Kenny, a naval aviator, was at that very moment piloting an A-4 Skyhawk fighter jet off the deck off an aircraft carrier over the skies of Vietnam. Her mother, glued to the evening news about the fighting in Vietnam, led the voice of concern. No one could understand the point of it all. By mid-1966, the American death toll was mounting daily. And now I am telling Joani that I am going back to do this all over again.

Our conversation was an emotional trip spiraling downward. I certainly had no intention of telling her about the typhoon or for that matter any story about my last four months. This was going to be really tough; I had no excuses. I had only one bit of good news. But it turned out that telling her how happy my stock broker was about the large sums of money being sent into my account at his firm, bore the weight of a feather against that of a rock on the scales of this debate.

She assumed all along that I had planned on just one trip. Would the next one be another four months? I had no answer.

"Well, do not call me back till you have an answer to that question!" Click!

Damn, you sure handled that well, the little voice of cynicism inside my head mocked.

Now you have even chased away the only sweet voice telling you that she missed you and wanted you home. Thoughts of asking for her hand in marriage were wafting away faster than gulls streaming out to sea in the winds under the Golden Gate.

Back on the ship, I found that nasty shipmate called loneliness waiting for me. Without asking, he had just barged into room with me in my tiny cabin. Trying to get rid of this unwanted visitor, I began thinking about the last time I had been homeported in San Francisco three years earlier. I had met and dated a charming young Stanford student named Lone Frederickson. (Lone, what a great Scandinavian name.) At the time, the two of us had talked for hours about great books to read. I had expressed a thirst to read every great book, and Lone had promised to have one of her English Lit professors put together a list of books I needed to read before I could declare myself educated and well read. I had kept that list with me, but had not taken the time to act on it. Now let's see…where did I put that list?

Armed with the Stanford list, I took off the next day to a huge bookstore on Market Street, buying a paperback copy of every book on the professor's list. My days of reading *Riders of the Purple Sage* were over. Oh the irony; Lone was going to be my antidote to loneliness!

The Merchant Marine Academy is a fine school; it will always have my deepest respect and admiration, but by purpose it is no Stanford. Now was the time to add depth with a humanities education. Soon I had read every book on the professor's list, and then began making my own list of the world's greatest authors, now my mentors, the men and women whose very writing and ideas shaped my desire and ability to think about writing works of my own. Lone never told me the name of the professor, but years later I was led to wonder if it might have been Wallace Stegner, the man at the very top of my mentor author list. In addition to winning the coveted Pulitzer Prize for fiction, he also taught creative writing at Stanford!

By the end of eleven days, the ship had filled out a new crew. Although Bernie's replacement was not a wingman match, we did get some promising young Academy grads, and we got orders to move. The chief engineer, the architect of our beer supply, had been taken off the ship due to severe gout, but our orders were to make his alcoholic logistics irrelevant. We were headed up the San Joaquin River to Stockton, where we would fill the holds of the ship with beer, whiskey, and PX sundries. The Pentagon knew what the troops wanted.

Why the tortuous winding trip up the San Joaquin River to Stockton to load non-essential PX cargo for the war when surely there were distributors in the Bay area nearby? No one had an answer to this question, but it is likely that a liquor wholesaler in Stockton was a financial supporter of someone in politics in California. We spent three full, twenty-four-hour days loading individual cardboard boxes on wood pallets with a variety of beer and hard liquor. Longshoremen spent those same three full, twenty-four-hour days opening many of those boxes, while hidden deep in the holds, drinking what they could on the spot, hiding bottles in every conceivable nook and cranny in the holds, and taking home as many bottles as could physically be carried beneath heavy overcoats. Why was this allowed? Because putting guards in the holds would have caused a wildcat strike by the longshoremen, and after all, one longshoreman's consumption is minor in the macro view of thousands of tons of beverage. It was deemed more important to get the ship moving,

Later, at the end of our crossing, the Army did put guards on the ship in Saigon, a waste of money as most of the Vietnamese longshoremen did not drink, nor would they have known a wildcat or a strike if it had bitten their Indochinese butt.

Voyage II

Sooner than usual, the load-out was complete: 9,800 long tons of PX supplies mostly in the form of alcoholic spirits. Time to wrap the ship up for sea. Checking for stowaways, a job I hated and always a waste of time on trips to a war zone, turned out to have unforeseen benefits that day. The longshoremen had left liquor bottles everywhere in hopes of coming back later, most of them still sealed. There turned out to be so many hastily-hidden bottles that we could be picky about brand labels to take back to our cabins for happy hour. This windfall came with consequences as the crew now had access to liquor in the holds, a problem soon to occupy the captain's full attention. Fortune had, however, smiled. Help in exercising authority had arrived in the form of a new officer, the junior third mate. This new mate, a recent grad from New York Maritime, was at least six and half feet tall, must have weighed 280 pounds, and was all muscle; we now had a "Bucko" mate. Later, I watched this mountain of a man lift two misbehaving, liquor-abusing, crewmen off the ground, one in each hand, and knock their heads together. He quickly had everyone's respect, and he was a teetotaler.

Finding a nice outside rail to watch a pleasant mid-February sunset, our winding trip down the San Joaquin into San Francisco Bay was idyllic. On a quiet evening framed by the twinkling lights of San Francisco, the *Exhibitor* slowed to drop off the pilot as my

The Faithful Sextant

midnight watch began. The sea was smooth, sheltered by Point Bonita and the massive cape at Point Reyes, as we made our way out past the Farallon Islands before setting the great circle course to Asia. Within an hour those sheltering points of land faded, giving the long winter North Pacific swells free run at our gentle motion. The first really big roller arrived to plunge our bow into its face, sending the ship into its first giant roll to port. With this plunge into the ocean came a noise I had never heard before at sea, it was the noise of hundreds of whiskey bottles rolling off beams in the holds to smash against hard things in the hold. Then all was quiet. But as all mariners know, with every roll to port comes an equal roll to starboard, bringing with it another smashing sound, that of all the bottles hidden on the other side of the ship. This sound continued as we took deeper and deeper rolls, until most of the pilfered bottles had been victimized by gravity. Within a few minutes, a strong smell of booze wafted through the ship, a smell so strong that it was reminiscent of holding your nose over a brandy snifter.

Days now found us employing an impatient dread of another long ocean passage balanced against the warm-blanket emotion of the certainty found in the ever-sameness of ocean transit routine.

Routine's bastard twin, change, showed up in an increase in demands and radio message traffic from the Navy Control of Shipping group sending Captain Winebrenner to seek my help. Aware that I had kept abreast of my Naval Reserve obligations, the captain asked me to take charge of corresponding to this leftover World War II Navy niche group. Trying to interpret the gobbledygook found in Navy messages was not my favorite chore. One afternoon, about mid-way in our passage, the radio officer brought me a Navy message, sharing his opinion that this one might be important. Reading it several times, I called the captain to the bridge to tell him that we were being diverted; the Navy was sending us to somewhere called White Beach.

"Where in Satan's blue hell is White Beach?" the captain asked.

"Never heard of it, Captain," I replied.

The second mate was called to the bridge, and the next two hours were spent plowing through every chart and publication on the bridge searching for somewhere named White Beach; this was way before the days of Google. Soon I saw the captain writing a plain language radio message to MSTS asking where the heck we would find White Beach. Seeing his frustration, I approached with the naval communication manual in hand. "Captain, do you want me to put that in Navy format?"

To which, without thinking of consequences, he shot back, "This will do. You can throw that damn book over the side."

I didn't think he really meant it, but what the hell, it sounded like an order to me. So I walked out on the bridge wing and threw the damn Navy manual over the side. In retrospect, jettisoning this unclassified though official publication probably could have gotten the captain and me reprimanded by naval officials, but what the heck, war is hell!

Four hours later our charter group at MSTS shot a message back telling us to look mid-way on the east coast of Okinawa. There we found White Beach.

Much more than just a cheap place to anchor a very low-priority, booze-laden cargo ship, White Beach turned out to be a small naval facility actively used to organize small Army units, Marines, and Navy Seals before insertion into Vietnam. In our eyes, however, what this was really about was the Pentagon saving money by keeping the *Exhibitor* out of the mythical war zone and avoiding the cost of war bonus pay to our crew. This penny-pinching bad news hit the ship rumor mill in minutes. To a man, we all took this as a personal insult.

Just like at Vũng Tàu on the last voyage, arrival in early March found the *Exhibitor* dropping anchor in the bay next to the Navy facilities at White Beach. But unlike the earlier anchorage, the Navy let us know that not only was coming ashore okay, they would even provide landing craft to take us back and forth on a schedule. This was no naval base; it was more like two piers and a few buildings left over from some WWII action, now being put back in service with the surge of troops entering Vietnam. Even after looking hard, there were few signs of any beach featuring white sand. Some American General must have named it, as the name White was never a word in the Japanese language.

Long ocean voyages gave most sailors an itch, and the scratch was going ashore for wine, women, and song; something we did not expect at this place run by the United States Navy. We were wrong. The small Navy facility featured two small buildings used as an informal Enlisted Club and an Officers Club. Additionally, just outside the perimeter of the Navy controlled base was a small Okinawan town whose entrepreneurs knew what American GIs and sailors wanted. They did their best to provide it. Services such as houses of prostitution were prohibited by the US military. We still controlled Okinawa as a protectorate; nevertheless delights of the flesh such as massage parlors were allowed. Typically found in these "full service" flesh mills was a price list posted at the door topped by the "Fleet Admiral Nimitz" massage: priced to include…well, the reader can imagine that all bells and whistles were included. Although military rules strictly prohibited sexual intercourse for hire (as tediously defined by long paragraphs in the Uniform Code of Military Justice), the girls in the massage parlors could and would clean the fluid out of every male orifice, including removal of earwax.

Our evening radio shack cocktail hour now moved ashore to the ad hoc Officers Club, featuring insanely cheap ten-cent drinks, a great jukebox, and two slot machines. This club was a raucous circus with new faces, running full tilt, seven nights a week. One evening something happened in that bar unlike anything any had ever seen. What happened could only have taken place in a wartime club full of wartime tested and alcohol-lubricated servicemen.

The military officers in the club, Marines with a scattering of Special Forces—Navy Seals—and a few displaced Army types, were all headed to Vietnam or rotating in and out of the zone. Calling these warriors uninhibited might have been a word used by a reporter; to me they were all rat-shit crazies.

Normal Navy O-clubs all have a small ship's bell by the bar, a bell that is often rung to celebrate special occasions. It can also be rung for quite a different reason, to alert patrons of some club infraction such as coming into the club without first removing your hat. When rung for special occasions such as a wetting down after a rank promotion, the promoted officer is expected to buy drinks for his party; offenses such as non-hat removal demand that the offender buy one round of drinks served to all present. Someone had hung a small ships bell at one end of the bar in this building.

Late one evening as I sat at a table near the back of the club with my happy hour partners, a Navy captain dressed in whites with a chest full of colorful ribbons and an entourage of lackeys came into the club, grabbed a seat at the bar, and began a serious talk with his aide. He had failed to remove his hat, visor sparkling full of gold braid (aka scrambled eggs). At the end of the bar, a junior officer instantly began ringing the ship's bell as hard as he could. At the same time the civilian bartender approached the captain to ask how he wanted to pay for a round of drinks, having broken the hat removal rule. The captain jerked his head towards the bartender and in his best John Wayne command voice, snarled at him, "Go to hell. This is no real Officers Club" and turned away to continue his conversation.

The noise became deafening as patrons pounded their glasses on the table demanding their free drink. The bartender shrugged that he could do nothing, the noise got louder, but no drinks were poured. Suddenly, from the back of the room, a Navy Seal Lieutenant JG, dressed in combat fatigue pants and a khaki-colored tee shirt sporting the Navy SEAL insignia, ran forward to the empty chair next to the captain, where in one smooth motion he snatched the captain's hat as he vaulted up to stand on the bar. Yelling obscenities in a drunken haze, he unbuttoned the front of his pants, pulled out his manly fire hose, and proceeded to piss in the finely starched white hat.

About that time, two of his buddies scrambled over the bar, grabbed him, and the three of them fled out the door as the young Seal tossed the now yellow-stained white hat back on the bar.

Right then it got real quiet, followed by the orderly departure of the captain and his retinue. The stained hat was left at the end of the bar. Things stayed real quiet for a minute. Then all returned to normal, dice cups slamming on the bar, guys yelling for drinks, and the two slot machines once again worked over, being cranked hard enough to almost break off the arm. It was just another evening in Dodge City.

Two days later I asked our boarding officer if he knew what had happened to the young Lt. JG Navy Seal. He said, "Oh him, nothing happened. His team was reinserted into the Mekong Delta on a secret op the next morning. Nobody gonna mess with one of the Seal Team One guys."

Wouldn't you know it, the very next night I too got kicked out of that sorry excuse for an "O" Club. My unceremonious ejection came as a result of an article I had read in Esquire magazine some months earlier telling how easy it was to jimmy old slot machines by waggling the handle in such a way that the first wheel could be locked on a winning slot, say two cherries, before letting the other two wheels spin. With the first wheel already locked on a winner, all odds of beating the machine overwhelmingly favored the player.

Guys yanking and pounding on these old one-armed bandits had of course worn the workings of these machines well past serviceable. It took only a few minutes for me to figure out how to use the system mentioned in the magazine. Before starting my winning run, I had scanned the room and with correct intuition, reckoned that no one in this club read *Esquire* magazine.

I was getting a winner two out of three pulls of the handle. After my third major jackpot in one hour, the manager of the club, not knowing what I was doing but figuring that it had to somehow be cheating, demanded my immediate departure, ordering that I not come back. He reasoned that only the slot machine was allowed to cheat; cheating by the player that cut into profits was strictly forbidden. What the hell, we were leaving the next day anyway. I bolted out the door, keeping the winnings.

Early the next morning we pulled anchor and headed out to the South China Sea for Saigon, knowing that this time we would only pause at Vũng Tàu to pick up a pilot; our same berth downtown was waiting for us.

Having a very homogenous cargo, this discharge was going to be faster than the last voyage. The weather had cooled in advance of the coming monsoon season; now we could sleep on the ship. And there was one more change. The ship now had a new crewmember, a four-legged furry one; the captain had picked up a small puppy dog in Okinawa.

We were old friends with the locals at our berth: the stevedore boss, the woman who would take your laundry, the beggars, the newspaper boy were all there to greet the ship. As we neared the end of the almost two weeks needed to discharge the cargo, the captain decided to give the cute little puppy to the newspaper boy; the Vietnamese kid seemed thrilled. The next morning the young boy appeared in the officer's salon carrying his usual armful of the *Armed Forces Newspaper*. Captain Winebrenner asked him how it was going with the dog, bringing a large smile to the youngsters face as he told him in Pidgin English that his family found the dog to be tender and delicious; the puppy had been put into a Vietnamese stew.

"You ate my dog?" the captain yelled. The young boy, a confused look on his face, quickly remembered, as he bolted for the door, that some Americans were real sensitive about eating dog.

The remainder of this trip would find Captain Winebrenner often mumbling, "I cannot believe it; they ate my damned dog!"

The next day the cargo on the ship was all but gone; the sailing board had been posted for midnight that evening. Our agent had recommended a nearby restaurant as having fine French cuisine, so Captain Winebrenner suggested that all of the officers should dine together for a farewell celebration. Most every officer said, "I'll drink to that," and we did drink, beginning at about four that afternoon. Some hours later saw a well-lubricated string of licensed mariners weaving across the quay to hoof it the few blocks to Madame Leccia's well-touted restaurant, the Guillaume Tell.

The restaurant turned out to be close, within walking distance from our friendly sandbagged, .50-caliber-equipped command post that guarded the main gate. Stumbling into the restaurant, the chances of good decisions were slim. The atmosphere permeating the Guillaume Tell was there to convince the diner that he had slipped into a nice place in the heart of Paris. It goes without saying that since we wished that this little ruse to be true, we slid easily into its fairytale, forgetting that we were on the waterfront of Saigon. Charlie owned this area.

We started by ordering raw clams, you remember…the ones we saw being caught fresh out of the cesspool Saigon River. From there we graduated to fine Gallic fare—that barely-cooked chef's special you find on the Champs Elysees, the kind of entree only a demented Parisian would allow down a human throat. Here we were in the Paris of the East, pretending we were in the Paris of the West, with Charlie the Cong dishing up the fare to his mortal enemy. How any of us survived that dinner is an amazing story of good fortune; but it was to get worse, much worse.

At about eleven, with just enough time to get back on board before sailing, we managed to weave our way back to the ship. As a group, we would have made Captain Joe Hazlewood of Exxon Valdez fame look as sober as a Mennonite parson.

On the ship, in working uniform, it was a good thing that the new junior third mate was sober, someone of skill had to supervise the anchor and bow lines. Sober or not, my watch began at midnight.

As we cast off, I was past slurring drunk, and the captain was drunk. The Vietnamese pilot appeared sober; a good thing for all involved as he was for sure going to have to get this ship down the dark river without much help from the officers.

The captain and I managed to stay upright until the pilot station at Vũng Tàu, when we set an ocean course. At that time, the captain gave me command of the ship and headed to his cabin—he did not look well. I was not well. Many things in my stomach wanted out, but that old ship did not have a john anywhere near the wheelhouse. About twenty minutes after the captain's departure, it was time for the second mate to relieve me, giving me a chance to deal with the cement mixer churning in my midsection. But the second mate did not show up. Finally, at 0400, I sent a sailor down to his cabin. Five minutes later the sailor returned to report, "Mate, he's not in his room, and there is vomit on his pillow."

I thought, *oh my God, this is not good, I am too sick to stand his watch*. Then it came to me. Every officer on this ship that ate in that restaurant is sick, drunk, yes, but perhaps much more serious…were we poisoned? I was now experiencing sharp shooting pains in my abdomen. There was nothing I could do; who was I going to call? Any kind of medical help was quickly receding into the night as the ship plowed ahead into the pitch-black South China Sea. If this mess was simply massive food poisoning combined with alcohol, turning the ship around for medical help at Vũng Tàu would have been beyond embarrassing; but if it was a Viet Cong way of saying goodbye… well, I guess we were screwed.

An hour later I sent a sailor from the 4-8 watch down to see if he could find his watch officer, the second mate. Arriving back on the bridge, he told me that the second was just getting dressed and would be up in a few minutes. He did not show for another half hour. He looked terrible, but agreed that he would be okay to stand the rest of his watch. We compared notes, agreeing that the illness seeming to hit all of us was more than alcohol related; we both hoped it would only be food poisoning. We had no idea what to do if it was more serious.

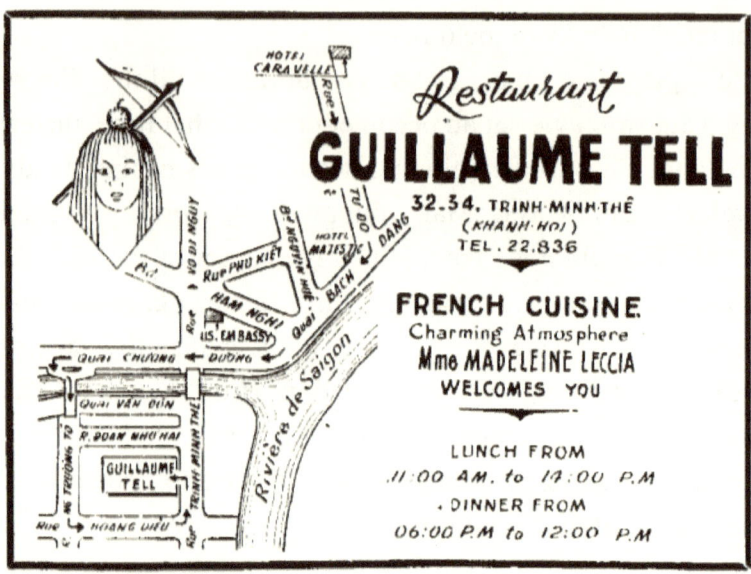

I slept though breakfast; food was the last thing on my mind. By lunchtime, I was still in severe pain but stumbled down to the salon to try a bowl of soup. That did not work, sending me to the john to throw it back up. This was going to be a painful recovery.

But recover we all did.

The ocean transit home was smooth sailing, the decision about voyage number three, not so much. On the plus side, spring was coming and the Pacific would become, well, Pacific. Also, I knew the ship and I liked the captain, he was staying for sure. On the negative, the Navy penny-pinching program of making us wait outside the war zone had cut deeply into profitability, and April was the beginning of monsoon season in Vietnam. One more not so small item, yet one I tended to ignore; this nasty little war for the hearts and minds of the people of South Vietnam was turning very ugly. North Vietnamese regulars were not "Charlie," they represented a real army supplied and supported by China and the Soviet Union. The money had been good and the experience life-changing…now might be the time to move on. Again, the old sailor's best advice, "The correct time to shorten sail before a storm is the first time you think of it!"

Penciling math on the back of an envelope showed that mates on voyages such as the Mediterranean, where overtime flowed like cheap Italian wine, made as much as the guys on war zone double pay. Let's set our compass to steer to the sunny straights of Gibraltar.

Berthing once again at an old pier in San Francisco, I headed for the pay phone at the pier head to call a certain blonde in New York to tell her that I would be on an American Airlines 707 into JFK tomorrow afternoon. It was May of 1966 and everyone was happy.

A year later, while in the scheduling office at American Export Lines, I asked the manager what had happened to the *SS Exhibitor*. Checking his ship schedule, he said, "After her third trip back to Saigon in May of 1966, we did not bring the ship home; instead, we sent her on to East Pakistan (Bangladesh today), where the crew was flown home and the ship was scrapped."

Oh, what a good decision I had made to leave the *SS Exhibitor* and sign on to the *SS Exporter* for voyages to the Mediterranean.

Millions upon millions of dollars spent to refurbish this ship for three voyages, two of which were to carry alcoholic beverages, and then it was cut up for scrap. A Caterpillar D-8 bulldozer flung overboard in a typhoon becomes a simple rounding error in the scheme of waste and abuse of national treasure, but what about the two men who lost their lives on her decks? There can be no price for their loss, but a pragmatist might say that it could have been worse.

Arlington

Now I have lost you, I must scatter
All of you on the air henceforth;
Not that to me it can ever matter
But it's only fair to the rest of the earth.

Now especially, when it is winter
And the sun's not half so bright as he was,
Who wouldn't be glad to find a splinter
That once was you, in the frozen grass?

Snowflakes, too, will be softer feathered,
Clouds, perhaps, will be whiter plumed:
Rain, whose brilliance you caught and gathered,
Purer silver have reassumed.

Farewell, sweet dust; I was never a miser;
Once, for a minute, I stood by your side;
Now you are gone, I am none the wiser,
I see the stones, but where did you hide?

Elinor Wylie
"Earthly Creatures"

First Lt. Frank Packer

It was hot. It was August. I was tired.

Long days of early mornings spent dispatching American Airlines aircraft from the gates at Washington National Airport followed by flying lessons to become skillful at crosswind landings, cross-country navigation, and cross instructors during nighttime flight drills, were all becoming quite a load.

This particular evening, I had much new stuff on my mind after several hours of ground school, simulator pilot training, as I unlocked the door to my tiny efficiency apartment. Efficiency-ha! Yes, it was efficient. How could it not be, everything was almost at arm's length. The bedroom was the living room with sleeping arrangements on a hide-a-bed—a long-term motel room with a small kitchen and no maid service. But, it was mine. It was my first living experience without family members or roommates.

Coming through the door, an envelope lying on the parquet wood floor caught my eye. Bending over to pick it up, I saw that the envelope was the distinctive yellowish Western Union Telegram using a cellophane panel to show a name and address. Additionally, this envelope was marked "American Red Cross" under the Western Union name. Turning around, as if a boy on a bicycle had slipped this missive between my feet, it was clear that someone had slid this envelope under my door earlier in the day. Holding the name and address panel tightly, I reread my name and address on the enclosed telegram three times before laying the unopened envelope on my small eating table. It was addressed to me!

I had never received a telegram. This could not be good. American Red Cross...They do not send an expensive telegram to ask for money. This is really not good. A small voice inside is now telling me that this day was not going to end well, not well at all!

❖

It's hard to say exactly what it was that was getting under my skin. The late October sky of 1966 offered sparkling fall weather to the Hudson River Valley as we returned from two voyages to the Mediterranean; where's the complaint? Any maritime officer would have bragged that there just was no better job than voyages on a "Stick Ship" freighter to the Mediterranean. Splendid sunshine warmed our every day, making for unique adventures as we found free time in tourist havens such as Lisbon and Venice or adventures behind the iron curtain in the Yugoslavian cities of Split and Rijeka on the Dalmatian Coast. Then there were the port cities of Italy: Genoa, Livorno, Naples, Catania, Taranto, Trieste and Venice, magical places where the Italians picked your pockets on the street but served the most special of dishes with a smile in waterfront bistros. After several days in Barcelona came the beautiful ports found along the Costa del Sol and Costa Bravos, followed by a trip through Gibraltar for days in the mystical Moorish city of Cádiz. We then ventured up the Rio Guadalquivir to Seville for Flamenco, bullfights, and the most delicious port made by caring monks. Days later found us tied up in Portimão or Lagos, tiny fishing ports on the southern coast of Portugal where we ate fresh anchovies and drank beer with the fishermen on the wharf. There were the two final stops, one in Lisbon to load cork (to make wine bottle stoppers) and the last in the Basque coastal cities of northern Spain like Bilbao. The crossing of the Atlantic to home usually sent us to Boston where we began the cycle all over again. Long days of cargo operations followed by nightly ship moves to a new port, although strenuous, nevertheless allowed enough freedom to enjoy overtime-fattened paychecks as we found time to drink, eat, shop, and fall in love alongside hidden fountains. Just what could be wrong?

Instead of going to Boston, this voyage sent us directly home to New York. Arrival day found my perky, blonde girlfriend waiting expectedly at the end of the dock as we berthed. Money made the year before in Vietnam had incented me to trade up my personal vehicle, now making her the mistress to a candy-apple red '66 Corvette. She and the car waited patiently, both engines purring. Joani had been meeting me at the end of distant travels like this now for almost three years, the holding of a candle for a distant beau becoming longer and more tedious. Our bond continued strong, but any half-wit could see the lemmings of a marriage proposal queuing up at the cliff's edge. My shore-side living arrangement continued to be a large house in a pleasant old German neighborhood in Queens, shared with academy grad roommates. The one roommate, Graham Hall, who had jumped ship for good, enjoyed having the four-bedroom house to himself as the rest of us floated to points unknown, that is, as long as our monthly rent checks arrived in the mail. The landlady, a German Frau in a German neighborhood of Flushing, looked after her boys by cutting deals on the rent in exchange for sexual favors (I was always occupied on those days, thank you Graham), making my share of the rent $37.50 a month. It seemed that our lives soared. Again, what was the complaint?

In spite of all of the above, it still felt like my life had gotten into a rut; I needed a change. Arriving back from our scenic Mediterranean voyage, my senses were assaulted as the ship maneuvered into its homeport dock in the bleak city of Hoboken, New Jersey. Slipping out of the Hudson River into a Hoboken dock, with the skyline of midtown Manhattan framing our stern, the *SS Exporter* was invaded by gangs of longshoremen who began discharging all of the cargo we had loaded throughout the Mediterranean voyage for transshipment to other ports along the eastern seaboard. Unloading everything in one place was unusual, as our normal routine would have sent us next to these same ports, where we would have dropped inbound trade to them, back loading cargo for Europe. But this time was different. We were now due for an annual shipyard maintenance cycle in Baltimore, and shipping laws required that the ship be empty of all cargo for that shipyard period.

The ship was going to be in the shipyard for almost two weeks, requiring the crew to be paid off, sent home, and told to be back to join the ship once the yard completed maintenance. Enjoying the thought of some quiet days off, I had called my parents, asking if I could spend our shipyard downtime with them at their apartment in Alexandria, Virginia, and would they be kind enough to pick me up in Baltimore. It was now late October of 1966; scheduling some down time away from ship schedulers and partying roommates seemed just the ticket to re-focus.

The *SS Exporter* sailed out of New York Harbor, her bowels empty, on the evening of November 2nd, for a leisurely transit down the New Jersey coastline, past Cape May, up the Delaware River, and into the Chesapeake and Delaware Canal, where on my watch, in the wee hours of the morning, we made transit into the Chesapeake Bay. By breakfast we were tied up at the Key Highway shipyard outside Baltimore awaiting our turn to slide into a floating dry dock. While eating breakfast, a serious conversation between the relief captain and our regular chief mate took place on the other side of the salon, the subject of which was to soon involve me. As I was to learn, they were discussing four pallets of cargo that had failed to be discharged in New Jersey, remaining stowed in a corner of the upper tween deck of number 4 hold, where it remained unnoticed until just this morning. Four pallets of cargo would not normally compel such deep discussion, but these four pallets just happened to contain cases of a popular alcoholic beverage.

The Faithful Sextant

Our next to last stop leaving Europe had been in the port of Lisbon, Portugal, where we had loaded hundreds of tons of a Portuguese sparkling Rosé wine. It turned out that the problem cargo sitting down in cargo hold number four was none other than one hundred cases of Lancers Rosé. Maritime law required our cargo holds to be empty.

The mid-1960s found large numbers of post-World War II American consumers just acquiring the joys of drinking wine. The sweet bubbly flavor of the Portuguese Rosé such as produced by two vintners, named Mateus and Lancers, nicely fit these novice taste buds, leaving a light, almost champagne taste that nevertheless gave a pleasant buzz. They had become huge sellers and were very popular, especially with the young ladies. To help market these wines, the manufacturers had designed nontraditional bottles, the kind which, once empty, were just too nice to throw away. These empty bottles were destined to sit in rows atop kitchen cabinets all over America, collecting dust until the fad faded. The Lancers bottle was a light tan pottery crock; it was everyone's favorite.

The chief mate had immediately called back to the tally clerks in New Jersey to ask them about this non-discharged cargo when he was informed that all wine unladen in Hoboken had exactly matched the required shipment as listed on the manifest. This cargo was overage, purposely loaded back in Lisbon to cover breakage and theft; the clerks in New Jersey wanted no part of it. "It's your problem, mate, just make it disappear," they told him. He replied, "Wouldn't you know it. The one time you want those damn thieving longshoremen to pilfer the booze, they let you down."

The captain informed the chief mate that the customs fine for having revenue cargo in a ship using special tax rules while in shipyard were steep, so they put their heads together and then called a meeting of the ship's officers. All of us were being discharged from the ship during its shipyard cycle and the captain wanted to know how many of us would have vehicles, and would any of us be interested in hauling away cases of free wine. The reception to this question was immediate and as any fool could guess, greeted by whoops of positive enthusiasm. The response also brought out an immediate streak of greed as two enterprising officers volunteered to rent a truck and take care of the problem in one swoop; whereupon the captain reminded us that this whole venture was illegal and if customs caught us sneaking untaxed cases of wine ashore, or worse yet, selling it once ashore, we could be fined, jailed, and lose our Coast Guard license. At first I was aghast that the captain was allowing, nay, encouraging this illegal behavior, but then as I thought about it, the chance of us getting caught was very remote. The ship and crew had cleared customs in New Jersey; foreign entry ships were never allowed directly into shipyards, and we were way off the beaten track, nowhere near normal customs clearance operations. The captain was savvy enough to understand that the truck idea could only have meant nefarious actions as he laid out ground rules for the disposition of this overage cargo. We would be split up in small units to be carried down the pier after working hours.

I ended up with five free cases of the most popular wine on the market. I called my father again, asking him to bring his car in through the shipyard gate to the head of the dry dock when he came to pick me up the following evening, and, oh by the way, please be sure the trunk was empty.

As soon as shipyard workers knocked off the next day, we began toting ashore one hundred cases of Lancers Rosé. We were breaking Baltimore City laws, we were breaking State of Maryland laws, we were breaking federal customs laws, but in spite of all of this, we were making sure that one law was enforced: The ship would have no cargo in her holds during the shipyard period. Our thinking on the subject: "Sometimes you have to break the law to enforce the law."

Spending over a week with my parents was relaxing: home-cooked meals, clean sheets, reintroduction of table manners; but then, as always, motherly inquisition began to get on my nerves. I needed to be back in Baltimore to sign back on the ship on Friday, November 18th, leaving only a handful of days to look up old friends from high school. Those of us who had gone to college would have by now graduated losing the 2-S student draft deferment, meaning for the men, that unless they had found some other deferment, my rat pack would all be away doing something in the military; that's just the way it was in those days.

However, my friend Charlie "Chas" Strauss and his wife Beth had children; always good for a permanent deferment from the draft. He would be home. I called Chas, telling him that I had a nice gift from Portugal, asking if I could see the girls and swap stories with him and Beth. A warm dinner invitation for Thursday night the 17th of November was received.

Arriving at the apartment of two of my closest friends, I could see that this would be much more than just a post-high school reunion; it would have the feel of the coming attractions short film for what just might become my own life, once I did decide to stop this globe trekking. As he answered the front door, I hefted a case of Lancers into Charlie's outstretched arms, an extravagance never seen among struggling twenty-somethings. Looking at the case of wine suspiciously, Charlie asked, "Ok Mac, where did you steal this?" Seeing no need to burden them with the truth, I told them that we got a deal on Portuguese wine in Lisbon and left it at that.

We wasted no time opening a bottle of the Lancers, followed by the routine consumption of gin and vodka. It had been years since the three of us had sat down together; many stories needed daylight. They had college stories, children stories, tales about mutual friends, and I had yarns about the Academy, life at sea, the trials of Vietnam… it was going to be a long evening.

Having put children to bed, we continued to drink and catch up on what looked to be a long night of "can you top this whopper," when sometime around ten o'clock the phone rang. The news

The Faithful Sextant

coming over those phone lines in the next minutes would change our lives forever.

Charlie answered the phone, and in very short order his face turned white as he listened, saying nothing. Finally, he interjected, "Well yes, ma'am, in fact, Bob is right here tonight. Let me put him on the phone." As he handed the phone to me, I was thinking, who the hell knows that I am in town?

Grabbing the phone, a little irritated at the interruption of a bulked-up sea story, I realized that Frank Packer's mother, Ann, was on the other end of the phone babbling and sobbing. Between sobs she blurted out, "Frank is dead."

Memories of the balance of that evening have forever fled with the blowing leaves of that autumnal evening.

Suffering alcohol-over-indulgent tears and depression, only instinct pushed me down well-worn streets back to my parent's apartment in Alexandria in the wee small hours of the worst evening so far in my young life. I had no idea what had happened to Frank except that there had been an aircraft accident in Florida, an accident that had killed him. There's no way…Frank could never be killed by an airplane…not a pilot of his skill. There was so much to learn, but in the meantime, I had to get back to sea.

The next morning I was up early, heading back to Baltimore to join the ship. Tugs pulled the ship out of the shipyard, where we set a course for the short trip back to New York Harbor. By this time in my career as a ship's officer, I was able to do all my navigation and ship-handling tasks by rote, and it's a damn good thing. I have no memory of making this trip back north. Arriving in Hoboken, Joani was waiting at the terminal where I explained details, as I knew them. We then drove back to Long Island. Dropping her at her home, I turned around and drove back into Queens where I picked up some clothes at my house and then aimed the 427 cubic inch Corvette south to Alexandria. I had told the port captain from Export Lines not to remove me from the active employment list; I had a funeral to attend.

The Faithful Sextant

A quick call to Charlie had informed me that the Air Force planned to bury Frank at Arlington National Cemetery on Monday afternoon, four days after his aircraft accident; there was no time to lose and no horses to spare as I broke multiple speed laws coming down the Jersey Turnpike. Arriving at my parent's apartment on Sunday afternoon, I began calling high school friends, most of whom had no idea that our class president had just become the first member of the class of 1960 to die. Without any idea where my high school steady Carole Pate might be, I called her parents. Carole's parents were shocked and saddened; everyone knew Frank.

Carole, they told me, had just gone through a divorce with her first husband, was in town, and would be happy (other than the news) to hear from me. Dialing her number I found my hands shaking. What the hell was causing this? Was it her or was it Frank? Carole answered my call, telling me quickly how glad she was to hear from me as she launched immediately into the story of the horror of her divorce, of how nasty her ex-husband had become, of how she really missed me, of how…

It was clear; she did not know!

I let her go on for a minute, finally stopping her by interrupting with a strongly worded "Carole." Then there was silence.

"Carole, Frank Packer was killed last Thursday in a fighter jet accident," I said after the pause. This was followed by the human emotion anyone expresses when faced with news that is outside any normal boundary of expectation.

Humans do not look at a clock to see what time it is…we look at a clock to see how far off the real time is from what we expect to see. The shock effect of terrible news, sort of like looking at a clock, is proportional to the width of the gap between what we expected to happen compared to reality of what actually did happen. Youth can never be ready to accept the death of peers; preparation is never available. Parents do not prepare us, society does not prepare us; death isn't covered in shop class or home economics.

Carole began crying. I began crying; this was no conversation. The vilest of all human emotion lies in the anguish found in the realization that the loss of a loved one is nothing more than the selfish, self-serving emotion of wallowing in self-pity. The loss of this person will make my life worse than when he was there to make it better.

Soon enough we gained some emotional high ground, as she demanded to know what had happened, leaving me to admit to a total lack of detail. All that I knew, I told her, was that Frank was to be buried tomorrow afternoon at two o'clock in Section 37 of Arlington National Cemetery. I would be there. She quickly asked if she could escort me, telling me that this was going to be harder than I might imagine and that she would be strong support. I agreed.

Monday, November 21st of 1966 turned out to be a slate-colored fall day in our nation's capital, just the kind of weather to attune all maudlin senses to the coming winter, to the death of youth, to the farewell of innocence, to society's most desolate and formal of all ceremonies, to the finality of love, to the coming of an empty space never to be filled.

Monday would bring another visit to the environs of the Tomb of the Unknown Soldier where the guards perform their never-ending twenty-one steps, twenty-one seconds/turn, twenty-one steps, twenty-one seconds/turn.... Frank and I had been to the Tomb. We had met the guards as Boy Scouts. They had showed us how to spit shine a shoe, how to caddy cloth a belt buckle, how to crease a uniform, how to respect the fallen; but they never told us what took place over the hill in Section 37. Monday would become the day for that experience.

Arlington is good at ceremonies; things move with well-oiled precision. Coming into the cemetery from a back road like the local I was, gave no special advantage as parking was regimented, just like everything else. Carole and I walked some distance following what became a large crowd of mourners. In spite of most surely knowing every person in the gathering crowd of mourners—Frank's family had been my family, Frank's friends had been my friends—the atmosphere was silent seclusion. I have no memory of speaking to anyone other than the lady in black who tightly gripped my arm.

Standing quietly next to a tree on a slope above the newly dug entombment, my attention became focused on the horse-drawn caisson carrying a flag-draped casket that now moved up the street. No one spoke, no birds chirped, only the clack of shod horses on the pavement and the rustic wheels of the gun carriage broke the silence. The caisson halted just below the crowd of mourners. Air Force servicemen in full dress uniform, who had trailed the caisson, then moved forward, removing the casket and with military precision, transferred it over to a stand at the burial site.

Now a chill wind began to rustle autumn leaves, the only other sound being that of clicking formal military heels and the rumble of the caisson moving off up the hill unburdened of its tragic cargo. Clouds had begun to darken the late fall afternoon with its solemn surroundings: the flag-draped coffin, the line of chairs covered in dark green velvet awaiting the close family members, the row of airmen standing at attention in perfect order near the casket. All I could do was stare straight ahead. I do not remember blinking.

Dignitaries circulated; family members found the velvet chairs; an ecclesiastical representative offered soothing words; rituals were carried forward.... I saw all of it but heard none of it; I was still staring at the flag on the coffin. All was quiet.

Next a first sergeant barked sharp a command.

Then a volley of rifle fire, immediately repeated twice more.

Then Taps.

Now I was back in focus. Several Air Force officers in dress uniform approached the casket, removed the flag, and folded it in a very exact manner, handing the precisely tucked-in triangle to an Air Force officer. This officer and arbiter of finality clutched the triangular flag, turned in practiced formality, strode in front of the family, and performed a sharp left turn in front of Toni: Frank's wife of barely two years. He bent over on one knee, speaking the well-rehearsed "Grateful Nation" speech, handing the flag to Toni.

I heard every word…I felt every emotion…I was fighting back the tears, and then I looked at Frank's mother and all was lost. She was way past emotional overload. I could see her anguish all the way up on the hill from where I stood. "It's mine. That flag belongs to me. I raised him, I am his mother, I am…I am…I am…it should be mine. Who is this woman? I am his mother. He is my son…he is my life…I get nothing?" All her unspoken emotion was there, exposed out in the open for everyone to see. Had Frank's mother ripped that flag from Toni's embrace, I doubt that I would have shown any trace of surprise. I would simply have nodded in understanding.

Then it was over.

Carole looked up at me. There were no tears, there was just numb. No one moved. No one spoke. No grief stricken words…just numb. Carole nudged me towards the sidewalk, a helpful jolt as my soul remained locked in place. It might have remained so for hours.

We said nothing as we wound our way through a maze of pathways between the regimented row upon row of perfectly aligned stelae, silent plinths marking the final remains of the guardians of our nation's heritage. I was trying to memorize the exact position of Frank's burial, thinking I would be back to say my own goodbye, but it all looked so much the same. Lost, we were zigzagging uphill through perfectly placed white markers, swimming in a sea of manicured green grass, bringing up many memories, none of which dealt with finding my car. Fortunately, Carole soon remembered where we had parked. Now, finally we could flee the Custis/Lee Farm, the Nation's home to military grieving: Arlington National Cemetery.

The dusk of a late fall day had arrived early as we merged into rush hour traffic, when suddenly a city bus full of commuters barged ahead, cutting me off, smashing into the right front fender of the Corvette. Quickly memorizing the number of the bus, I watched as it sped away into evening traffic, my mind hardly registering the severely cracked fiberglass fender of the beautiful, candy-apple red sports car.

After I dropped Carole at her place, I wandered back to my parent's apartment. My mom and dad had just arrived home from the Arlington ceremony. They had been very close to the Packer family, and we spent some time speaking to the events of the day; I had no memory of seeing my own mother and father at the graveside ceremony. There was very little about peripheral details I remember from that day.

Several weeks later, back in New York, before I could reach a settlement with the bus company about my smashed fender, some of New York's finest wise guys stole my Corvette out of a parking lot at the subway station in Queens, never to be seen by me again. My "rule of threes" was in full force: When it starts going bad, the shit just keeps piling on, needing three personal calamities before the ship of life rights itself to an even keel. Losing my car was now number two. And funny thing, once the "threes" are in effect, there is no avoiding peeking over the shoulder looking for the final blow. Man—the superstitious animal.

Back in New York City it began. Self-imposed or external, the pressure mounted. The question of my settling down, the question of finding a job, the question of marriage, the question of how to forget Frank. Taking a slice out of the money pie saved from shipping out, I went alone down to the diamond district of Manhattan and selected a dazzling two-carat unmounted stone to be placed an hour later in a Tiffany setting. This stunning ring had the desired effect of later finding an excited, faithful, young blond girl yell yes, yes, yes as she assented to become engaged. We set no date, perhaps only delaying the decision about becoming man and wife. Continuing to make good money, I began serving on Export Lines ships as a night mate: a relief officer giving the regular officers a chance to spend some time at home while the ship loaded and unloaded in port, a puffed up, albeit well-paid, night watchman. Regardless of high pay or boring security, the time had come to turn the pages for a new chapter in my life. Returning to the even higher-pay, over-the-top-excitement voyages to Vietnam rang up hollow as a plan for career enrichment.

The drive to change direction led to some interesting job interviews, all of which resulted in offers—all of which meant living in New York City. One was a job selling cellophane for Dow Chemical. (Who knew there were fifty-two kinds of cellophane?) Another was with a small naval architecture firm with a direct line to becoming a partner in the company. In spite of pay and promotion incentives, there had to be a more interesting future than a vision of riding the corporate train while riding the commuter railroad between suburban lawns and Manhattan granite walls.

At the top of the list of plans for a new career was to follow in my father's flying footsteps: becoming an airline pilot, leading me to begin lessons in a Piper J-3 out on Long Island. These sessions were expensive and left me with no clear path to the future. Every way I sliced this plan, it made sense to move back to Alexandria where flying lessons were cheaper. There, I would find the added benefit of a father nearby as an instructor, a man who had spent a lifetime teaching rookies to fly, a man with access to free multi-engine, government-owned aircraft

The decision to begin flight training back on my home turf carried huge risk to marriage plans. A little voice told me *she will never leave Long Island.* We talked about it…she cried…I cried, but we went ahead with the plan, a sparkling two-carat hostage serving as an insurance policy that I would return.

Thus it was that the big page in the book of the life of Bob was turned over. I packed everything in my apartment and moved back to Alexandria. My worldly belongings fit nicely into a rental car, (oh, for those old days) allowing me to take up residence in the second bedroom of my parents' apartment, even knowing this would be a short stay as my father had just been promoted again. This promotion was to soon take them to Brussels, Belgium where he would be attached to the US Embassy, serving as the FAA liaison to foreign airlines needing to understand government rules to land in this country. Not wanting to hinder my parents as they began plans to move abroad, I rented a small efficiency in the same building and settled into my new life. My father gave me the keys to his classic MG-A, thus solving my lack-of-wheels predicament, while relieving him from shipping this car to Europe. On February 24th of 1967 I applied for and was issued a Federal Aviation Agency Student Pilot License, signed by my own father as the FAA executive.

Two months later, a car loaded with drunk men whizzed though a stop sign in Alexandria, removing the front end of the little blue MG-A, again showing that superstitious belief in *bad threes in a row* easily extends to larger numbers. The next week, again dipping into the pie of savings, I trooped into the Chevy dealer and bought a shiny, new, gun-metal-blue Corvette off the showroom floor. It was time to change my luck, though a more pragmatic person might have reminded me that I was damn lucky that the drunks had narrowly missed broadsiding me in that flimsy little top-down MG.

Meanwhile, I began a new routine of building skill and experience in a cockpit. Twice a day and some evenings found me over the skies of Maryland and Virginia, filing flight plans, learning to understand curt controllers, trying to remember that pulling up on the lever put the flaps down, a counter intuitive action, one holding possible dire results if done backwards. I had contracted with a flying school located at a small airfield near Friendly, Maryland, a short twenty-minute commute from my apartment, to get me through all of the required licenses. I would be flying in a Cessna 150, a tough as nails, two-place aircraft featuring up-to-date instruments and radios—a perfect platform for what I needed to learn. It was clear to me that I needed many new skills, and yet some pilot skills such as navigation and weather should be a lay-down, considering previous experience at sea.

The flight school had assigned a female instructor, who was perhaps ten years my senior, not exactly what I had in mind as she too was working through the hours needed for the licenses to become an airline pilot, making her seem more like competition than a mentor. Even my father refused to fly with me until I had been certified for cross-country solo flight. Disassembling the reasons for my urge to fly came to me only years later when it struck me that it may have had some deep-seated component—if Frank can't become a pilot, then I will.

Arriving back at my apartment one evening after a full day of pilot training, I could hear my phone ringing even before I came through the door. Picking up the receiver, I found my mother, who was only days away from moving to Europe, on the phone. She was crying. *Now what in the hell*, I was thinking.

"Bob" she wept, "I really do not want to be the bearer of bad news, especially considering what you have just been through, but there is no other way…Frank's mother, Ann Packer, died this morning."

This appalling news was a kick in the stomach every bit as distressing as the phone call just weeks earlier from this same lady telling me her son Frank was dead. How could this be? Mrs. Packer had been beyond distraught at Frank's funeral, but she looked healthy; she was only fifty-two years old. I hurried upstairs to my parents apartment, where my mother shared details of the evening before, a story beyond bizarre.

The very previous evening my parents had invited Frank's parents over to their apartment for dinner, a nice thoughtful way to tell them how sorry they were about Frank, how much they were thinking of them, and to say goodbye before they headed to Europe for several years. These two couples had, after all, been next-door neighbors as their respective six kids grew up. They had shared fourteen years of pet dogs, four pet burros, pet alligators, a coop full of chickens, trips to the hospital, and even a couple of summer vacations on the shore of the Chesapeake Bay. These two families had indeed been through a large part of what is the heart of a human's family life, the time when you bring up your children.

Fine food, old friends, many stories to relive, one overarching subject just lying in front of everyone that evening, like the extra serving of pudding you shouldn't have eaten: How could this have happened to Frank? As a lifelong pilot, my father wanted to know how it happened, but his empathy for the feelings of the other family would have prevented technical questions. Alcoholic drinks had proven emotionally problematic for both women. I had learned that later, as the evening wore on, Frank's mother and my mother passed the emotional tipping point, leading Frank's father to call it a night about ten o'clock.

Later that evening, once the Packers had arrived home, sometime in the small hours of the next morning, Mrs. Packer began having stomach distress, followed by a trip to the hospital in an ambulance. She died later that morning of a poorly diagnosed disorder of the stomach.

Had stress and poor health triggered some unknown embolism? Had she drank too much at dinner and finally just given up to the tragedy of losing Frank? Had she literally died of a broken heart…or was it something else? My mother felt terrible, over and over reliving the dinner party, trying to find a cause for the untimely tragic event.

My mother called two days later to tell me that a memorial service had been scheduled for Wednesday, March 29th at the Mount Vernon Methodist Church, the very church in which both of our families had worshiped; the church that lists both families as founders and charter members; the church in which my sister had been married the previous June; the church where Frank and I had been baptized.

I did not attend.

Surrounded by this unexpected death left me feeling like one of the young Marines in a landing craft on the beach at Tarawa, where the normal progression of death following eighty years of life was repealed. As I thought about Frank and his mother, it seemed that usual laws of the universe were being broken right and left, leaving no wiggle room to bring it all into life's regimen. I was then in a place of grieving, a place I had never before visited. On some level I understood that someone close to me could die, leaving me to intuit that such an unexpected tragedy would bring shock, but there was no way to prepare for the one-two punch coming from the loss of Frank followed by my other mother—his mother!

This army of grief supported by mysterious circumstances of the death of my childhood friend and his mother continued to haunt my thoughts daily as I forged ahead with my new life direction. I had expected that getting through his funeral would be a serious test, but had no idea that this supposed healing balm would heal nothing.

Now, for sure, my "rule of three calamities" was complete; there would be no further need to peek over my shoulder. Or so I thought!

One week later, in a spring rainstorm, I soloed in the Cessna 150. Two weeks later while on a solo cross-country flight to a small airport near Fredericksburg, Virginia, I just barely escaped a head-on collision in my little Cessna 150, when I landed on what I believed to be an active runway at the same time that a larger twin-engine Beech was landing on the same runway from the opposite direction. I saw him first and swerved off into the grass with no damage or injuries, other than to my ego once I learned that he was right and I was wrong. I shook off the whole thing, knowing that with learning would come mistakes, also reminding myself that the "rule of three calamities" has on occasion run farther than just three.

Then finally the weather of bad fortune changed; my father had introduced me to the head pilot at American Airlines and he had accepted me into their pilot training program, provided I accomplish my instrument rating and commercial pilot's license within six months. With the Vietnam War eating up military pilots, the airlines were crying for trainees. Concurrently, American offered me a job as an agent at their gates so that I could begin building company seniority while I worked to obtain the needed licenses to start the company-sponsored pilot training.

Playing in the background of this worldview redirection, however, was the unfinished chapter in the book of Frank. There were just so many things I needed to understand about the loss of my friend, my classmate, my alter ego. Thus it was that I began turning over and over the six years since our high school graduation. Somewhere there had to be a key to unlock the how of this tragedy, to unlock the void of never again trekking down a dusty road to an excellent adventure with my childhood friend.

Parting ways in the summer of 1960 to attend federal service academies, we had vowed to stay in touch, and indeed we had written letters exploring the challenge of making it through plebe year. Our hope had been to see each other during summer breaks, even to the extent that I brought my academy roommate, Steve Woycke, down to Alexandria during my second-year summer to stay with Frank's family at their house, borrowing his stored scuba equipment to go diving in the quarries of West Virginia, reliving our great adventure. His mother was like a second mother to me, even though her son's academy schedule prevented his being there with us. In spite of our best efforts, the rigorous schedule thrown at us by our service academies was to doom our ability to fly in formation until we finished up with the regimentation stuff.

While at the Air Force Academy, Frank had dreamed of owning a vintage airplane, leading him and a couple of friends from the academy to scrape together start-up money. This began a search of old barns until they were able to locate a very beat-up old Waco UPF-7 biplane, purchasing it as junk. Now, his days of model airplane building were over; he owned the real thing, even if it did need refurbishing from propeller to rudder. We had joked many times that Frank should have been born into my family, where flying small aircraft was a rite of passage, and indeed, most surely Frank's love of aviation had been fertilized by the man who lived across the street: my father.

Bringing his limping biplane back to the academy, where he talked his way into some unused hangar space, Frank began spending all of his free time searching for spare parts and putting this classic aircraft back in working order. By the beginning of the summer break in 1963, between junior and senior year, the plane was flying like a champ. He and his partner decided to fly the Waco back to the East Coast during the summer break.

Before he departed Colorado, Frank had written asking if I could make it down to Alexandria for some serious screw-off time in the new biplane. Once again, our rigorous academic schedules showed no matching weeks off. (The United States Air Force Academy used semesters, we were on a quarterly program.) Nevertheless, I optimistically told him that some chance floated for my early release. Additionally, I spread whipped cream on top when I upped the optimistic ante by reminding him that I now had a sports car at my disposal since, as a result of a promotion in the FAA, my parents were planning to move from Minneapolis to New York that summer, so I would have my father's A model British MG at my disposal. Several more letters and my summer began shaping up to be rock star quality.

As June approached, it all began to fall apart. Our academic year and the class of 1963 graduation slipped to the end of July, forcing me to call Frank's parents, asking them to pass on the bad news, as by now Frank and his buddy were well into their cross-country expedition.

Not being able to get together that summer, I heard after the fact about Frank's legendary escapade.

Arriving on the East Coast, Frank's academy buddy departed to see friends and family, leaving Frank to begin looking for a flying partner among old friends from Alexandria. Soon he was able to connect with a member of our high school rat pack, Dee, who himself had been flying for several years and was waiting for an opening at Braniff Airlines. The two old friends hooked up with an agenda to find some spare parts to retrofit the fuel metering system on the

Waco, soon locating an airport up in Pennsylvania where they got a promise of help. So with a six-pack under the seat and a smile on their faces, the boys turned over the prop, brought the Waco to life, and set a course north in the vintage biplane.

The trip to Pennsylvania looked like it might be successful. A guy running an aircraft maintenance facility seemed to understand the problem and working with care around the aviation fuel system, thought he had licked the fuel starvation problem. The two boys refilled the fuel tank on the Waco, turning south for the trip home.

They had just crossed the Potomac River, coming over the city of Arlington, when something failed in the just-repaired fuel line. Without fuel, the engine quickly died, turning the Waco into a two-winged glider.

Frank yelled at Dee, "Take the stick, I'm going under and see if I can fix this. Oh yeah, you might be looking for a place for us to land!" Dee later related that he was crapping in his pants…what the hell was Frank doing; they were only at 3000 feet and while the Waco had a gentle glide path, there was almost no time before…well, before there was no time. Dee calmed himself down, remembering, that as a pilot, his first duty was to find an emergency landing spot. In the distance he spotted a golf course that later turned out to be the Washington Golf and Country Club. Dee decided right then would be a good time to bank right and line up one of the straight fairways in the event that a fix for the fuel line was not found.

Dee could hear Frank banging on the fuel line with a wrench just before Frank yelled up to Dee to turn on the ignition in hopes of diving the aircraft and "windmilling" the prop to get the engine started. Dee yelled back, "Frank, get back up here, we are too low to dive. I have us lined up for a golf course, but it's your shot."

Jumping back up from deep in the tubular fuselage, Frank took the stick, observing right away that while the plane was lined up nicely on a golf course fairway, they were too high to make a landing on the chosen fairway without a steep dive; a maneuver leaving them with way too much airspeed for a safe unpaved, short field landing.

Dipping into his pilot skills, Frank began to skid the biplane by slamming the rudder over while banking in the opposite direction; a kind of stall maneuver used by glider pilots to drop altitude without picking up much forward airspeed. Falling out of the sky, where one wing is dipped steeply towards earth as the aircraft skids sideways, requires skill and more than a little balls as this maneuver can suddenly snap into a stall skid, where the nose of the aircraft falls quickly or the aircraft flips, a situation certain to doom the biplane.

Frank was able to erase just enough altitude before leveling the biplane with a straight shot and a reasonable glide path down to the golf course fairway. Frank's execution of the slip maneuver would have earned him an A+ from an Academy glider instructor, however, abruptly a new problem appeared: a foursome of golfers had just teed off on this hole and were now walking down the fairway. These golfers had no idea what was happening about 200 yards behind them and about 100 feet over their heads as a gliding aircraft makes only a slight whisper of noise. There was no way for the boys to warn the golfers. Ordering Dee to yell "Hey, watch out" would be as useless as yelling "Fore!" Frank gave a sharp pull up on the stick to be sure he cleared the golfers and then dove for the ground.

Frank's landing was spot-on in the middle of the fairway, but he had used up almost half of its length by making sure he missed the golfers. At this point the boys were hurtling down the fairway at an alarming rate of speed, headed towards the center of the green right where the flagstick would be located. Both Frank and Dee were literally standing on the brakes.

Waco had designed this tough little biplane for just such rough landings on unpaved runways. The oversize disc brakes went to work immediately, slowing the wheels to where they could be stopped; a desirable feature for the pilot in distress, a not so desirable feature for the manicured grass found on golf courses..

Fortunately for Frank and Dee, the green on the 7th hole at Washington Golf & Country Club had no front-facing sand trap, as they were never going to get stopped before running up onto and over the immaculately groomed green. The aircraft did finally come to a stop several feet in front of the flagstick, two ugly gashes extending from behind the biplane in parallel across the green and back several hundred yards on down the fairway.

The two boys were quite shaken until they realized that it was all over and they were safe, at which point both of them began to laugh. Frank later told me it was the same kind of laughter we had experienced the night after our high school graduation when we had beat the crap out of each other in a drunken brawl on the grass in front of the Jefferson Memorial.

Meanwhile, the four golfers had by now sprinted to the green, thinking that they may be pulling a pilot out of a terrible aircraft crash. But when they approached the two laughing hyenas, their concern turned quickly into anger, especially by the golfer who had hit his best shot of the day, right up near the green on this par four rated hole, but now found his second shot blocked by a two inch trench and a biplane…a story he would later relish for years until every guy in the club bar had heard it four times, demanding that he never tell it again on pain of having to buy drinks.

What a superb piece of flying. The shiny silver biplane looked as if it had been placed on the green by aliens as a joke to golfers. A fix to the fuel pump was found, leaving the aircraft ready to fly, although the FAA drew the line at letting the boys attempt a takeoff from the golf course. This dilemma required a plea from Frank to his father for the money to have the wings removed and have the aircraft trucked out.. Fortunately, my father was by then in New York, heading flight safety standards for that region of the FAA, otherwise he might have been involved in investigating Frank as the pilot of this ill-fated landing.

Within a short time, the Waco was ready to fly again; the fairway and the green had been repaired, and life went on. Frank and his Air Force buddy then took the repaired aircraft back across the country to Colorado, where they began studies for their last year at the Academy.

Such was the story told me of the adventure I had missed the summer of 1963. In January of 1964, Frank wrote a letter, enclosing a picture of the Waco, with more news. He had come home for Christmas on a commercial airliner, leaving the Waco in Colorado in the care of one of his academy flight instructors, an older officer with over 10,000 hours of flight time. The instructor had taken his biplane out for a joyride and wrecked it. He noted that although the airplane was now a wreck, he and some friends planned to have it rebuilt by summer. Frank was not a skier, so what the hell else was there to do in Colorado Springs in the winter?

Then he had more news...news that requires a little background. The five federal service academies have a little tradition: allowing seniors the privilege of having a car at the Academy, usually about one hundred days before graduation. This has turned into a feeding frenzy with the blood in the water provided by cheap, quick auto loans from the likes of Navy Federal Credit Union and anxious auto salesman making bargain deals on Corvettes, Mustangs, Camaros, GTOs, etc. You get the picture...the inmates have been locked up without cars or girls for four years; in about one hundred days they will have a guaranteed job with a guaranteed income, so turn them loose. This is one of the big events of the year for sales of new muscle cars.

This little over-the-top tradition comes with troubling side effects. The boys, most of whom turned twenty-one during the year, who as mentioned have been locked up without cars or girls, had also been without adult beverages for lo those four years. Now mix high horsepower cars, unused driving skills, and free flowing adult beverages and you have a formula for new red Corvettes plastered around trees, diminishing graduating class sizes while wasting taxpayer dollars training bright young officers for four years only to lose them in auto accidents. But the author digresses...this is a problem for the academies.

Also, (another digression) the reader might note that the author was driving a new candy-apple red Corvette as an upgrade from a Mustang...leading to the thought that it is sort of disingenuous to cast stones at others when he himself drove a chick magnet; to which the author answers, noting the wonderful line from the movie *Terms of Endearment*. This famous line comes in a scene in which actor Jack Nicholson, who plays a retired playboy astronaut, is showing prudish next-door neighbor actress Shirley MacLaine the imposing 'brag-wall' in his family room, highlighting all of his awards and accolades from his years as an astronaut. At that point in the movie, Shirley sarcastically says to him, "Why, I bet you have this 'stuff' on the wall JUST to get young girls in bed." To which, in astonishment, Jack replies, "Are you kidding me, sometimes all this is not enough!"

People who knew him just had to know that Frank would do it differently…and he did. He filled out the application for a loan from the Credit Union, put on his best sales pitch, and convinced them that instead of a shiny new Corvette, he wanted to buy another airplane. They said okay! Frank then went out and bought a used Stearman. He sold the Waco, refurbished the Stearman—removing the crop dusting gear—and flew it home after graduation.

Some thirty years later, while I was attending a dinner sponsored by our Joint Service Academy alumni group, I stood talking to a Boeing executive who was also an Air Force Academy grad. I noted on his nametag that he was from the class of 1964, leading me to ask if he remembered Frank Packer. His eyes lit up and he said, "Of course I remember Frank. He was the pilot icon of our class."

There it was. The guy would rather buy a beat-up but flying Stearman that he could refurbish than buy a Corvette chick magnet. This guy had only one goal; he was going to be the best pilot in this country's Air Force. I already had him pegged to be an astronaut and a general for sure. He now owned two biplanes, and although he had no steady girlfriend, that too was going to change.

His letter from January, again just before we were to graduate, went on to say that he had two months off after graduation before reporting to his first duty station in Alabama and that he planned to fly the Stearman back home. He then went on to say that this year we were for sure going to get in some hell-raising flying.

The stars however, were still not in line. Frank graduated in the first week of June of 1964, and my graduation from the Merchant Marine Academy came some eight weeks later on the 27th of July. Once again there would be no adventures in the sky over Virginia in a biplane.

The summer of 1964 was magical. I had graduated from a fine, though rigorous, federal academy, finally making the dean's list in my last quarter. On my arm was a delightful blonde—a charmer by any standard. The world was my apple. Now was the time to pick its fruit and take a bite. There was no need to rush into the workplace; in my skill-set there were jobs everywhere; heck, I could always go into the Navy as an ensign.

Several days after graduation, Frank called with ground-shaking news. Arriving home in early June from graduation, he had met one of his younger sister's high school classmates; they had dated exclusively and Frank had fallen in love. On August 5th of 1964, in the Washington Post newspaper, Mr. and Mrs. Stephen J. Donchez announced that their daughter, Toni, was betrothed to 2nd Lt. Frank C. Packer, recent graduate of the United States Air Force Academy.

This news from Frank was like the "looking at the clock" simile. The news I heard bore no semblance to what I expected. Aerobatics in a Stearman was what I expected to hear; wedding bells is what I heard. What threw me off so was a line from his letter a mere six months earlier describing his two weeks at home over the Christmas holidays, "…girl-wise, the old place seems kind of deserted…." He had nothing going on in his love life, and now in a short eight weeks, he was getting married…Wow!

Then he told me that they had planned a big engagement party. Could I make it down? I told him, "I will be there."

Toni and Frank had a different kind of engagement party. I had been told that Toni's father was a senior executive at the CIA, requiring that everyone attending the event pass a mild security check. What a damper it put on young adult friends when the party was run by a bunch of mean-looking men dressed in blue suits with dark sunglasses, who were staring with suspicion at every guest.

Stories and exaggerations shared by several of my old high school teammates were the highlight of this gathering, but overall it seemed a somber affair. I met Toni for the first time, and even though we had graduated from the same high school, we had never met. She had arrived at Groveton High the beginning of her senior year, thus never meeting guys who graduated two years earlier. She knew none of the stories and adventures this rat pack had shared, nor do I think she wanted to know. A week later it is doubtful if Toni could have picked me out of a lineup at the local police station, but what she needed to know, what was the only thing that mattered, was that if Frank loved her, then she was our princess.

After the wedding, Frank and Toni headed to Craig AFB, where he began to fly the Air Force way. I headed out to sea as a third officer on a huge troop ship headed to Germany. My voyage across the Atlantic was to cause me to miss their wedding. Later, Frank was to mail to me formal pictures of the more-than-attractive bride and groom.

I spoke to Frank again a year or so later, after he had been assigned to the 319th Fighter-Interceptor Training Squadron based at Homestead AFB in Florida. He told me about becoming a father and about his life in the sky over Florida. It all seemed like a big lark: days spent in maneuvers learning to shoot sleeves towed by training aircraft until they were only flapping rags. He was getting paid to do what he loved and family life was great. He laughed and said, "Bob, it doesn't get better than this."

I headed to Vietnam; he continued boyhood dreams of shooting down enemy fighter jets. Homestead AFB—located just south of Miami—and the "man strapped on rocket," F-104 interceptor were both strategically located as near as possible to Cuba. This country still had reverberations from the fallout of the Cuban Missile Crisis.

The two years following the engagement party found the two of us charging down paths directed by the mission statement from our respective academies: me to move up in the ranks as a ship's officer on voyages spanning the globe, Frank to experience all that could be learned about flying small, fast military aircraft. The loop connecting us then closed with that dreadful phone call from his mother late one evening. Our next and last meeting would be back on our boyhood turf at Arlington.

The first stories about this accident told of the Starfighter flaming out, causing Frank to eject. Somehow a parachute malfunction allowed him to come out of the harness and free fall to his death. For years I went through guess after guess about what had happened, and then a confluence of technology and age cleared the picture. Aging guys began to write stuff down, just like I am doing.

Frank was always a star baseball player; he was born with incredible vision and hand-eye coordination. He was the only guy in our senior class to letter in four sports, serving as our high school football quarterback and the spark plug to the baseball team. At the Air Force, Frank found a position in the outfield, where his ability to throw a ball was described as "an arm like a cannon." One of Frank's good friends on the Falcon baseball team was the catcher, a guy named Al McArtor. Al had also wanted to fly the F-104 Starfighter, and he was in the 319th squadron at Homestead the day Frank was killed. Here paraphrased is what Al said about the accident.

"Returning from a training mission, Frank found his Starfighter flying on 'bingo' fuel. Lining up in the base turn for an approach to the Homestead main runway, his huge General Electric J79 single gigantic engine, starved of fuel, suddenly flamed out."

A Starfighter is not a Stearman. No pilot can glide the Starfighter; its wings are just little seven-foot stubs designed to let it to knife through the sound barrier. Without thrust from the engine, the pilot must eject and he must eject immediately. Frank ejected. Witnesses saw a good parachute opening and the eject looked normal when about twenty-five feet above the ground the parachute riser released, sending Frank to the ground, where he hit tail first. His survival kit had not released, making the landing harder than it should have been.

Crash trucks and medical assistance were on the spot immediately, but Frank's back and neck were broken; he was dead before they could help him.

Are there a limited number of close calls a guy can have in a lifetime? Had Frank finally exceeded that number? Was it poor cockpit management to let the fuel level drop below acceptable levels? Were the German Air Force pilots spot-on nicknaming this aircraft the "witwenmache" (widow maker) after it killed many a fine fighter pilot? Erich Hartmann, the world top fighter ace, who commanded one of post-war Germany's first jet fighter squadrons, was on record as saying the F-104 was not safe and unfit for the German Air Force. Investigative reporters later followed the trail of a $10 million dollar bribe from Lockheed, just enough to change the right German minds about this purchase. Was the Starfighter an unacceptably difficult aircraft to fly, or was it just a bad design from the start?

Space is unavailable in this book, or for that matter in a bookshelf of books, to adequately indict Lockheed and its problem-plagued F-104 Starfighter, but Frank's death while piloting this technological misfit requires a few statistics and anecdotes. However, had our enemies wanted to impair this country's strategic air capabilities, they could have done no better than to have left a fleet of shiny new Starfighters lined up at the ready line of one of our airbases, free of charge.

Weapons platforms used by militaries have one goal: kill or destroy the enemy and his resources without killing your own servicemen. How did the Starfighter fare during the years it served in our active duty Air Force? Records show that not one enemy aircraft was ever recorded as shot down by this interceptor; not one enemy soldier on the ground in Vietnam was a solid confirmed kill as a result of attack action by this aircraft. On the other side of the coin, this platform began killing pilots early and continued killing them at an accelerated rate until the aircraft was retired or sent to foreign allies. Years later, after the early retirement of this aircraft, many of them were mounted on pylons near the main gate of military bases, garnering constant comments about how sexy they look; finally a good mission.

The last day Frank flew, his training flight would last only about thirty- to forty-five minutes before he ran out of fuel, depending on how he was flying. It was noted that he returned in "bingo" fuel (landing on fumes). This situation was neither unusual nor thought to be dangerous, as the landing characteristics of this "almost wingless" aircraft rewarded a light aircraft—that is with little fuel and no ammunition. A heavy aircraft landing meant that landing speeds had to be kept above 200 miles per hour to avoid a deadly stall. In simplistic terms, the lighter the aircraft, the less chance of a deadly stall.

Frank had the aircraft light for a smooth, lower-speed, no-stall landing. It just turned out to be too light; it ran low enough on fuel to flame out, where upon it became a sleek, pointy rock. Safely flying this sled was an awful lot to ask of a young man, even one as skilled as Frank.

As I finish these thoughts I can almost hear some of Frank's fighter jet classmates say, "Lighten up, McEliece, it was the parachute that killed Frank, not the Starfighter," and it's true, I am looking for somebody or something to blame for this untimely, uncalled-for death. Nevertheless, my intensive study of this event would seem to validate my criticism of Lockheed.

Everything had been about speed. As the fighting/flying platform evolved, each step-up in speed seemed to bring a corresponding benefit in success of mission while avoiding the danger of being shot down by the enemy. The Starfighter may have looked to be the next logical step in this hunt for speed, but to me, after a great deal of study, it now looks as if engineers took one step too far. Today, some almost fifty years later, it could be argued that two of our military's most successful aircraft, the A-10 Warthog and the Predator Drone—both slow, both ugly, both deadly, both platforms guaranteed to expose fear in the hearts of enemies while performing as mission superstars—are better answers. And about pilot safety: the Warthog has a fine record. The drone pilot, an officer seated in an air-conditioned room somewhere in Nevada, need only worry about lack of exercise and dietary fat.

Frank's death continues a lazy orbit around my consciousness to this very day. It pops out for a stroll around my active thoughts frequently, some days coming for a visit several times, the regularity depending on the happenstance of triggers lighting off some memory. For example, speeding down the highway in my new, more-than-fancy, high-powered luxury car, my iPhone prompting bluetooth to randomly send the Everly Brothers screaming "Bye, Bye Love" though my nine-speaker sound system, brings Frank and me to life, remembering warm days whistling down a country road, the top down in his 1955 Ford Fairlane convertible, heading off to some sort of new teenage mayhem.

"Frank," I suddenly say as I begin a conversation in real time with my long lost friend, "can you even begin to imagine the wonders of what has happened to the world of cars and radios in the sixty years you have been gone?" Then I plunge into a truth serum session about Frank.

Remaining a close friend to Frank Packer had its difficult moments. It was hard to be close when he always needed to be first in everything, not just one or two things…everything. And he was always number one. He was always the leader, a position from which he could direct the show such that he would outshine everyone around him.

Frank was not my only friend. There were times when we both needed a break. But at the end of the day, living across the street did insure the inevitability of seeing each other along a shared path. Our experiences became irreplaceable, yet many was the day of over-the-top competition as he proved up to the task of securing a place as tall or taller, as strong or stronger, as brave or braver than the other boys of the pack, that I wished he would just take a damn day off. Frank always excelled, a trait bringing with it the role of alpha male.

Being always at the top of his game must have been tedious for Frank. From my close vantage point, I got to see times when the magic fell short. The day of our infamous "hedgehog scuba diving incident," as told earlier, when he deserted me, his diving partner, as we ran out of air at the bottom, remains a hard-to-excuse lapse. The events of that day probably should have cost me my life. The reader of this memoir may recognize that I think of that day often.

Frank's departure to the Air Force Academy brought with it two big changes. First, and most amazingly, he went into a late-teen growth spurt, putting on several inches of height in just a year; he no longer had to prove up to the tall guys. Secondly, Frank was now an alpha male living in a pack of carefully picked alpha males; he was just one fish in a big Air Force Academy ocean. These two changes adjusted down his ability and desire to demand the lead dog position.

But back in my shiny modern car, as the Everly Brothers wind down their classic song, an old cliché floods my mind. "The one with the most toys at the end, wins." And I think, *Frank, I finally won! I am the lucky one who ended up with the cars and boats and big house and beautiful family and rewarding careers. Finally, I am number one, the dog at the head of the sled team.* At which point a tear rolls down my cheek as clarity returns: It was never really about winning. It was always so much more. We were always traveling down life arcs in our own direction, but I suspect that had we both lived to complete those semicircles; had we grown to maturity with the time to reconnect our semi-circular paths, we would have discovered a track locking them into a circle, connecting two lives well played. We would have been closer than ever.

Time that we did have together was way too brief; nevertheless, it will always be part of the oil on the canvas of the painting of who I am.

❁

Many, many questions linger about the loss of Frank. One thing for certain…the world had lost the kind of fine leader it cannot easily replace. I had lost the best kind of friend a man can have, our high school class of 1960 had lost its president, a wife had become a widow, and two children were now fatherless.

And about Frank's mother, my questions about how a woman this young could die so suddenly have never been answered. She had begun drinking heavily once her children left home, and she had stopped taking care of her health—all contributing factors. Trying to understand her untimely death, coming so soon after her supernova son's death, was so unexpected and so bizarre as to lead me sometimes into dark and unsubstantiated guesses about the truth of its cause.

Frank's father, Dr. Donald MacGregor Packer, continued his cutting-edge work in physics, chemistry, and rocketry. Dr. Packer had been at the top of the chain of physicists working on the Manhattan Project, creating the first atomic bomb and later working at the Naval Research Lab, where he was instrumental in the Vanguard rocket program. He was a man of few words. There is a strong memory of an evening in mid-October of 1957 when Dr. Packer rounded up the four boys, my brother and me along with his sons, Greg and Frank, to come into the pasture next to the chicken coop. Checking his watch carefully, he aimed a pair of binoculars into the dark evening sky, where he found and showed us the passing dim light of Sputnik as it soared over our heads in the heavens.

"There, there is your challenge," was all he had to say as he pointed to the Soviet spacecraft; only he would have had the unpublished coordinates to find this faint speeding light among the stars. I have never met another person who can say in honesty that they viewed the orbiting Sputnik during its short three-month lifespan, but, see it or not, it was to change the life direction in some way for most youngsters of my generation. Dr. Don Packer was to continue his cutting-edge research, quickly becoming re-married to his secretary and later settling into retirement near a golf course in Sarasota, Florida, where he lived to the grand age of 102.

There is no guarantee for anyone of our womb to tomb time. Frank's father lived over four times as long as his superstar son, playing thousands of rounds of golf over his lifetime with a kind of golfing religious fervor, landing many a golf ball on fine greens but never landing a biplane on one! Both Frank and his father were men of great achievements, leaving us to wonder why some are given so much more time to realize those accomplishments.

My own father, a man who lived a healthy prosperous life past the age of ninety-three, had his interest in airplanes diminish in later years to be replaced also by daily rounds on the golf course. Too late, it came to me that reacquainting these two accomplished men on the golf course would have produced interesting observations.

Frank's death brought with it a loss of innocence, a loss of youth, a loss of leadership to my high school rat pack, and a loss of a key member of our Bengal Seven group. Moving on with the journey to maturity, all of us assumed that this was a one-off event, a not to be repeated anomaly surely to fade in memory, an event not-to-be-repeated until that time of life beyond imagination: old age. We were oh so wrong.

Cpt. James McEliece

The Vietnam War managed to slam into my life as seen from the deck of the *SS Exhibitor,* yet after that episode, the war in Indochina slid into my everyday background. Frank's death, though it preceded the now heavy Vietnam buildup, had put me on notice that incoming fire was possible; the men of my generation were no longer assumed safe. The mangroves of the Saigon River, the back alleys of Saigon, and the helicopter-darkened sky above South Vietnam had permanently erased any childish thoughts that war was exciting, a new wild experience, anything except a dirty, needless, political morass destined to chew up the elite of a generation of American males, American female nurses, and young South Vietnamese. This thing was taking big bites out of my generation for what even the least imaginative guys could see was just some giant Asian game of Weiqi (Go), where surrounding the enemy tile so often resulted in our own encirclement. Even straight-up young men could see that the loss of face and honor from purposely impregnating and marrying a girl or fleeing to Canada might make a better choice.

Guys like me who had experienced the leading edge of America's Asian experiment in 1965 (some thirteen months following the Gulf of Tonkin incident) assumed it would get worse, but I am not sure anyone thought it would reach the level of intensity that we were seeing in 1968. The guys who were over there at that time found themselves in a dangerous quagmire unlike any expectations, much more serious than I had ever seen in '65.

Oh, my life in the August heat of 1968 in Alexandria felt intense, working a ground support job at American Airlines (AA) and pushing though flight training to get the licenses needed to enter American's flight school. But even I could see that the guys I was meeting on the flight line, having fulfilled their draft commitment and 365 days in 'Nam, had a different look in their eye than I saw in '65.

Stepping into my small apartment, having completed a full day of working at AA and pushing through a couple of hours in a ground flight simulator, my over-occupied mind was suddenly diverted at the sight of a Western Union Telegram lying on the floor of my apartment. Has this war in Vietnam come back to visit again?

"What if" thoughts about this telegram began to race around like fruit flies over a rotting banana. My parents were in Brussels, but if something had happened to one of them, surely a staff member from the Embassy, where my father held a position, would have telephoned their family. My sister with her baby daughter had lived in Brussels with my parents for several months while her husband, Cpt. Peter Clay, served with the Marine Corps in Vietnam. She had returned to live north of Baltimore with her husband's family, awaiting his return from the war. Had something happened to her or her husband in the Marines, someone would have called.

My mind was beating around the bush, purposely ignoring the yellow envelope, purposely ignoring the obvious because it did not want to inspect the obvious. No force had been enlisted to muster the will to walk over and open that damned yellow envelope. It did not want to deal with the fact that Jim, my only brother, a 1965 graduate of West Point, was on his second tour in Vietnam, serving as a company commander to a mounted Cavalry (CAV) unit driving Armored Personnel Carriers (APCs) around in some of the worst fighting in the nasty Iron Triangle area north of Saigon. The choices had narrowed to no choice.

No other rational choice existed for a coward's escape; this Red Cross Telegram had to be about Jim.

Have a drink; maybe that will give courage. So I had a martini… then four. The trip from the living room of my efficiency apartment to the refrigerator for ice took me by the dining table. I stared; the envelope did not move.

Two servicemen coming to the front door had largely replaced World War II-era delivery of the deadly telegram informing the family that a loved one was dead or missing. This would become a familiar event within another two and a half months when my friend Karen Powell received her very personal two-man visit.

But that meant nothing to me. I was only an older brother. Then again, maybe brothers only rated a telegram informing them of their loss.

This game went on for several hours until I was quite soused, whereupon I stormed over to the table, heart pounding, and ripped open the envelope. The little piece of yellow paper with child-like, pasted-on print, a glued together little puzzle message torn right off the Western Union teletype, looking for all the world like a ransom demand sent from the Unabomber, screamed at me that one Captain James H. McEliece Jr., United States Army, had been wounded by enemy fire in Vietnam. He was hospitalized.

He's alive!

That's all that came in focus for some time.

The message was very short, only telling me that Jim had been hospitalized. It sounded good. Later I was to learn that celebration time was far into the future. There was good news: Care for wounded in Vietnam was far better than it had been in the Civil War, which was good news. But there was bad news: Germs and bacteria in the jungle battlefields of Vietnam sometimes bested even the most modern of antibiotics.

Jim, it turns out, had been treated in a field hospital in 'Nam and then flown out to a hospital in Japan, the renowned Zama. Years later a book written by a Maj. Ronald Glasser, MD titled "365 Days" became one of the most stark and striking books written about Vietnam. Dr. Glasser retells seventeen stories related to him by wounded GIs who passed through his hospital at Zama. My brother was to arrive and depart Zama Hospital two weeks before Dr. Glasser arrived for duty, otherwise his story might have been one in the book. At one point the group of Army hospitals in Japan were handling six to eight thousand wounded boys from Vietnam a month.

Once Jim was deemed fit to travel home, the Army elected to fly him back to his closest point of home address in the States; they chose Andrews AFB outside Washington, DC. Why the Army selected Andrews AFB remains a mystery.

In early September, I had been invited to be a dinner guest with my sister and her mother-in-law in Maryland. We were both unaware that our brother Jim was being transported back to the States on a military hospital flight at that very time.

Arriving back at my apartment in Alexandria about nine o'clock after dinner, the phone began ringing minutes after I stepped through the door. It was my sister, with whom I had just enjoyed dinner, telling me that she had just received a phone call from Jim. He was in town; he had called from a ward at nearby Andrews AFB.

"We have to go see him tonight," she demanded. I told her that I would bring an ice bucket and a bottle of Scotch and would meet her there.

With military base stickers on both our cars, we drove directly through the front gate at Andrews, directly over to the hospital. Ginny had brought her sister-in-law, Patti Clay, along with a neighbor friend and some plastic glasses; we were set to have a party.

By now it was at least eleven, well past visiting hours, a triviality to our determination. Finding Jim wide awake in an upper floor room of a somewhat rustic WWII hospital ward, we pounced on him, breaking out Scotch on the rocks for all. Our welcoming committee was just getting started on our third drink, when suddenly the military equivalent of Nurse Ratched walked into the room, a stern look twisting her face and not a wrinkle showing on her well-starched, white uniform. Being well-indoctrinated military officers, my brother and I quickly noted her collar devices to check for rank, smiling upon realizing that we both outranked her.

We immediately introduced ourselves to the nurse as Army Captain McEliece and Navy Lieutenant McEliece, fine upstanding officers just slightly senior to the nurse.

"Nice to meet the two of you," she scowled. "Now just what the hell do you think you are doing in my ward at midnight? And I certainly hope that is not an alcoholic beverage in those glasses," she added.

Quickly gulping down the remaining Scotch in my glass as I slid the ice bucket under the bed with my foot, I began to tell her the dire circumstances of my brother's near-death experience and how he had just come back in from Vietnam.

"I know where he came from, and I am aware of his wounds, but that doesn't answer the question," she spit back. "What are you people doing in here breaking five or six of our hospital rules?"

People, I am thinking. *We are not just some people, we are military officers; in fact, we are military officers senior to you Nurse Ratched.* Then I made my first big mistake, I tried to pull rank on her!

She ignored me as if I was one of those incessant beeping hospital alarms as she began citing hospital rules as well as some obscure Uniform Code of Military Justice rules. After a pause, and in her best voice of authority, she commanded, "Will it be necessary to get some MPs up here on the double?"

It was then that I learned a never-to-be-forgotten tactical lesson: On duty military nurses carry the rank of general; doctors have the rank of God.

We said a hasty and heartfelt goodbye to Jim, taking off down the stairs with the ice bucket and the half-empty bottle of Scotch in its brown paper bag. Once in the parking lot we were laughing and hugging as the four of us finished off the bottle of Johnny Walker Red.

Jim was to recover fully from his wounds, never, however, recovering a pear-shaped chunk of his calf muscle, a permanent reminder of the cost of close arms combat. He went on to fill in a thirty-year career in the Army, making it to colonel while earning a PhD.

As for me, I assumed his incident with a combat injury would close out the books on Vietnam…again I was wrong.

Cpt. Joseph Powell

By the fall of 1968 my life in northern Virginia had begun to firm into a stage from which a career would emerge; the chrysalis was forming. I had decided that piloting an aircraft was little different than piloting a ship; just that the vessel moved faster, and the fast trips meant you were not away from home as long. Sure, airline pilots carry more prestige, but the pay was about the same. On the negative side, airline pilots face about thirty-five years of living out of a suitcase in hotel rooms, eternally in jet lag—occupational hazards not suffered by maritime officers. These important considerations for career planning were not the big game stoppers.

Number two on the decision tree about pilot training involved a physical shortcoming bringing with it an impending end to my flying career. I had developed, and still have to this day, difficulty processing information though my right ear, which shows up most strangely and strongly when using headphones. I can hear all the discrete decibels of sound, I just cannot make sense out of the words coming into that ear.

This little physical idiosyncrasy jumped up to bite me hard one day on a cross-country solo flight. As I sat alone behind the stick of my Cessna 150 at the end of the runway at Baltimore International Airport, a snarly air traffic controller had needed to repeat takeoff clearance instructions to me four times before I understood them.

Simply guessing at air traffic control (ATC) instructions that you did not clearly understand is a sure formula for disaster. You must understand and repeat the instruction back to the controller. As I remember it, the ATC guy that morning hinted that student pilot of Cessna N7368Y (that's me) might do better in another career.

But topping the list, even more important than ATC flubs, was the worldview of what I wanted out of life.

As a ship's officer, I had performed some truly artistic feats of navigation. These Picassos of navigating skill were artistically expressed on charts as lines of great circle routes, saving hundreds of miles, or as lines showing passages through rocky narrow straits or as sextant star sights in mid-ocean with a seven-star pinwheel: artwork of a true master of his profession.

But there would be no framing or gallery exhibit. The end of each voyage brought crushing repudiation of this artistic aptitude when it became my duty to take a large red eraser and scrub away the pencil lines of every one of these Renoirs. My God it was painful, had no one any respect or appreciation for what had gone into this masterpiece?

Of course not. The only navigator who is remembered is the one who fails to pay due respect to his profession. This is, for example, the third mate who allowed the Exxon Valdez to run up on Bligh Rock, creating a story now forever in maritime dialect. These disaster-prone officers have their charts saved forever in the files of Coast Guard Review Boards and the offices of maritime lawyers.

Airline pilots are no different. Even the best pilot ever born leaves little behind but empty holes in the sky as tracked by flight plans stored in cyberspace. The pilot's Picasso is only as good as the next takeoff, his Renoir: a safe landing. There had to be more creativity and fulfillment than a lifetime of sky holes.

❦

The Faithful Sextant

There was one more moving part to my life that could not be ignored, my fiancée Joani. The ruse of no wedding date, of no living together, of being together only for short, intense romantic trysts featuring a dreaded deadline for her return to New York or mine to Alexandria, was taking its toll. Now without plans for flying or plans for sailing or making firm plans to start a family, the empty holes in my life became filled on a daily basis with more trivial pursuits.

The only meaningful action I had taken was to join the Naval Reserve, where I associated with career-driven officers who all had busy lives and clear goals. It was a good decision; now positive role models once again filled at least one part of my life.

The one segment of my social calendar endlessly empty and always lonely was Sunday evenings. Filling this void found me often calling married friends, groveling for a home-cooked meal and some family time; my own family having fled to the far corners of the earth. So it was with gratitude and anticipation that one particular Saturday I accepted a Sunday dinner invitation from my old friend Charlie Strauss and his wife Beth.

Charlie and Beth had come a long way in two years, moving into a house in the suburbs. In addition to a growing house, their family had now swelled to three girls, Allison, Susan, and Lee. Three more picture-perfect, charming little girls could not be imagined as again I was smacked in the face with the diorama of the rewards of family life that was missing from my shallow, unengaged-engaged but-not-sure-about-the-future existence. Arriving early for dinner, now down to poverty-level gifting with a cheap bottle of wine rather than a case of Lancer's Rosé like two years before, I was, nevertheless, warmly greeted by my two old friends and a tribe of hooting and hollering young girls.

Eight years had passed since our high school graduation, enough time for hard-fought college degrees, decent paying jobs, and a firm trench of suburban family life. Usual routine set in with a round of chilled martinis and a banishing of the children to play in another room, when Charlie walked over and dropped a folded-over copy of the Washington Post in my lap. He then turned and walked back to the kitchen where Beth was preparing dinner.

Mildly irritated that some cracking-good bullshit story of mine was being interrupted, I moved the newspaper out of my lap to a side table and continued on with my story of amazing, single-guy drivel. Charles listened from the kitchen for a few minutes then returned to the family room, stared me down until I shut up, and then said, "Mac, you might want to read that page I had opened in the newspaper!"

Okay, I get it, some big deal from the Washington Post rag.

Grabbing the folded quarter page, I noticed it was the obituary section of the paper, a slice of the news never visited by young guys. My eyes flashed the page, seeing nothing of interest, and just before throwing it on the floor; a name caught my attention…POWELL, JOSEPH LEWIS Jr., Captain USMC.

Here we go again with the clock thing: me expecting some minor trivia, my eyes reading, my eyes sending, my brain rejecting, my eyes sending again, the brain rejecting again, the eyes insisting, then sending the information elsewhere, upstairs for further processing, none of it making sense. The eyes continued to read. The eyes continued to send new information. Single words now leaped headlong off the page at me…South Vietnam…Helicopter…Marine Corps…Shot Down…Pilot…Killed…Twenty-Five Years Old…Alexandria…Mrs Karen Powell…Leaves Behind…Arlington National Cemetery.

Now signals of panic are bouncing around everywhere as the eyes again read the story, adding in all of the little words, connecting those big horrible words, turning the shock words into a story. The story read like a news article yanked from the daily front-page nastiness of the war in Vietnam; what was it doing back here in the obit section? Obituaries are for old people.

I had never seen an obituary for a friend or contemporary; we were too damn young. Frank's death and burial happened so fast that

I am unsure an obituary was ever written; I never saw one. Here I was staring at this death notice surrounded by a war story, trying desperately to make sense of the whole thing.

I looked up at Charlie asking, "Is this some sort of sick joke?"

"No Bob, Joe was shot down and killed over a week ago while flying a Med-Evac Helicopter in Vietnam near Khe Sahn," Charlie said.

The real absurdity of it all—and what I thought at the minute was a taste of irony—was that exactly two years earlier, a dinner invitation from my friends Charlie and Beth had included a phone call to tell us that Frank had died. Was this proof that parallel universes exist? Was I now visiting this other universe where time had been set back, forcing a replay? I did not yet know, but before this evening was to end, the irony of this parallel universe would be strengthened.

Still confused, I saw the obituary said that Joe would be buried at Arlington the next week on Monday November 4th. Again re-reading the obit and seeing that Joe had been killed in Vietnam on October 17th, it all became clear. Unlike Frank's burial where the time from accident to interment was a short four days, the screwed up mess in Vietnam would have taken much longer. Frank had a very clean and "whole" death, it was doubtful there had even been any spilled blood, but it took little imagination to visualize the ugly job of picking Joe's remains from the burned-out cockpit of the CH46 helicopter, placing what could be found into a body bag, all the time while under fire from enemy snipers.

Joe had arrived in Vietnam on May 1st of 1968 and was assigned to HMM-161, MAG-39 of the 1st Marine Air Wing. The big push to hold the position at Khe Sahn in the Quang Tri Province had ended just before Joe arrived in that war zone, but hostilities and our military's desire to shut down the Ho Chi Minh Trail had continued to make this a very hot area. Joe's squadron had inserted at the Phu Bai base in Quang Tri as a new unit, bringing in the new "D" model Sea Knight helicopter with them. A helicopter of many missions, the CH46 was a good machine called on to do recon, insertion, evacuation, and medical evacuation. Joe's operating area had become a major transit point for well-trained North Vietnamese regulars equipped with the newest of Soviet or Chinese weapons, ragtag Viet Cong volunteers plinking off shots from antiquated French hunting rifles having melted into the jungle or melted in our napalm. A hovering helicopter was a very inviting target.

In his award-winning stark book *Dispatches*, author Michael Herr talks about a scene following a firefight in Vietnam where some two dozen deceased soldiers had been stacked together in body bags at a landing zone (LZ) prior to transport back to a rear base for identification and processing, when suddenly the LZ came under attack by North Vietnamese. A mortar shell tragically landed amid the stacked corpses, blowing the bodies and bags all to hell. Later, after the LZ was secured, legs, arms, and torsos of the corpses awaiting shipment were found everywhere. Human imagination cannot grasp the psychological damage done to the soldiers assigned to match all of the parts, some of who may have been close friends, zipping them back into fresh body bags.

It is understandable that it was going to take eighteen days to get Joe back to Arlington. Joe's funeral was going to be a closed casket.

As an only child, Joe held a special place with his parents. It is likely that his parents were responsible for placing the obituary for Joe in the Washington Post, allowing folks like me to know about Joe's ceremony in Arlington well before it happened. Joe's father was the Assistant to the Under Secretary of Defense, meaning there would be many people attending this Arlington funeral; I would be one of them.

Just after we completed our tear-sodden dinner, Charlie and Beth's doorbell rang. It was the next-door neighbor…she had a very sad look on her face. She asked Charlie if he had a guest who owned a dark blue Corvette. Charlie turned around and yelled for me to come to the door. It turned out that she had backed out of her driveway, not seeing the low profile of my dark sports car, and smashed into the front fender.

Just like after Frank's funeral when the bus smashed the fender of my red Corvette, now it had happened to my blue one…just after learning of Joe's death. It was enough to make a man believe in other worldly fates and devils.

Again, I was so overwhelmed by Joe's death that this became only a buzzing annoyance. I remember only shaking my head and saying, "Well, at least it was the left fender this time!"

Back at my apartment, again suffering a world-class hangover after another night of crying with Charlie and Beth—déjà vu from hell—it felt as if I was being punished. Having been through this drill two years earlier with Frank, I began the same trail by picking up the phone to call friends from high school. As a lesson learned from Frank's graveside service at Arlington, I was going to need an escort.

One option for an escort was a schoolteacher living on the seventh floor of my building, a young lady named Fran Matthews. In my quest to find company between visits by my New York blonde betrothed, I had met Fran at a party. In a twist of irony, Fran taught the fourth grade at the elementary school I had attended, at the same school Joe had attended, and in a further over-the-top coincidence, she had become best friends at this school with Mrs. Maude Gray, the woman who had been my sixth grade teacher so many years earlier. It is beyond weird and uncomfortable to find yourself on a double dinner date with your sixth grade teacher, her husband, and another of the younger teaching staff you just happen to be seeing. It seemed as if I was breaking some universal generational law of appropriate etiquette with one's sixth grade teacher. Would Miss Manners approve?

Fran would have been a rock of emotional stability serving as an escort to my upcoming return visit to Arlington, but her friend and fellow teacher, Mrs. Gray, had also been Joe's sixth grade teacher. This was more moving parts than I could handle, so I decided to go it alone.

The fall weather on Monday, November 4th, 1968, opened up undistinguishable from that experienced two years earlier on November 21st, also a Monday. I had come to expect this kind of cloudy, chilly day to be the norm for burying best friends at Arlington. Continuing the string of parallels, Joe was to be buried in Section 13, the section abutting Section 37; for all eternity my two friends would be near each other. Unlike Frank's ceremony, Joe's was to begin with a service in a chapel at St. George's Episcopal, a fine church located less than a mile from Arlington.

Arriving a few minutes late and remembering to keep my newly purchased replacement Corvette away from buses, I wandered into the small chapel through a side door. The room was packed from wall to wall. This was nothing like the group of people who attended Frank's ceremony. In no time I began to feel uncomfortable. It was my preconceived notion that I would know most of the people attending, but that was not the case, not at all.

My eyes immediately fell on Karen, standing on the other side of the room in a long black dress with a black veil over her head and face. Working my way towards her, it felt as if the doors to Filenes Basement had just opened to the arrival of tour buses from New York, strangers groping for Karen, her beautiful black dress having just been marked down 50 percent.

Who the hell are these people? I am thinking. *They were not there the day Joe came to my rescue at the Mexican food table in the fifth grade, saving a new, Kansas farm kid from taco humiliation. They hadn't shared a sandwich when no food came with the team to an away high school track meet. They didn't throw an arm around your shoulder in the days after a tragic high school, steady girlfriend breakup. They had never slithered into a football stadium at night, carefully avoiding county guards, to lime a football field of a rival team. They were not members of our elite high school alliance.*

Who were all these self-important adults nodding as if they knew all along this would happen, now seen hovering as if to confirm that knowledge? These people did not know the Joe I knew; I could see it in their eyes.

And they did not know the Karen Vest Powell I knew so well. The girl who had sat next to me in dreaded French language laboratory laughing at my silly jokes until Mrs. Croom, the teacher, chastised us for not telling the joke *en Français*. Karen was the girl who followed our Junior Varsity team as a cheerleader. They could not know that!

I quietly backed away from the commotion surrounding Karen. This day was not about me. Looking around the room, I was not sure it was even about Karen. I was there not because it was the family thing to do, not because it was the neighborly thing to do, not because it was the correct move for office politics or even because it was the polite thing to do; I was there to say goodbye to the president of the student body of my high school, to my classmate, to my teammate, to my fellow Bengal Seven member, to my fellow Vietnam warrior. I was there to say goodbye to a lifelong friend. I quietly backed out the door until the procession left the chapel for the trip over to Section 13.

The graveside ceremony took much longer than Frank's had taken; the Marine Corps, as well they should, puts on a more formal ceremony for their own fallen from enemy fire. For the rifle salute, they had brought along a full platoon of Marines in dress uniform.

As before, I found a tree on raised ground, allowing me to view all without interacting among the mourners. Following the "Grateful Nation" speech and flag presentation to Karen, the setting sun and chilly autumn air sent many of the mourners to their autos as soon as was respectful. Karen's parents had escorted her away as soon as they could, leaving just a few folks speaking among themselves, mostly about the tragedy of what was now "Lyndon's War."

After a time there remained only the workers from the cemetery, Joe, and myself. I had made a promise that for Joe's service there would be no leaving until time was allowed for a proper talk. Dusk had by now come to visit when at last I reached down for a handful of fresh graveside dirt, dropping small clumps and pebbles on to the lowered coffin, making a thumping sound that reverberates loudly between my ears even to this day, as I said goodbye to Joe for all eternity. From there it was a lonely drive back to my apartment where a full bottle of Johnny Walker Red patiently awaited my solemn return. I had not spoken to Karen.

The Faithful Sextant

Three days later, I called her.

Hearing my voice brought a lapse of silence. We always start phone calls with the trite, the banal, the question that wants no answer, "So how are you today?"

What the hell, everyone knew how Karen was today…she was not okay. But I had rehearsed this call before dialing the number. This call required a leap right to the heart. I boldly asked, "Karen, it was not possible to talk to you at Arlington. Can I come over and tell you what I could not say then?"

In a soft voice she replied, "Yes, of course, Bob. I would love to see you. Tomorrow morning would be fine."

Thus began a journey unlike any I had ever experienced.

The next day, over a cup of coffee, Karen talked about Joe's last mission; she talked about dealing with the Marine Corps; she talked about what to do with Joe's uniforms in the closet; she talked about the paltry $10,000 life insurance granted to the now-growing sisterhood of Vietnam widows. During a pause, as Karen caught her breath between emotions, she slowly stood, crossed the room, and turned on her record player, dropping the needle in the center of the LP album already sitting on the turntable platter to the most haunting of tragic ballads: Richard Harris singing the Jimmy Webb song, "MacArthur Park."

Sipping coffee ended; conversing ended; rational thought ended …and so began the Richard Harris-fueled crying sessions. Some folks are of the opinion that "MacArthur Park" is a much too long, maudlin, sappy ballad, but for those who have not been where we were, I defy them to tell me that Jimmy Webb and Richard Harris have not crafted an arrow to the exact center of the heart of human tragedy.

Karen and I hugged each other with tears streaming, neither of us understanding who was comforting whom. Little two-year-old Sean stood in the middle of the room trying to understand why his mommy and this strange man were crying, finally running to his mother to join in.

I was to come over to visit Karen and Sean maybe four or five more times. We took Sean to the Zoo, only to find ourselves sitting on a bench crying. We went out to dinner, never making it to dessert before leaning on each other crying. People in public places stared at us crying. Our age, our torment, the headlines in the Washington Post said it all. The older ones knew right away why the anguish. They wanted no part of stepping up to ask if something was wrong; they knew what was wrong. No human with a heart knows what to say to the widow of a fallen warrior.

Between crying sessions, I had tried to help Karen organize her life. The intimacy of our shared grief was manifesting itself in raw emotions. We were mistaking what felt like a bond of love for each other with the all too recent disappearance of our ability to bond with another loved one, of the anguish found in the absolute permanence of death, of our most human need to replace that bond of love for another, a place now filled by an empty void. In truth, my presence had become more an anchor to the past than a signpost to the future.

Karen's parents could see all of this. They booked a several-week trip for the family to the Caribbean to remove her, even if temporarily, from the ghosts of the past, leaving me to decide that it might be best if I left Karen and Sean to make their own future.

Karen was to marry again and she and I were to stay corresponding friends for life.

Some years later, Joe's father was buried alongside Joe in Arlington.

And once again, it crossed my mind that at least now the book on Vietnam had reached the end…and once again I was so wrong!

Joani

I had driven to New York in 1969 to see Joani as part of our long-distance romance. This would become a fateful trip. Joani had just returned from escorting a close friend on a one-way airplane trip to Indiana. This friend, facing great stress, was pregnant and heading off into the unknown for a hurry-up wedding to the infant-to-be's father. Joani must have had great anguish as she sat on the airplane flying home thinking, *That could very well have been me!* Unaware of the emotional cost of her ordeal, with my mind off on a tangent about our future, I had suggested that it was time for her to drive with me down to North Carolina to meet my grandmother and cousins. My request to meet family members must have seemed insensitive to her deep recent feelings. She was mentally comparing our path to that of her friend, while I, testing out the men are from Mars and women from Venus thing, was blissfully planning a ratchet up in our future plans.

Her answer to this stress was to stop the clock until she could closely inspect our relationship to be sure we weren't traveling the same path as her friend. We agreed that our romance was still strong, and that we would continue to be a couple. But as I drove back to Alexandria a day later, a shiny, two-carat diamond engagement ring nestled deeply in the pocket of my pants, there were many questions unanswered. Our engagement was either on hold or over. It was hard to tell which.

But we were to keep visiting each other; the New York to Virginia loop continued.

In early 1971, having planned a trip to go skiing in Utah with friends, I picked up the phone at work and called Joani, asking her to join us on what I thought was a rock star ski trip. She answered the phone with a strange tone in her voice and paused for some time before informing me she would not be skiing; she was going to marry another man.

Neither of us could ever again figure out exactly what went wrong.

Two virgins seeking love, Joani and I had become the "first" for each other, a rather Victorian and exclusive life event. Perhaps it was this bond of primacy that held us together, or perhaps our needs had drifted while we were not looking. I did not know, but one part of this I did know; there would be no discussion, she had made this decision for me. Then it hit me, this is not the decision I wanted.

Sure, I could make decisions, big decisions about what I was not going to do. I was not going be a pilot…I was not going to work and commute in New York…I was not going back to sea. Negative decisions are no way to run your life; it leaves indecision as a replacement for positive decisions. But a wise man once said, *There is no such thing as indecision. Failure to decide is really a decision to do nothing.* Doing nothing was what I became good at. I had begun a life of searching, framed in short-term, lackluster goals and sybaritic living. Weeknight barhopping, Friday night singles parties, and Saturday night dates would continue, that is until a prairie princess was to come into my life and turn it around.

First Lt. Larry Greene

Years later, in a time when memories of Vietnam had faded, my brother Jim related a story in an "oh, by the way" tone, about meeting the father of one of our football teammates and mutual friend from Groveton High. Jim had been on a duty tour in Japan, where he ran into a General Greene, the father of Larry Greene…aka "Mean Greene Number Eighteen."

My yearbook picture of the Groveton High Varsity Football team posed Larry as the only guy pictured sporting a full-toothed smile, but then Larry was always smiling. As a member of the class of 1961, Larry fit in as a classmate of my brother, and indeed, they were close friends, double dating and pulling drinking trips to DC. Larry lived only a few blocks from our house, making him a close friend of mine as he came by to see Jim and, of course, we were football teammates, always a male bond. My ever-penny-pinching parents had made my brother and I share a yearbook at the end of my senior and my brother's junior year, forcing us to share pages for autographs and messages from friends. Larry Greene had filled the entire front cover page with a message to my brother, remembering daring-do BS stories from the romping he and Jim had done. The front inside cover was the favorite page for eternal messages, and now this twerpy friend of my little brother had used the whole damn page to memorialize a lot of teenage, testosterone-driven hooliganism.

The Faithful Sextant

Not only was that page gone, but after I went off to the Academy, the yearbook itself disappeared. I had assumed that it had been lost in one of the many moves made by my mother and father. But lo and behold, some twenty-two years later, my wonderful wife, Maye, while visiting my brother and his wife, noticed this supposedly lost, joint-owner Groveton High senior yearbook resting in a bookcase in brother Jim's staff mansion at West Point (Yes, Colonels get small mansions). Quick as a fox, without letting anyone know, including me, she liberated the two-brother yearbook. She knew that I had been desperately searching for this book for years, and after all, the book embodied my senior year, not my brother's, and besides, he had now held possession of the book for half a lifetime; it was time to share. Her clever swiping of my senior yearbook only reinforces the old wisdom to always check your guest's luggage before they depart, especially your most trusted guests.

That yearbook has been a major resource in the writing of this memoir.

All that about messing up my yearbook was silliness, I loved Larry; he was a Groveton Tiger!

After graduation from Groveton High, the Army, in its usual way, moved Larry's father to Ft. Knox, so Larry tagged along, making that his hometown during college. After college, Larry followed in his father's footsteps by becoming commissioned in the Army as an officer, almost insuring that he would be sent off to Vietnam, and he was. Larry arrived in country (South Vietnam) on August 10th of 1967, about the same time that my brother Jim had arrived and about a year and a half after my departure. Larry had made first lieutenant, assigned to Delta Company, 4th Battalion of the 503rd Infantry, a ground-stomping recon unit in the Phû Yen Province, about half way up the coast of South Vietnam.

General Greene sadly informed my brother Jim that his son, Larry, had stepped on a mine during a firefight and had died on January 30th of 1968. Larry's body had been recovered and buried in Arlington several weeks following his casualty. Shockingly, neither Jim nor

I had known of Larry's death. He was buried at Arlington National Cemetery in Section 1, site 164A.

Researching this event revealed that Larry's father, General Greene, upon his passing from old age, was also buried in Arlington in Section 1, site 166B right next to Larry.

Now it was coming together at Arlington. Frank was buried in Section 37, Joe in Section 13 and Larry in Section 1. Though not intuitive, it turns out that these three sections all border each other in the very western side of the National Cemetery. The plinths marking the graves of my three friends who lost their lives while on active duty for this country form a nice little triangle bonding them in hallowed ground for all eternity.

The Custis and Lee families would never know what a national treasure their beautiful plantation now provides for the military veterans, their families, and the people of this country.

Epilogue

Young people ask me all the time, "What was the big deal about your generation and the war in Vietnam?"

It is a valid question. Our country has now been fighting a war of ideology in Kuwait and Iraq and Afghanistan and Syria and Yemen and Somalia and Libya and on our own home turf in New York and Washington, DC, for longer than we fought in Vietnam. And it is every bit as ugly. Korea was ugly. World War I and II were on a scale far larger than Vietnam. And yet this part of our history continues to capture imagination in ways unlike any of these other events…at least in the minds of my generation.

There have been enough books written about the Vietnam experience to fill a small library. I have several shelves of my home library devoted to nothing else. When first writing this memoir, I had thought of providing the reader with a lengthy reading list of my favorite books but elected instead to scatter book names throughout this memoir in sections where they fit. Never intended to be a history book, no bibliography and footnotes will be found in *The Faithful Sextant*. Besides, who really reads either? So my answer to the question of what this war meant can only be couched in terms of what it meant to me personally.

No posttraumatic shock syndrome (PTSD) lurks here. No VA psychologists or psychiatrists have had their time wasted by me. But then I was no warrior. I never experienced eyeball-to-eyeball terror such as my brother experienced. I was only a spectator seated in the front row where the sweat from the passing actors sometimes flew off in my face. But the heat and feel and smell of that sweat hitting my face was damned strong.

Here is what was a big deal. First came the sorting out of the whole experience. As a lifelong charter member of organized living, putting this chaotic clusterfuck into a neat little package was never going to happen. It did not happen as I stared at it from the deck of the *SS Exhibitor,* and it never happened in the years to come. Maybe it's like that in all wars, but this was my first one and it in no way resembled the Hollywood war movie as portrayed by John Wayne or Henry Fonda.

Then there was the surprise awaiting all of us returning home from Vietnam dressed in some form of service uniform. The folks on the street, having been swayed by the likes of Tom Hayden, Jane Fonda, and the anti-war protestors, treated us with contempt. I was never spat upon, but there sure was a tone of disrespect. We were treated as if we'd been clueless clods duped into performing heinous acts by warmongering leaders or worse yet, savage war lovers filled with the thrill of splattering the blood of innocent women and children. The vision of the classic Pulitzer Prize award-winning photo showing a severely burned naked nine-year-old girl running for her life from an American plane dropping napalm became imprinted on the back of the retina for many Americans. And I represented the guy who provided the napalm (which in a way was true).

Upon moving to Alexandria, curiosity sent me into Washington, DC on two evenings at the height of the anti-war marches. By then I had buried Joe in Arlington, making me no fan of the way our government was prosecuting this war. I wanted the damn carnage to stop as much as the hippies surrounding me on the mall, however, a chasm of difference in outlook separated me from them. The lyrics from a song made famous by the rock group Stealers Wheel reverberated in my ears: *Clowns to left of me, jokers to the right, and here I am, stuck in the middle....*

Perhaps the most telling of differences could be seen every Tuesday when I appeared at an evening formal military training meeting dressed as a naval lieutenant, defender of United States military policy.

By far the largest impact of the Vietnam War was the big personal loss, the loss that comes with no closure or expiration date, the loss of my friends, my rat pack. As years have gone by, I have communicated with two of their widows, but that has been a sandwich with little meat in the middle. Understandably, they have moved on with life, seeing no need to open old wounds. The children of my deceased friends want no part of learning about my good old days with their long-gone father. They grew up without these men, and even knowing that these warriors left behind the genetic material of their soul does not change the view of him as a picture on mom's wall of some man who was in another life of hers.

The grief I personally inherited from my generation's war did not, unfortunately, end with the burial of my friends. The search for a lady to become a life companion, subsequent to my broken engagement, was to place me in the company of a widow of a pilot killed in action, then with a woman who cut the ties with her husband while he was still in Vietnam, and finally with a lady who had been an Army nurse in a field hospital in Vietnam. In all three cases, I knew nothing about their Vietnam War baggage until a committed relationship had formed. All three relationships ended poorly.

I had begun to believe that I was star-crossed...that I would never escape the gravitational pull of my generation's involvement in this war. Then it happened, an event that would change my life.

It all started with the termination of the life of my second Corvette, the gun-metal-blue one. I had stopped for gasoline at a filling station where a giant tandem trailer tanker had just refilled the underground tanks. Water, dirt, and gunk, being heavier than gasoline, will sink to the bottom of a tank in a filling station where it harmlessly stays until professionally removed. That afternoon, the tank truck had stirred up the gunk and water at the bottom of the underground tanks, and it had not had time to settle. I then, unknowingly, filled my dry-as-a-bone empty Corvette gas tank. About three miles later, this water and gunk invaded the sweet 327 V-8 engine of my Corvette, where this contamination caused it to shut down. The engine never was to run properly again, incentivizing me to sell the car to some boys who seemed not to mind the knocking. It came to me much later, that this had been a signpost to the future. My Corvette days were over. It was time to move on with so many more things than just a fancy vehicle.

A very attractive, very smart and talented, blonde haired, blue-eyed lady with a cute little Chevrolet Vega came to my rescue. This lady was Mabel Lucille Johnson, a name that speaks loudly to her Swedish, Protestant, prairie fundamentalist background. Maye, as she was known to all, was a lady founded in those Midwestern values, a most giving lady sent to turn my life. She was to remove me from my self-imposed, sybaritic, directionless life. We would find each other and become happily married for the next forty years (and counting).

But for me, there often remains a missing part. What would my deceased friends talk about today were we able to pick up the phone or have lunch over a couple of beers? Is it fair to say that mourning and remorse over the loss of a friend or loved one is another form of self-conceit or egocentric sorrow over something has been taken away from us? That dose of honesty, however, is just not as strong as the loss. Most of my rat pack from high school and three of my five academy roommates have predeceased me, and while all of them are sorely missed, there will always be a special place for the three lost serving their country.

On the plus side of what Admiral Lord Nelson called the "butcher's bill," I did not lose my brother Jim nor brother-in-law Pete Clay, both warriors, both serving to save the democratic rights of the people of South Vietnam. They served in danger and some would say were lucky to have returned. But dear reader, if you take nothing else from this story, remember, in war there is no lucky, there is no unlucky. War demands its dead and its wounded and its permanently, psychologically changed, and at the end of it, either you are one of these or you are not.

The pin of the Vietnam War pricked just about everybody in this country who lived through its plague. Whether Kent State survivor, Woodstock protestor, limping POW pilot struggling off a plane from Hanoi to unknown children and an ex-wife who decided not to wait, or a member of the sisterhood of widows, everyone agreed that a monument should be erected to memorialize the dead. Demand for some sort of monument or shrine to those lost in Vietnam was fertilized and grew until it could not be ignored. From the roots of a small verbal group, this memorial grew into a contest of design and a contest of wills. Out of this fray came a long, low V-shaped wall, the design of a young Chinese American girl studying at Yale. The wall was to have the names of those who died as American combatants inscribed on its face.

The design would be constructed of a highly polished, dark gabbro, an igneous stone with large crystals of pyroxenes and olivine, giving it an otherworldly, greenish midnight sheen. Nearby monuments and buildings erected of bland white granite now reflect off the wall as if begging to share some of its recognition. Instated on the Mall grounds of Washington, DC under what had been the temporary US Navy headquarters during WWII, this memorial instantly took on a haunting life much greater than the sum of its whole.

Controversy continued to follow the Vietnam Wall. Not the least of which came from fellow veterans from our wars in Korea and World War II, both fought earlier and both lacking a comparable monument in Washington. Committees were formed, funding was found, and both earlier war memorials received outstanding designs. Designs, in fact, more demonstrative, more elaborate, and more expensive than this plain, ordinary wall of gabbro sunk in the ground in the northwest corner of the Mall. Veterans from the Korean War and the great World War now come to visit their new memorials, and they are pleased to have been remembered.

Meanwhile a steady flow of folks visit the wall. Children of the deceased come, widows come, veterans come, and just ordinary tourists come. I have been there twice with the same result. I had to know. I had set out to find the why of it in the story of their service, set out to discover how a middle-aged, middle-class man, a man who held together his volunteer fire department yet knew how to char grill a steak to perfection and who had raised three children, sending them to college…what would drive this man to dig out his old green camouflage jacket, climb on a Harley, and drive cross country, where he would find a quiet spot on the Mall of his nation to cry his eyes out in front of strange people and a stranger black wall.

I peek at the older tourists as they look away, trying not to get caught up. More veterans wearing unit patches make no pretense… they sometimes have to sit to get control of emotions. My times there, I wear dark glasses, trying to hide my face so no one would see the salty liquid being mopped up by a handkerchief. It is the wall of bawl!

And no one comes without touching. Everyone touches…it is impossible not to touch. Not to feel every name. Not to feel the sacrifice. Many visitors leave something on the raised shelf in front of the wall. So much stuff has been left that the Park Service now fills a warehouse, refusing to throw any of it in the garbage. No one knows what to do with the left-behinds, but all know it is not garbage.

The greenish-black wall exudes a power, a kind of Stanley Kubrick magical power of a plinth frightening the apes and perplexing the astronauts. It spooks all who stand near it, even those believing they have no investment of loss as enumerated in the list of names.

How to explain this?

War victimizes so many people in so many ways. Ways that the war lover, the political policy maker, the Hollywood movie producer, the Ivy League philosopher have no equivalent life experience to offer understanding or give meaning to. I had experienced the heat and the smell and the stories of Vietnam but was never equipped in any way to deal with the emotion of the cost in human loss and…

- Sorrow
- Grief
- Suffering
- Misery
- Woe
- Anguish
- Pain
- Distress
- Agony

The reader gets to choose here. Looking back, however, it seems to me that any of these adjectives will work.

My generation has been called the generation of whiners. War is war, and looking back from history's perspective, none were worth the sacrifice. Our newest veterans from Iraq and Afghanistan will find their own peace, and no one who experienced the Vietnam era would ever take anything from their sacrifice. Leave us alone to cry over our losses and soon enough we too will be forgotten.

But would I go back to the youthful joy of the late 1950s? The era of teenage fantasy, of drive-ins with foamy shakes and Mighty Mo burgers, of youthful romance, of boyhood testing on the playing field, of friends and memories for life? Would I erase the bleakness of the loss of innocence, of the loss of childhood, of the loss of friends for life?

"Not for a moment," as Wallace Stegner so poignantly ended *All the Little Live Things:* "I shall be richer all my life for this sorrow."

Acknowledgment

Relying on the human memory is much like the editing of a book. Every time the author opens a chapter file to inspect and change the wording is similar to asking the brain to reopen a memory. Once the save button is clicked, then all those memories are pushed back into the gray matter with new changes and variations. I was fortunate to find memory help from friends and family. For this I want to thank Ginny Clay, Dr. Kate Avery, Beth Arbogast, Charlie Strauss, Dr. Karen Gravelle, Dr./Col. James McEliece, Sarah Shuler, Toni Packer, Karen Dickson, Joan Deters, and beta readers Jeff and Rebecca Krida. Factual assistance from classmates of the 1964 graduating classes of the United States Air Force Academy and the United States Merchant Marine Academy was invaluable.

I am indebted to the many authors who have gone before to tell the story of Vietnam and must name two who changed everything for me, Bernard Fall and Michael Herr. Two authors who have personal connections, Patrick Davis (USAFA) and Dick Couch (USNA) allowed me to see that Academy guys could learn to write. In learning to write, I must thank Prof. Brooks Landon of the University of Iowa for showing how to write a sentence and Prof. Mary Karr of Syracuse who taught me to write the truth no matter how much it hurt.

I also appreciate the help given by Erica McEliece in proofreading the final draft. I would have struggled and may not have succeeded without my knowledgeable business partner Christine Keleny. She was always cheerfully available with great editing advice and corrections as we pushed through several edits. Through her publishing Company, CKBooks Publishing, she made it possible for us to get a striking book out to readers. None of this, however, would have been possible without the patient support of my wife Maye. Her help and loving care through the birth of what was sometimes known as "That Damned Book" cannot be understated.

About the Author

Born with a head of the blondest hair ever seen, Robert Devereux McEliece passed through his primary education known to all as "Cotton." A four-year education at one of the finest Service Academies, Kings Point, imprinted him with the standard nickname for Scots/Irish of "Mac." Remaining active for over thirty years as a reserve officer in the U.S. Navy, he was promoted to Commanding Officer of three different units. At the end of that time he was known as Captain McEliece.

Bob has written a second book, soon to follow this, his first. He lives with his wife, Maye, near Seattle, where there is still a scent of salt in the air.

If you enjoyed reading this book, please leave a review on your favorite book website.

Thank you

www.ingramcontent.com/pod-product-compliance
Lightning Source LLC
Chambersburg PA
CBHW020055020526
44112CB00031B/182